W9-AJO-521

PRO/CON VOLUME 11

FAMILY AND SOCIETY

Fluvanna County High School
3717 Central Plains Road
Palmyra, VA 22963

Published 2003 by Grolier,
a division of Scholastic Library Publishing
90 Sherman Turnpike
Danbury, Connecticut 06816

© 2003 The Brown Reference Group plc

Library of Congress Cataloging-in-Publication Data
Pro/con
  p. cm
Includes bibliographical references and index.
  Contents: v. 7. The Constitution – v. 8. U.S. Foreign Policy – v. 9. Criminal Law and
the Penal System – v.10. Health – v. 11. Family and Society – v. 12. Arts and Culture.
  ISBN 0-7172-5753-3 (set : alk. paper) – ISBN 0-7172-5754-1 (vol. 7 : alk. paper) –
ISBN 0-7172-5755-X (vol. 8 : alk. paper) – ISBN 0-7172-5756-8 (vol. 9 : alk. paper) –
ISBN 0-7172-5757-6 (vol. 10 : alk. paper) – ISBN 0-7172-5758-4 (vol. 11 : alk. paper)
ISBN 0-7172-5759-2 (vol. 12: alk. paper)
  1. Social problems. I. Scholastic Publishing Ltd Grolier (Firm)

HN17.5 P756 2002
361.1–dc21

                                                                      2001053234

All rights reserved. No part of this book may be used or reproduced in any
manner whatsoever or transmitted in any form or by any means, electronic or
mechanical, including photocopying, recording, or any information storage and
retrieval system, without written permission from the copyright owner except in
the case of brief quotations embodied in critical articles and reviews. For
information, address the publisher.

Printed and bound in Singapore

SET ISBN 0-7172-5753-3
VOLUME ISBN 0-7172-5758-4

For The Brown Reference Group plc
Project Editor: Aruna Vasudevan
Editors: Sally McFall, Chris Marshall, Fiona Plowman, Lesley Henderson
Consultant Editor: Angela J. Hattery, Assistant Professor of Sociology, Wake
Forest University
Designer: Sarah Williams
Picture Researchers: Clare Newman, Susy Forbes
Set Index: Kay Ollerenshaw

Managing Editor: Tim Cooke
Design Manager: Lynne Ross
Production Manager: Alastair Gourlay

GENERAL PREFACE

*"All that is necessary for evil to
triumph is for good men to
do nothing."*
—Edmund Burke, 18th-century
English political philosopher

Decisions

Life is full of choices and decisions.
Some are more important than others.
Some affect only your daily life—the
route you take to school, for example,
or what you prefer to eat for supper—
while others are more abstract and
concern questions of right and wrong
rather than practicality. That does not
mean that your choice of presidential
candidate or your views on abortion
are necessarily more important than
your answers to purely personal
questions. But it is likely that those
wider questions are more complex and
subtle and that you therefore will need
to know more information about the
subject before you can try to answer
them. They are also likely to be
questions where you might have to
justify your views to other people. In
order to do that you need to be able to
make informed decisions, be able to
analyze every fact at your disposal, and
evaluate them in an unbiased manner.

What is *Pro/Con*?

Pro/Con is a collection of debates that
presents conflicting views on some of
the more complex and general issues
facing Americans today. By bringing
together extracts from a wide range of
sources—mainstream newspapers and
magazines, books, famous speeches,
legal judgments, religious tracts,
government surveys—the set reflects
current informed attitudes toward
dilemmas that range from the best way

to feed the world's growing population
to gay rights, from the connection
between political freedom and
capitalism to the fate of Napster.

The people whose arguments make
up the set are for the most part
acknowledged experts in their fields,
making the vast difference in their
points of view even more remarkable.
The arguments are presented in the
form of debates for and against various
propositions, such as "Is Pornography
Art?" or "Is U.S. Foreign Policy Too
Interventionist?" This question format
reflects the way in which ideas often
occur in daily life: in the classroom, on
TV shows, in business meetings, or even
in state or federal politics.

The contents

The subjects of the six volumes of
*Pro/Con 2—The Constitution,
U.S. Foreign Policy, Criminal Law
and the Penal System, Health, Family
and Society*, and *Arts and Culture—*
are issues on which it is preferable
that people's opinions are based on
information rather than personal bias.

Special boxes throughout *Pro/Con*
comment on the debates as you are
reading them, pointing out facts,
explaining terms, or analyzing
arguments to help you think about
what is being said.

Introductions and summaries also
provide background information
that might help you reach your own
conclusions. There are also comments
and tips about how to structure an
argument that you can apply on an
everyday basis to any debate or
conversation, learning how to present
your point of view as effectively and
persuasively as possible.

VOLUME PREFACE
Family and Society

The traditional view of the family has changed in the last few decades. The so-called "nuclear family"—a married heterosexual couple living in a house with their children—no longer seems the norm. Many more people choose not to marry, and 50 percent of those who do end up divorced. Many children are now born to unmarried parents, while the number of single-parent families is also rising. What has brought about all these changes to the family unit? Should we be worried by new attitudes toward family life? Should the state intervene to preserve traditional family values?

Changing attitudes

Just a few generations ago men and women had very different roles in the family unit. The man was seen as the breadwinner and provider, while the woman's role was as a homemaker and a childrearer. This view began to change in the second half of the 20th century. As more and more women got jobs, they no longer needed to rely on the support of men. Many women started to reject their traditional roles as mothers and housekeepers, opting instead to pursue a career.

The sexual revolution of the 1960s also had an enormous effect on family life. Increasing numbers were put off marriage until later in their lives. Many more chose to live together rather than marry. The number of children born to unmarried parents soared.

The media, too, have played a major part in deconstructing the traditional family model. A good example is the award-winning television show *Murphy Brown,* in which a female character decided to have a baby out of wedlock. The show prompted criticism from former Vice President Dan Quayle and sparked a nationwide debate.

Asking questions

All children need love and attention as they grow up. But must a child have more than one parent to meet this need? Does the adult have to be the child's biological mother or father? Is a gay father or lesbian mother any less of a parent than a heterosexual one?

Many people believe that single-parent families and gay and transracial parenting reflect today's egalitarian society. Others feel that the modern family lacks traditional values, which has contributed to rising levels of juvenile crime, delinquency, teenage pregnancy, and drug use. If parents find it difficult to instill in their children acceptable morals and values, whose responsibility is it? The school? The state? While schools often step in to promote a sense of responsibility and reinforce family values, many people do not feel comfortable with parenting techniques such as corporal punishment. Many others are equally uncomfortable with state interference in family affairs.

Family and Society deals with 16 issues concerning the family—what it means to be a parent, the issues young and old people face in the United States, and the role of the family in society. By presenting both sides of the arguments clearly, this book will help you form your own opinions about a range of family-related topics.

HOW TO USE THIS BOOK

Each volume of *Pro/Con* is divided into sections, each of which has an introduction that examines its theme. Within each section are a series of debates that present arguments for and against a proposition, such as whether or not the death penalty should be abolished. An introduction to each debate puts it into its wider context, and a summary and key map (see below) highlight the main points of the debate clearly and concisely. Each debate has marginal boxes that focus on particular points, give tips on how to present an argument, or help question the writer's case. The summary page to the debates contains supplementary material to help you do further research.

Boxes and other materials provide additional background information. There are also special spreads on how to improve your debating and writing skills. At the end of each book is a glossary and an index. The glossary provides explanations of key words in the volume. The index covers all twelve books, so it will help you trace topics throughout this set and the previous one.

marginal boxes
Margin boxes highlight key points of the argument, give extra information, or help you question the author's meaning.

summary boxes
Summary boxes are useful reminders of both sides of the argument.

further information
Further Reading lists for each debate direct you to related books, articles, and websites so you can do your own research.

other articles in the *Pro/Con* series
This box lists related debates throughout the *Pro/Con* series.

background information
Frequent text boxes provide background information on important concepts and key individuals or events.

key map
Key maps provide a graphic representation of the central points of the debate.

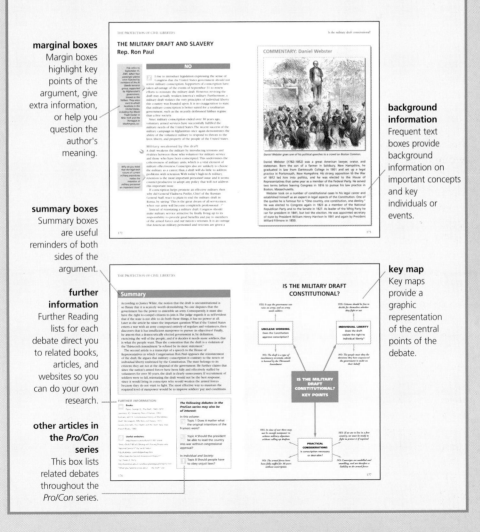

CONTENTS

PART 1

THE FAMILY

INTRODUCTION

According to *Merriam-Webster's Collegiate Dictionary,* a "family" is a "group of individuals living under one roof and usually under one head."

This definition is in keeping with the traditional meaning of a family, made up of a married heterosexual couple living together in the same house with their children. Up until the 20th century this was generally the "normal" family situation.

In the last 30 years or so, however, the situation in the United States has changed. From the 1970s onward the proportion of married couples with children decreased, the numbers of single mothers grew, and the average age of first marriages also increased.

Today the concept of family has a variety of meanings. The number of marriages has declined, while the number of divorces has risen, and many households are headed by single people, often women; adoption by single people and gay individuals or couples is also more common.

Effects on family structure

Several factors influence how a family household is structured. Changes in marriage, cohabitation, divorce, and fertility rates are all significant. Similarly, as a society develops, its ideas on what is considered the norm may change, and its values, laws, and even the economy itself can be affected—all of which may influence family structures.

The United States, for example, saw great changes after World War II. More women entered the workforce and were able to support themselves and their families on their own income without having to be dependent on a male partner.

The feminist movement of the 1960s also brought great developments, as did the availability of contraception. Society became more sexually liberated, and people began to live together rather than marry, resulting in a growth in the number of children born out of wedlock and a corresponding change in how "illegitimate" children were perceived.

The U.S. family today

According to the 2000 Census, there are around 10 million single mothers in the United States, in contrast to the three million that existed in 1970; in the same period the number of single fathers also increased, from 393,000 to two million.

Supporters of these changes in the familial structure argue that the rise in single-parent families is a reflection of a more modern, egalitarian society. Critics, however, respond that falling marriage rates have led to a corresponding decline in family values, and that in turn has had an adverse effect on juvenile crime, delinquency, and teenage pregnancy rates. The results, they argue, just prove that the family is, in fact, in trouble.

Family values

The family is more than just a group of people living in the same house. Historically, the family provided its members with a sense of responsibility, morals, and values. These factors were reinforced by society—by the school, the church, and the peer group, among others. The reality today, however, is sometimes very different.

Topic 1 examines the issue of whether society does enough to support family values. Jennifer Ballen and Oliver Moles, in the first article, claim that society can help parents by being there to reinforce family values and helping combat problems such as

Prejudice

Many people, however, argue that the existence of couples like Etheridge and Cypher shows that the United States is a liberal society, accepting of relationships that once would have been taboo. Others say that there is still too much prejudice in the world; and since prejudice is a learned and not an inherent trait, the fault must lie at least in part with the family. But is that fair? Topic 2 examines the relationship between the family and prejudice. M'Lynn Hartwell, in the "yes" article, argues that as the family itself is the source of people's prejudices, they find it too painful to confront them.

"The strength of a nation derives from the integrity of the home."

—CONFUCIUS

---

drugs, alcohol, and violence in young people. They claim that mentoring programs, summer schools, and actions by community organizations, religious bodies, and schools also help strengthen families and provide a backup for parents and children in need. William J. Bennett, in the "no" article, looks at the state of marriage and the family. He uses the example of the relationship between rock star Melissa Etheridge, her former lesbian partner Julie Cypher, and their two children to show how family life has broken down. Bennett argues that Etheridge and Cypher are the "21st-century family" not only in the liberal definition of their family, but also because their relationship failed.

Clayton E. Tucker-Ladd, however, claims that matters are not that simple and that other factors instill prejudice.

Marriage

If the family is responsible for teaching values, does marriage really make a difference to the family unit? In the "yes" article of Topic 3 Family First states that marriage is the remedy to "a host of other social ills" and that the government should do more to promote it. The "no" article is an interview with media personality Rosie O'Donnell, also the lesbian mother of three adopted children. The article says that children can be happy in a variety of family circumstances and that prejudice should not prevent this.

Topic 1
DOES SOCIETY SUPPORT FAMILY VALUES?

YES

FROM "COMMUNITIES: COMMUNITIES CONNECT FAMILIES AND SCHOOLS"
STRONG FAMILIES, STRONG SCHOOLS
NATIONAL FAMILY INITIATIVE OF THE U.S. DEPARTMENT OF EDUCATION,
SEPTEMBER 1994
JENNIFER BALLEN AND OLIVER MOLES

NO

FROM "THE STATE OF MARRIAGE AND THE FAMILY"
*THE BROKEN HEARTH: REVERSING THE MORAL COLLAPSE OF
THE AMERICAN FAMILY*
WILLIAM J. BENNETT

INTRODUCTION

The family is traditionally responsible for educating children in the customs and values of the society in which they live. Parents teach the desirability of qualities such as kindness and compassion, honesty, trustworthiness, moral integrity, loyalty, tolerance, respect, and good manners. Those are the values on which society is theoretically founded. They are reinforced by the education system, by most religious codes, by media images —and by the behavior of most people much of the time.

The model is sometimes far removed from reality, however. Families themselves can be damaged in many ways: by broken marriages, by abuse, by addiction, by unemployment, or by poverty. But is a damaged family as able to inculcate positive values in its children as the model version?

And do changes in society make those values in any case out of date? If, as some people believe, society is becoming more violent, more selfish, and more dangerous, might not teaching a child traditional values of trust and openness do them more harm than good? How do "family values" relate to real life today?

The question is complicated by the ambiguous meaning of the phrase itself: What are "family values"? Most people would agree that they include the qualities already listed. In the second half of the 20th century, however, another meaning emerged. The phrase acquired political undertones. To many conservative commentators and religious leaders "family values" provided a useful shorthand for a range of beliefs that contrasted with what they saw as "alternative." In this instance family values come to imply being against abortion, gay rights, feminism, and sexual permissiveness.

Many of those who believe that family values are alive and well, and that society reinforces them, often reject the politicized view of family values championed by their critics. They point instead to more general ethical attitudes and behavior, such as that the majority of Americans are still honest, respectful, and so on, and that although a minority may act in an antisocial, violent, or criminal way, that does not necessarily mean society itself is becoming any less moral.

"It takes an entire village to raise a child."
—AFRICAN PROVERB

Advocates argue both that deviant influences have always existed and that the situation is no worse now than before. Most children grow up surrounded by positive role models on which to base their social behavior.

Critics who condemn society for failing to support family values, on the other hand, perceive a decline in the country's standards. They point to, among other things, repeated scandals involving senior politicians—the conduct of former President Bill Clinton, for example—or to the ethnic hostility or misogynistic attitudes adopted by some rock stars as evidence of a moral decline.

Critics often trace that change back to the steep rise in the numbers of divorces, single-parent families, adoptions, and surrogate parenting.

They wonder where, for example, the son of a single mother will learn values connected with being an adult male. The best answer, they believe, is from his father or from another paternal figure. They also look to other mentor figures in society—teachers, public officials, entertainment and sports stars—to set examples. Some even argue that society should use legislation or other methods to preserve the traditional family, such as by giving tax breaks to couples who marry.

Opponents argue that marriage breakdown is a fact of life, and that families cannot be kept together involuntarily. They say that family values must evolve to keep pace with the new shape of the family itself. They also point out that the so-called nuclear family—the model of father, mother, and a few children—is in many ways a comparatively recent development. Family values have changed in history as the family structure has changed, they argue. In the Middle Ages marriage was usually based less on emotion than on real estate or political alliances. The same remains true of societies in which families arrange marriages, often between men and women who have never met. Similarly, many people still choose to leave their babies in the care of nannies and send their children away to school. There is not much evidence that any of the above practices damage the child's appreciation of so-called family values.

The following articles look at two different aspects of the debate. Jennifer Ballen and Oliver Moles argue that parents can turn to communities to reinforce values and counter dangers such as drugs. However, William J. Bennett describes what he sees as the consequences of broken marriage.

COMMUNITIES: COMMUNITIES CONNECT FAMILIES AND SCHOOLS
Jennifer Ballen and Oliver Moles

The authors begin their piece with statistics that lend authority and credibility to their argument.

✓ Forty-eight percent of Americans believe that people need support from their local communities, beyond their immediate families, to help raise their children. This proportion rises to 60 percent when those asked are single parents or lower-income persons.

Community efforts to strengthen parental involvement can have far-reaching benefits. According to research on this topic, parents who are involved with their children's education are more willing to pay tax money to fund schools. The overall life in a community often improves, and juvenile delinquency may go down. Residents with a greater stake in the community stay longer, and better-educated residents attract higher-paying businesses and increase local tax revenue.

Service organizations and agencies, religious groups, and individual citizens are working to make communities safer and drug free, to reinforce skills related to good parenting, to encourage people to serve as mentors, to extend learning opportunities, to link social services with educational programs, and to train parents in leadership and child advocacy. Some organizations have a long history of activities; many have demonstrated their worth. All focus on critical needs. Communities can be a powerful influence on parents and children. There are a variety of ways that community groups can help increase family involvement in their children's learning.

Do you think good parenting skills can be taught? What do you think makes a good parent?

Combating alcohol, drugs, and violence

Monitoring the Future is an ongoing study that looks at the behaviors, attitudes, and values of American secondary school students, college students, and young adults. For further information on this study go to http://monitoring thefuture.org/.

Each year, thousands of our youth become involved in the use of alcohol and other drugs and engage in violent behavior.... Data from the University of Michigan's *Monitoring the Future* study indicates that slightly more than one-quarter of high school seniors, almost one-fifth of 10th-graders, and almost one-tenth of 8th-graders reported some use of marijuana in the past year. After declining for several years, the use of other drugs, such as inhalants, LSD, and stimulants, is also on the rise.

However, some prevention programs have been successful, and communities can play an important part in these programs. The most promising prevention programs are those in which parents, students, schools, and communities join together to send a firm, clear message that violence and the use of alcohol and other drugs will not be tolerated.... Solving the drug and violence problem is a tremendously complex enterprise that requires the cooperation of the entire community.

> Are drug taking and violence the main problems in society? Do you think that improved family values would help reduce them?

Reinforcing successful child-raising skills

Programs for parents may offer classes, literacy training, career preparation, early childhood education, monitoring of children's health needs, and referrals for services. High-quality programs engage parents early, sometimes before the child's birth, and stress the critical early years of a child's development and the parent's primary role in nurturing that development. Communities can encourage these types of programs. ...

A growing number of programs focus specifically on getting fathers more involved with their children. Several of these were highlighted at a July, 1994, conference on fathers led by Vice President Gore. One of these, the Philadelphia Children's Network, operates a Father Reengagement Initiative, which helps men engage in activities with their children and begin to provide emotional and financial support for their children.

> In 1994 then Vice President Al Gore held the Third Annual Family Reunion Conference on the "Role of Men in Children's Lives." Gore advocated the role of men as strong and positive role models in their children's lives. The "Father to Father" initiative was set up as a result. It brings together fathers, local communities, and agencies to help strengthen the relationship between fathers and their children.

For school-age children, the National Urban League directs Partners for Reform of Science and Math (PRISM), a comprehensive national initiative to get parents involved in local school reforms. A network of parents serve as advocates for ways in which families and communities in the state can be involved in children's education. Attractive materials for parents depict strategies for promoting reforms, using community institutions like museums and science centers, and strengthening home learning environments. Leader's guides and videos also have been developed.

The MegaSkills Program created by Dorothy Rich (1988) is designed to help parents help their children develop broadly applicable skills and values like confidence, effort, and responsibility.... More than 4,200 parent workshop leaders from 45 states and more than 1,000 school districts have been trained. The MegaSkills Program has also been adopted or sponsored by 96 businesses for their employees and the community. Several studies show increases in the understanding of parents' role in education, time spent with children on schoolwork, and children's school performance. A recent extension of the MegaSkills Program focuses on both the classroom and the family to ensure that children receive consistent, mutually reinforcing information about the importance of skills and attitudes to school success....

Several local communities have also created resource centers that are devoted primarily to families of children with disabilities. Such centers lend toys and books and provide parenting information and workshops on parents' and children's rights in special education legislation....

Provide mentor programs

In mentor programs, interested persons—from college students to senior citizens—offer emotional support, guidance, and specific assistance to young people. Because of changes in families and communities, many youth have few opportunities for contacts with adults who can help them develop into responsible adults. A number of mentor programs sprang up in the 1980s to address this need. A study of Big Brothers/Big Sisters of America, which has organized mentors for many years, noted the importance of detailed screening and supervision of mentors to assure high rates of interaction....

In 1971 the Teaching-Learning Communities (T-LC) Mentor Program in Ann Arbor, Michigan, was established using older volunteers to give potential dropouts the guidance and motivation they need to stay in school. The program proved so successful that today T-LC operates in 12 elementary, middle, and high schools in Ann Arbor. More than 200 mentors are working with students on a one-on-one basis from one to five times a week. The majority of the mentors are senior citizens, many of whom are recruited into the program by community organizations and by enthusiastic friends who are already mentors....

Offer summer learning programs

Summer learning programs, which expand the scope of learning and employ less-formal procedures, are particularly important for low-income children who, studies show, suffer serious academic losses over the summer, largely because low-income families and communities have limited academic resources. A number of successful summer programs with similar attributes have been identified. One in Oak Lawn, Illinois, works with 100 entering high school freshmen for six weeks each summer. In addition to helping students directly, outreach workers visit homes to build strong

The Greek goddess Athene assumed the identity of Mentor, a noble, to act as a guide to Telemachus, son of Odysseus. Traditionally a "mentor" is a more experienced person who provides guidance to someone junior in order to help them progress further in their career or education. Does your school have a mentoring program?

Big Brothers Big Sisters of America (BBBSA) was established in 1904. Today it provides one-to-one mentoring by adults to children from predominantly single-parent families through over 500 different programs. To find out more about BBBSA, go to www.bbbsa.org.

communication between families and schools. A full-time home-school coordinator also works throughout the year in this... secondary school program.

Link social services

Because unmet health problems and welfare needs often limit children's ability to learn, there is growing interest in making sure that parents know about and have access to community services for children and their families. A recent review shows that successful coordination of services can result in the provision of convenient and comfortable facilities, increased focus on prevention, a sustained commitment from various specialized agencies, and more participation by families in the planning process.

A step-by-step guide for local development of a "profamily system" of education and health services, based on the experience of seasoned practitioners and researchers, describes several community efforts. The range of services available is an issue that the local communities and parents should decide. Some communities prefer locating social services in schools; some prefer links to facilities near schools; others prefer for schools to make referrals only....

Neighborhood organizations need to understand the concerns of young people and their parents and to involve families in planning and directing activities for youth in inner-city areas. In a three-city study, McLaughlin noted that leaders of successful neighborhood groups were flexible, provided a wide range of personal services and personal development opportunities, and offered a sense of security despite violence in the neighborhood....

Encourage parental leadership

[V]arious aspects of the community—school systems, local community groups, religious organizations, individuals, and national organizations working locally—can help strengthen children's safety and achievement and families' ability to help their children learn. Some organizations work directly with parents to build their skills and leadership. Others do what parents are unable to do: volunteer during school hours, tutor and mentor youth, or run summer learning programs. Some programs deal exclusively with education, while others address concerns about the safety and welfare of children—concerns that must be resolved before learning can take place.

All provide important supports to families in difficult circumstances....

Do you think it is difficult for people to know what social services they are able to apply for? How do you think they could improve their ways of disseminating information?

The authors argue that outside institutions can help children and families; but if that is so, why are there so many episodes of juvenile violence and crime?

THE STATE OF MARRIAGE AND THE FAMILY
William J. Bennett

The author uses celebrities as an example and thus immediately gets the attention of his audience.

David Crosby was a founding member of the 1960s band the Byrds, but was most famous as part of the group Crosby, Stills, and Nash.

Do you think Crosby meant that fatherhood should be taken lightly?

NO

For years, the rock star Melissa Etheridge and her partner, the filmmaker Julie Cypher, had been asked to name the biological father of their two little children, Bailey and Beckett. Tired of keeping it a mystery, Etheridge and Cypher (who had left her husband in order to live with Etheridge and who then bore the two children) revealed their secret in the February 3, 2000, issue of *Rolling Stone*: The father was the fifty-eight-year-old rock legend David Crosby.

Not a big deal

As Etheridge and Cypher explained, several years ago, while vacationing in Hawaii, they had dropped in to visit Crosby and his wife, Jan. During the conversation, Etheridge and Cypher mentioned their wish to have a child. Jan Crosby volunteered, "What about David?" Crosby, who concedes that he did not know the couple well, immediately agreed. "I don't even think it should be a big deal," he said later.

In the magazine interview, Etheridge said: "I know that because of the procreation of our species, that it was man and woman, and that's the way it was all built. But two loving parents—that's all a kid needs. Two men, two women, a man and a woman, whatever."

In a subsequent television interview she added: "I do not believe that my children will be wanting in any way because they didn't have a father in the home every single day. What they have in the home is two loving parents. I think that puts them ahead of the game." Besides, interjected Cypher, "The definition of family is changing and evolving in our society so quickly."

Twenty-first century family

Crosby, who has not assumed any parental duties toward the two children, agrees: "Maybe it's a good thing for a lot of straight families to see that this is not something strange.... If, you know, in due time, at a distance, [Bailey and Beckett] are proud of who their genetic dad is, that's great."

At the end of the *Rolling Stone* interview, Cypher went to retrieve a photo album. "Look at this," she said, producing a photograph of a smiling group of people, including the two youngsters. "There's David, his son, his other son, his daughter-in-law … his granddaughter … his daughter."

"And there's my mother," added Etheridge.

On the back of the photograph, Cypher had written an inscription: "Twenty-first-century family."

Melissa Etheridge and Julie Cypher, embodiments of twenty-first-century ideas in more ways than one, and role models for countless young Americans, have since broken up.

The case of Claire Austin

Two years ago, the British press reported on events surrounding the birth of twin girls, Danielle and Emma. The story began with the desire of a wealthy Italian businessman and his Portuguese wife, living in France, to have a third child. (They were already parents, via surrogate births, of a son and a daughter.) The couple asked Claire Austin, an English surrogate mother, to bear the baby for them, and then went looking for donors of sperm and eggs. The latter came from an anonymous Englishwoman, the former from an American man. On February 28, 1999, a doctor in Athens carried out the procedure of implantation.

Twenty weeks into the pregnancy, Miss Austin learned she was carrying twin girls. Her doctor was appalled: The couple wanted a boy—one boy. Miss Austin was told she should terminate the pregnancy. She was unwilling to do so, but she had no formal agreement to appeal to (surrogacy is illegal in France). Nor did she know to whom the children belonged— after all, they were genetically related neither to her nor to either member of the commissioning couple. Eventually she found Growing Generations, an adoption agency based in Los Angeles that specialized in "unconventional parents.

"The agency located a couple living in Hollywood: Tracey Stern, a scriptwriter for the television programs ER and Buffy the Vampire Slayer, and Julia Salazar. Stern and Salazar agreed to adopt the twins, who are now being looked after— by a nanny from Puerto Rico.

Do you think that in using another example involving celebrities, the author may have reduced the impact of his argument?

What anecdotes suggest, research confirms: Over the last four decades, marriage and family life have undergone an extraordinary transformation, yielding arrangements as temporary and as fragile—and as widespread—as those detailed above.

"The scale of marital breakdown in the West since 1960 has no historical precedent and seems unique," exclaims the

Lawrence Stone (1919–1999) was an eminent social historian who wrote on the family.

distinguished historian Lawrence Stone. "At no time in history, with the possible exception of Imperial Rome, has the institution of marriage been more problematic than it is today," adds the demographer Kingsley Davis. In the judgment of James Q. Wilson, America's preeminent social scientist, we are witnessing a "profound, worldwide, long-term change in the family that is likely to continue for a long time."

Postmarriage society

Scholars now speak of an ongoing trend toward a "postmarriage" society, one in which commitments to spouses and children are increasingly limited, contingent, and easily broken. Marriage itself is far less permanent, and far less of a social norm, than ever before in living memory. Concomitantly, Americans have seen a stunning rise in (among other social indices) divorce, out-of-wedlock births, unwed teen mothers, abortion, the numbers of children living in single-parent homes, and the numbers of cohabiting couples. In many of these categories, our country now has the dubious honor of leading the industrialized world.

The author uses irony to emphasize his point that the traditional family unit is in decline in the United States.

A little later on, I will be tracing the devastating effect of these trends on all sectors of our society, and especially on the poor and the defenseless among us. But I should note right at the outset that not everybody agrees the effects have been devastating; that, to my mind, is part of the problem. A few years ago, for example, Shere Hite, the author-researcher of the *Hite Reports* on human sexuality, urged upon us "that the breakdown of the family is a good thing" (emphasis added) and that today's "new living arrangements" may be "one of the most important turning points of the West." Last year, *Time* magazine published an article by the influential feminist Barbara Ehrenreich on the desirability of institutionalizing the crack-up of the family by formally replacing yesterday's "one-size-fits-all model of marriage" with a different and better model: "renewable marriages, which get re-evaluated every five to seven years, after which they can be revised, recelebrated, or dissolved with no, or at least fewer, hard feelings."

Shere Hite is a cultural historian and feminist internationally recognized for her work on psycho-sexual behavior and gender relations. She published a series of articles on sexuality, family, and gender relationships that became collectively known as the Hite Reports. For further information go to www.hite-research.com/.

What is family?

These voices … suggest is that when it comes to marriage and family life, everything is now up for grabs. More so than at any other time in human history, we share no common understanding of marriage and the family.

Marriage itself, detached from any objective foundation, is seen by many as possessing little or no intrinsic worth but as being a means to an end: the end, that is, of "personal happiness" or "fulfillment." In the quest for fulfillment, spouses and children are often looked upon not as persons to be loved and valued for their own sake but as objects to be acquired, enjoyed, and discarded.

Bennett argues that marriage and children can sometimes be seen as acquisitions. Is that a harsh comment on society?

Deconstructing family life

Like the breakdown of the family itself, this cultural deconstruction of family life and its purposes has no historical precedent. It has left us open to doubts about some of our most basic understandings: about the parent-child bond, about marital permanence, about the link between marriage, sex, and procreation.

It has already dragged innumerable children and adults into the very opposite of "personal happiness," and it threatens to undo altogether a precious historical achievement.

Summary

Does society support family values? Jennifer Ballen and Oliver Moles, analyzing various programs that complement school education for children, argue that it does. They suggest that the community includes resources— from mentors and role models to senior citizens—who can help parents inculcate values in young people. Around half of all Americans, they argue, believe that social support is necessary to help parents combat the rise in antisocial behavior connected with alcohol, drugs, and violence. They quote examples of various successful programs around the country to support their argument.

William J. Bennett, in an extract from a longer book on the state of marriage in America, argues that the rising number of broken marriages suggests that the very notion of family values is under threat. Marriage has changed, he suggests, and often no longer reflects the kind of values that society needs. He cites the case of a lesbian couple who have had a child. It seems that personal happiness, rather than community feeling, shapes people's actions today. While it is not possible to predict the results of such an unprecedented development, Bennett argues that individual lives have already been affected by the decline in marriage. It is possible that the very foundations of the society he calls "a precious historical achievement" are also under threat.

FURTHER INFORMATION:

Books:

Lasch, Christopher, *Haven in a Heartless World*. New York: W.W. Norton & Co., 1995.

Useful websites:

http://www.statelocal.gov/index.html
U.S. State and Local Gateway site, which has useful statistics on family, divorce, drug abuse, and so on.
http://monitoringthefuture.org/
Site featuring the *Monitoring the Future* study.
http://www.ncoff.gse.upenn.edu/
National Center on Fathers and Families, includes information on recent initiatives.
http://www.ed.gov/PressReleases/10-1997/edchild.html
Article on former Vice President Al Gore's promotion of father and family relationships.
http://www.bbbsa.org/about/aboutimpact.html
Big Brother Big Sister Association site, featuring details of the mentoring system, recent news, and how to get on to the system.

DOES SOCIETY SUPPORT FAMILY VALUES?

YES: No one can become a responsible member of society without the kind of values that families teach children

YES: Despite changes in society, most people still have the same basic values, such as honesty

VALUES
Are family values really important?

OUT-OF-DATE
Are family values still the same as society's values?

NO: There are many different places to learn about positive values, such as at church or even from the media

NO: Society has become more violent and selfish. Values like trust and honesty are naive in a society in which so many people are dishonest.

DOES SOCIETY SUPPORT FAMILY VALUES?
KEY POINTS

YES: Children from a broken home only have one role model. It is better to have as many role models as possible.

YES: It is not coincidence that the rise in divorce in the United States parallels a decline in community values in the nation

HAPPY FAMILIES
Does the breakdown of the traditional family inevitably lead to a decline in values?

NO: A broken home is a more positive environment for a child than living with parents who are always fighting, or where the family is dysfunctional

NO: Many single parents raise children with strong value systems. There are also many sources of support for child raising, such as community groups and education-based projects.

Topic 2

IS THE FAMILY THE SOURCE OF PREJUDICE?

YES
FROM "LESSONS: UNDERSTANDING PREJUDICE"
WEARETRAVERSECITY.COM
M'LYNN HARTWELL

NO
FROM "DISLIKING OTHERS WITHOUT VALID REASONS: PREJUDICE"
CHAPTER 7, ANGER AND AGGRESSION
PSYCHOLOGICAL SELF-HELP
CLAYTON E. TUCKER-LADD

INTRODUCTION

Merriam-Webster's Tenth New Collegiate Dictionary gives the following definitions for "prejudice": "a (1): preconceived judgment or opinion (2): an adverse opinion or leaning formed without just grounds or before sufficient knowledge b: an instance of such judgment or opinion c: an irrational attitude of hostility directed against an individual, a group, a race, or their supposed characteristics." Racism, sexism, ageism (discrimination on the grounds of age), religious intolerance, even snobbery are all forms of prejudice.

One glance at the television news or at the daily newspapers shows how widespread prejudice is. According to the National Criminal Reference Service, in 1999 there were 7,876 hate crime incidents reported to the FBI, and figures for previous years are similar. Hate crimes are offenses motivated by prejudice such as racial bias (4,295 of the reported incidents

in 1999), religious bias (1,411 incidents), sexual orientation bias (1,317 incidents), ethnicity/national origin bias (829 incidents), disability bias (19 incidents), or a combination of these biases (5 incidents).

There are many organizations and initiatives against prejudice. For example, the Juvenile Diversion Project is the Anti-Defamation League's alternative sentencing program. Alongside or as a replacement for imprisonment it tries to change the attitudes and behaviors of young people convicted of hate crimes and turn them into activists against prejudice. Statistics support the program's policy of concentrating on young offenders. According to the Justice Department's Bureau of Justice Statistics (BJS), of about 3,000 hate crimes recorded in around a dozen states from 1997 through 1999, 31 percent of the perpetrators were aged under 18.

But where do our prejudices come from? Are they passed on from family member to family member, or do they develop elsewhere as a result of outside influences?

History shows us that prejudice is not new. The Jews, for example, have long been a persecuted group. The most extreme example of the persecution was during World War II (1939-1945), when the German leader Adolf Hitler (1889-1945) had approximately six million Jews exterminated in death camps. Hitler's National Socialist (Nazi) Party recognized the importance of the family in spreading its anti-Semitic message. Children were indoctrinated with Nazi philosophy at school and by their families. They were also given nursery books filled with anti-Semitic imagery.

> *"Never try to reason the prejudice out of a man. It was not reasoned into him and cannot be reasoned out."*
> —SYDNEY SMITH (1771–1845), ENGLISH ESSAYIST

Black people have also suffered from prejudice. Part of the reason that slavery lasted so long in the United States was that the white community was educated through schooling, books, the media, and the family to believe that blacks were inferior to whites intellectually, socially, and morally. Such examples of bias are greater in scope and destructive effect than most of the prejudice encountered from day to day but often not different in principle.

Prejudice takes root in our belief system—the principles on which we act, whether consciously or not. Where do these principles come from? The noted psychoanalyst Sigmund Freud (1856-1939) believed that most of our character is formed in very early infancy. Others—for example, the celebrated English poet Philip Larkin (1922-1985)—suggest that childhood (rather than just our very early infancy) is the most formative period of our lives. In his poem "This Be the Verse" Larkin consequently suggests that your parents mess you up, adding, "They may not mean to, but they do/ They fill you with the faults they had/ And add some extra, just for you."

While the family may have some responsibility in passing on certain viewpoints on race, gender, or religion, for example, some educators argue that other factors enter the equation. Clayton E. Tucker-Ladd, for example, suggests that deprivation can lead to prejudice. He goes on to explain that prejudice has been created under experimental conditions by designating people as "haves" or "have nots" or as "powerful" or "powerless." Prejudices may also be perpetuated simply because they are financially rewarding.

The following two extracts examine where prejudice comes from. In the first M'Lynn Hartwell suggests that the family is a cause of prejudice. She proposes that one of the reasons prejudices instilled by the family often remain is that even as an adult, it is too painful for an individual to confront the sources of those prejudices, his or her family. In the second article, however, Clayton E. Tucker-Ladd argues that other factors help form prejudice.

LESSONS: UNDERSTANDING PREJUDICE
M'Lynn Hartwell

YES

☑ I have described some of the attitudes and ideas that are used by people to justify their hatred. What I have described are their prejudices.

Providing a definition of a key term or concept, particularly one from a dictionary, is a very good way to begin your argument.

One dictionary definition of prejudice is:
An adverse opinion or leaning formed without just grounds or before sufficient knowledge; an irrational attitude of hostility directed against an individual, a group, a race, or their supposed characteristics.

Since prejudice is defined as an attitude that is irrational, hostile, and without basis in fact, why would people hang on to such ideas? Of course, they don't identify their ideas as irrational, hostile, or unfounded. To the contrary, such ideas often form the cornerstone of an individual's, a family's, a community's belief system—that set of ideas and attitudes that influence the standards by which people conduct their lives.

Unless there is a reason to be analytical about one's belief system, and more often than not there isn't, the fact that prejudices are passed from generation to generation gives them an aura of authority and truth, even when they are products of folklore and fantasy with no grounding in reality.

Take a moment to analyze your belief system. Can you think of any ideas that you hold that might owe more to fantasy than fact?

You have, no doubt, been exposed to ideas in your own family that you later discovered to be more about superstition than fact. It is unlikely that you will pass on those ideas as gospel, but possibly fragments will get integrated into your thinking, since the hold that family custom has on us all can be very strong.

What compels individuals to stay invested in their prejudices?… It makes life easier to have beliefs that appear to define what's okay and what isn't about other people's behavior, and more importantly, about one's own behavior.

A "stereotype" is one group's oversimplified view of what people in another group are like.

Prepackaged judgments about right and wrong feel safer because they are shared with other like-minded people—there is the endorsement of majority thinking and a reason not to have to do the hard work of figuring out the morality of every situation life presents. The problem is that in this process stereotypes and the other hallmarks of bigotry are perpetuated and sanctioned by religious and political groups with self-serving agendas.

COMMENTARY: Racial segregation

A group of white supremacists protest against integration in Alabama.

The segregation or separation of people according to race began in the United States after the Civil War (1861–1865). In the South state legislatures made discriminatory practice official by enacting the Jim Crow Laws—"jim crow" being a derogatory term for a black person. Those laws required black people to use separate public facilities from those used by white people. For example, black people had to travel in special sections on public transportation and attend black-only schools and colleges. Although strongest in the South, segregation also occurred elsewhere in the United States. Opposition to segregation began around World War II (1939–1945), and President Truman outlawed segregation in the U.S. armed forces in 1948. In 1954 the National Association for the Advancement of Colored People (NAACP) was instrumental in persuading the Supreme Court to declare segregation in schools unconstitutional. That decision triggered a federal move to end educational segregation, often in the face of violent protest. From the late 1950s the civil rights movement under the leadership of Dr. Martin Luther King, Jr., campaigned for racial equality. The movement helped bring about the passage in 1964 of the Civil Rights Act, which outlawed discrimination in many areas of life, and the Voting Rights Act (1965), which enabled black people to register to vote without being the victim of discriminatory tactics such as literacy tests. That legislation gave the federal authorities weapons with which to break down segregation, but even at the end of the 20th century a certain amount of separation along racial lines still existed in the United States.

A major conduit of prejudice is the family. Where strong prejudices exist in a family their influence becomes part of the socialization of the children. Will these individuals retain their prejudices once they reach adulthood? Many of us grew up in prejudiced families.

The draw of attitudes originating in the formative years is very powerful. It is only when equally powerful ideas impact our belief system in adulthood that prejudices learned early will likely be moderated or relinquished. How close one stays to the family culture is the key.

A response to unfounded bigotry

In my experience, gay and lesbian people who have left the family fold to live their adult lives have been able to move away from family prejudices as well. Having been exposed to unfounded antigay and lesbian bigotry, you probably have also learned to reject intolerance more quickly than your heterosexual counterparts.

Has Hartwell made a convincing case that gays are less prone to be prejudiced than nongays, or should she have provided evidence to back up her statement?

This is not to say that gay and lesbian people have no prejudices. One need only to look at the tensions between the greater gay and lesbian community, their minority brothers and sisters, or some of the religious fundamentalists, to know that prejudice is alive and well in the gay world. But I believe that in the main gays are less likely to be co-opted by the prejudices learned in their families because lesbians and gays tend to move away from the family culture more often, and more quickly, than non-gay people tend to do.

Strict rules of Mormonism

A form of Christianity, Mormonism was founded in the United States in the 19th century by Joseph Smith (1805–1844). Its largest branch, the Church of Jesus Christ of Latter-day Saints, is based in Salt Lake City, Utah, and had about 10 million followers worldwide in 2000.

One family culture that people have particular trouble moving away from is that based in the Mormon religion. Mormon families impose strict rules on how their adult children should live their lives. If these children as adults do not move away from the Mormon culture, the likelihood is that all learned prejudices will be kept intact along with everything else that is part of the Mormon family's teachings.

While the lessons of Mormonism are largely about healthy living, much of their teaching is highly prejudicial to anything that does not follow the Mormon religion. To ask these people to question their prejudices is to challenge the monolith of Mormon theology.

Even when a given family culture is not as binding as that of the Mormons, some adult children never grow independently of the family, never become truly self-defining individuals. Such people need to continue to please mom and dad, either directly, or as they have internalized them.

These folks spend the rest of their lives courting parental approval by not deviating from what they were taught as children. To ask these people to question their family's prejudices is to ask them to defy and rebel against their loved and feared parents.

A third condition that often insures adults will have the same prejudices as their families has to do with the way they were disciplined as children. If their parents were harsh disciplinarians, using authoritarian methods to teach obedience, it is likely the adult child will have an authoritarian personality —what social psychologists identify as the "prejudiced personality"—rigid thinking, intolerant, and punitive.

Another version of the prejudiced personality results when individuals are taught obedience by parents who threaten the withdrawal of love as a major means of discipline. The child's life is spent figuring out how to earn affection and avoid abandonment. These people grow up feeling insecure and fearful, angry at parents but unable to express that anger or, often, to even admit it to their own consciousness.

Prejudice down the generations

These are the candidates to become hard-core haters—full of unresolvable rage, ready to displace their hostility on any group. They hate Jews, blacks, "women libbers," fags, dykes, queers, all foreigners, anyone different from them and identifiable as "dangerous." Their reservoir of anger is never depleted because they don't get to express it to the appropriate people —the parents who caused their anguish in the first place.

These are the kinds of people who are most likely to perpetuate an unbroken cycle of bigotry generation after generation. They replicate the culture they grew up in, usually complete with the kinds of discipline and the rules of love they experienced in their own families. Their prejudices are embedded in their view of the world, a view they pass on to their children. This is prejudice as legacy, unquestioned because to do so would be to confront fears too deep to fathom, or resentments too threatening to deal with.

Do you agree that children do not want to challenge their family's values? What about children who rebel against their parents?

Go to www.google.com, and see if you can find any evidence to support the argument that violent criminals are sometimes the product of strict family upbringings.

DISLIKING OTHERS WITHOUT VALID REASONS: PREJUDICE
Clayton E. Tucker-Ladd

NO

Where do prejudices come from?

Prejudice is a premature judgment—a positive or a negative attitude towards a person or group of people which is not based on objective facts. These prejudgments are usually based on stereotypes which are oversimplified and overgeneralized views of groups or types of people. Or, a prejudgment may be based on an emotional experience we have had with a similar person, sort of our own personal stereotype. Stereotypes also provide us with role expectations, i.e. how we expect the other person (or group…) to relate to us and to other people. Our culture has hundreds of ready-made stereotypes.…

Do you agree that these values represent standards in society? What other examples are there?

When we are prejudiced, we violate three standards: reason, justice, and/or tolerance. We are unreasonable if we judge others negatively without evidence or in spite of positive evidence or use stereotypes without allowing for individual differences. We are unjust if we discriminate and pay men $\frac{1}{3}$ more for the same work as women or select more men than women for leadership positions or provide more money for male extra-curricular activities in high school than for female activities. We are intolerant if we reject or dislike people because they are different, e.g. of a different religion, different socioeconomic status, or have a different set of values. We violate all three standards when we have a scapegoat, i.e. a powerless and innocent person we blame for something he/she didn't do.…

Gordon Willard Allport (1897–1967) was an eminent U.S. psychologist who wrote several books, including The Nature of Prejudice, *published in 1954. William Edward Burghardt DuBois (1868–1963) was a U.S. sociologist, writer, and editor and cofounder of the National Association for the Advancement of Colored People (NAACP) in 1909.*

Allport, DuBois, and other thinking on prejudice

Gordon Allport (1954) has deeply influenced psychologists' thinking about prejudice, namely, that it is a natural, universal psychological process of being frustrated or hostile and then displacing the anger from the real source to innocent minorities. This explanation implies that prejudice takes place in our heads. On the other hand, ninety years ago, a great black scholar, W. E. B. DuBois, reminded whites that prejudice doesn't just spring from the human mind in a vacuum (Gaines & Reed, 1995). It is exploitation, not just a mental process, that contributes to prejudice against the minority and to self-doubts within those discriminated against....

Following DuBois, many sociologists see prejudice as caused by social problems, such as over-crowding in urban areas, overpopulation, unemployment, competition between groups, etc. It has been found, for example, that persons who are low in socioeconomic status or have lost status are more prejudiced, perhaps because they look for people to blame—for scapegoats. Rural and suburban America have always looked down on the poor, urban dweller—80 years ago it was the Jews, Italians, and Irish, today it is the blacks, Mexicans, Puerto Ricans, etc. In effect, the victims of city life were and are blamed for the crime and deterioration there. That's not fair, is it? Also, competition between groups, as we will see, increases the hostility: Jewish and black businesses compete in the slums, black and white men compete for the same intensive-labor jobs, men and women compete for promotions, etc.

Experimentally created prejudice

The Zimbardo "Prison Experiment" created negative, prejudiced attitudes just by placing some people in power over others who were powerless. One might wonder if the same thing happens between management and workers in industry? There are other examples of instant prejudice. One third-grade teacher in Riceville, Iowa, gave a lesson in discrimination. The teacher divided the class into two groups: blue-eyed and brown-eyed. Each group got the same special privileges and praise on alternate days. On the days their group was favored, the students felt "smarter," "stronger," "good inside," and enjoyed keeping the "inferiors" in their place. The same children on the deprived days felt tense, unsure of themselves, and did poorer work. They learned within a few hours to feel and act negatively toward "friends." Humans seem much better at learning prejudices than math....

This experiment was conducted by Philip G. Zimbardo and other researchers at Stanford University in the summer of 1971. The researchers studied the behavior of a group of volunteers who had been arbitrarily designated as "prisoners" and "guards." Go to the experiment website at www. prisonexp.org to find out more.

Psychologists have other explanations

Psychologists suggest we learn prejudiced attitudes via several other processes. Examples: We may learn to discriminate because prejudice pays! Slave owners certainly profited greatly from slaves. In the past, parents profited from having lots of obedient children. Factories profit from low paid workers. Bosses profit from bright, able secretaries who work for 40% less than males. We can impress certain people and curry favor with them if we are prejudiced, e.g.

a prejudiced parent, friend, or boss likes us to hold the same views....

Belittling beliefs are just as destructive as being hit with a tire tool or refused a job; yet, the beliefs were learned and used without realizing the ignorance and unfairness involved. This unthinking conformity to beliefs of our social group happens frequently.... [T]hese stereotypes are resistant to change. By their unpleasant, hostile nature, stereotypes discourage intimate contact with the "target" persons so that one doesn't discover what individuals of that type are really like. However, if one does have contact, the prejudice may become a self-fulfilling prophecy....

Are stereotypes always hostile? Can you think of any "positive" stereotypes?

Personality and prejudice

What kind of people would follow an aggressive ... prejudiced leader? The classic book on this topic is *The Authoritarian Personality*. [The] authors described several traits of authoritarian leaders, like Hitler, and their followers, like the German people:

The author refers to a highly respected source to reinforce his argument. The Authoritarian Personality was written by Adorno, Frenkel-Brunswick, Levinson, and Sanford and published in 1950.

1. Rigid, unthinking adherence to conventional, middle-class ideas of right and wrong. The distinction has to be made between (a) incorporating ... universal values and (b) having blind allegiance to traditional social-political-religious customs or organizations....

2. Respect for and submission to authority–parents, teachers, religion, bosses, or any leader. This includes a desire for a strong leader and for followers to revere the leader, following him (seldom her) blindly....

3. They take their anger out on someone safe. In an authoritarian environment (family, religion, school, peer group, government), the compliant, subservient, unquestioning follower stores up unexpressed anger at the authority. The hostility can't be expressed towards the authority, however, so it is displaced to an outsider who is different—a scapegoat....

4. They can't trust people. They believe "people who are different are no good." ...

5. Because they feel weak, authoritarian personalities believe it is important to have a powerful leader and to be part of a powerful group. Thus, they relish being in the "strongest nation on earth," the "master race," [and so on]....

6. Over-simplified thinking. If our great leaders and our enormous government tells us what to do, if our God and our religion directs our lives, then we don't have to take responsibility for thinking or deciding....

7. Guard against dangerous ideas. Since the authoritarian already has a handle on the truth, he/she opposes new ideas, unconventional solutions, creative imaginations....

8. I'm pure, others are evil. The authoritarian represses his/her aggressive and sexual feelings, then projects those traits on to stereotyped persons in the outgroup....

"Ethnocentrism" means taking the attitude that everything belonging to one's own group is superior.

9. Ethnocentrism: Everything of mine is better than yours—my country, my religion, my kind of people, my family, my self....

This picture of an authoritarian isn't pretty. How many of these people are there? Zimbardo's "prison study" suggests that the potential for authoritarianism may be quite high, given the right circumstances. It is estimated that at least 80% of us have prejudices. Hostility (especially the you-are-not-my-equal and I-don't-care-about-you type) abounds in the world....

The author suggests that eight out of ten people have prejudices. Do you think that anyone can be truly without prejudice?

Summary

M'Lynn Hartwell suggests that the family is a major influence in the creation of prejudice. She contends that "the fact that prejudices are passed from generation to generation gives them an aura of authority and truth," and the retention of these beliefs is linked to how close a person stays to his or her "family culture." People who move away from the family to live their adult lives, she observes, can discard family prejudices. Some children, though, never gain the ability or willingness to question their beliefs later in life. Some children, as adults, never stop wanting to please their parents, and children of authoritarian parents are likely to grow up "rigid thinking, intolerant, and punitive." Additionally, the author suggests, children whose parents threaten to withdraw their love as a punishment grow up angry at their parents, and this anger, instead of being directed at the parents, finds expression as prejudice.

Clayton E. Tucker-Ladd acknowledges the theory of displaced anger but also argues that many sociologists view social factors as being to blame for prejudice. For instance, he suggests that persons of low socioeconomic status blame others for their perceived predicament. Economic competition between groups also creates hostility. The author goes on to report that prejudice can seemingly be created by placing people in a position of power over powerless individuals. He also states that according to psychologists, people have learned that prejudice can pay off financially, citing examples such as the slave trade and inequalities in pay in the modern office. The author also looks into the "authoritarian personality" and lists characteristics required by a prejudiced leader and his or her followers.

FURTHER INFORMATION:

Books:

Adams, Maurianne, et al. (editors), *Readings for Diversity and Social Justice: An Anthology on Racism, Sexism, Anti-Semitism, Heterosexism, Classism, and Ableism.* New York: Routledge, 2000.

Stern-LaRosa, Caryl, and Ellen Hofheimer Bettmann, *The Anti-Defamation League's Hate Hurts: How Children Learn and Unlearn Prejudice.* New York: Scholastic, 2000.

Webster-Doyle, Terrence, and Rod Cameron (illustrator), *Why Is Everybody Always Picking on Us? Understanding the Roots of Prejudice.* Trumbull, CT: Weatherhill, 2000.

Useful websites:

http://usinfo.state.gov/usa/race/
State Department page on U.S. race and ethnic diversity.
www.aclu.org
Site of the American Civil LIberties Union.

The following debates in the Pro/Con series may also be of interest:

In *Individual and Society*:

Topic 1 Is inequality a problem?

Topic 2 Is it possible to live in a nonracist society?

Topic 3 Are women still the second sex?

Topic 6 Should affirmative action continue?

IS THE FAMILY THE SOURCE OF PREJUDICE?

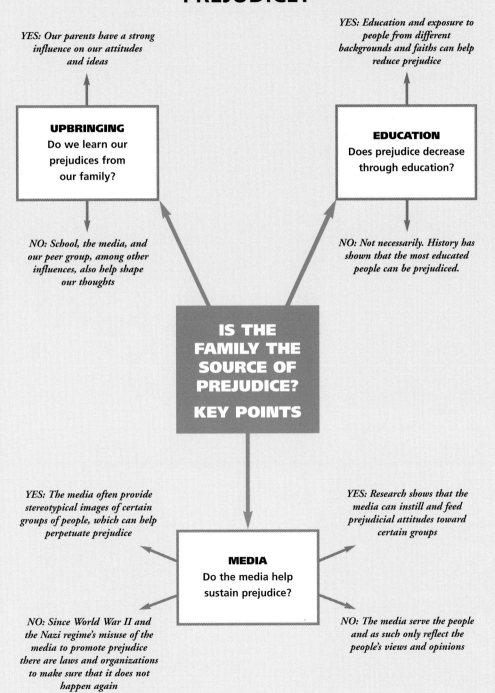

YES: Our parents have a strong influence on our attitudes and ideas

YES: Education and exposure to people from different backgrounds and faiths can help reduce prejudice

UPBRINGING

Do we learn our prejudices from our family?

EDUCATION

Does prejudice decrease through education?

NO: School, the media, and our peer group, among other influences, also help shape our thoughts

NO: Not necessarily. History has shown that the most educated people can be prejudiced.

IS THE FAMILY THE SOURCE OF PREJUDICE?

KEY POINTS

YES: The media often provide stereotypical images of certain groups of people, which can help perpetuate prejudice

YES: Research shows that the media can instill and feed prejudicial attitudes toward certain groups

MEDIA

Do the media help sustain prejudice?

NO: Since World War II and the Nazi regime's misuse of the media to promote prejudice there are laws and organizations to make sure that it does not happen again

NO: The media serve the people and as such only reflect the people's views and opinions

Topic 3
IS MARRIAGE ESSENTIAL TO THE FAMILY UNIT?

YES
FROM "THE IMPORTANCE OF MARRIAGE"
WWW.FAMILYFIRST.ORG/CAPITOLWATCH/0899.SHTML
FAMILYFIRST.ORG

NO
FROM "ROSIE'S STORY"
ABC NEWS.COM, MARCH 14, 2001
REBECCA RAPHAEL

INTRODUCTION

Marriage is the socially and sometimes legally acknowledged union between a man and a woman, whose resulting offspring are seen as the legitimate children of those parents.

Marriage exists in a variety of forms in different societies. In Western countries "monogamy," in which a husband or wife has one partner, is most common. "Polygyny," in which a man may be married to more than one wife at one time, is acceptable in Muslim societies. Traditional communities, such as the Nayars in India, practice "polyandry," in which one wife is shared by a group of men, usually brothers—but that is quite rare today.

The modern family unit encompasses a variety of parent-child situations. They include the traditional nuclear family headed by a heterosexual married couple, single-parent families, cohabiting couples with their own or step-children, and gay people parenting foster or adopted children. Thus marriage does not necessarily form the basis of most families today.

In recent years marriage has actually declined in industrialized Western countries. That has resulted in a lot of discussion about whether marriage is important to the modern family unit.

According to "What's Happening to Marriage," an article published by the National Marriage Project, marriage remains "an important life goal. Indeed, the vast majority of Americans will marry at least once in a lifetime." But the 2000 Census showed that fewer than a quarter of American households were made up of married couples with children. *The New York Times* also noted that in the 1990s the number of single-mother families with children had grown nearly five times faster than the number of married couples with children.

Changing demographic patterns have contributed to the decreased incidence of marriage. Historically, many marriages were arranged for economic, social, or political reasons, but in the last hundred years or so that type of arrangement has declined—although it still exists in many developing countries and in ethnic communities living in Western countries today. For many centuries women were economically dependent on their husbands. But after the Industrial Revolution more women began to enter the workforce, a fact exacerbated by World Wars I and II, when women were called on to perform traditionally male jobs.

> *"A man and a woman marry because both of them don't know what to do with themselves."*
> —ANTON CHEKHOV, 19TH-CENTURY RUSSIAN DRAMATIST

Greater educational opportunities also opened up certain previously inaccessible jobs to women, enabling more of them to become financially independent. As a result, some chose to concentrate on their careers and marry later, if at all. Economic well-being also resulted in more people choosing to leave unhappy marriages—today around 40 percent of marriages end in divorce.

Feminism and the sexual revolution have also meant that single-parenthood is no longer viewed as a sin. Thus more women are choosing to raise

children on their own—although some critics argue that this has more to do with the welfare system, which has encouraged the growth of single-parent families. Others argue that the current decline in marriage has less to do with economics and more to do with the fact that marriage has lost its religious significance.

Most orthodox religions believe that the purpose of marriage is to procreate and to enable men and women to live together in mutually supportive relationships. Christians, for example, believe that marriage is important since it is not only a gift from God, but a relationship in which men and women can support each other and be faithful while providing a stable framework for children to grow up in. Muslims similarly believe that Allah created "mates" for men and women and that out of that union "sons and daughters and grandchildren" would grow. Since marriage is perceived as such an important relationship, many religious groups now hold premarriage seminars and marriage guidance sessions.

Yet many children are currently growing up in nontraditonal families. In 2000 the General Social Survey (GSS) of the National Opinion Research Center at the University of Chicago found that although 73 percent of children lived with married parents in 1972, that percentage had dropped to 51.7 in 1998. It also found that marriage was "less central and cohabitation more common." The World Congress on Families also reported that by 1995 almost 50 percent of women between the ages of 25 and 29 had lived in nonmarital cohabitation.

The following two articles examine the issue in greater depth.

THE IMPORTANCE OF MARRIAGE
Familyfirst.org

YES

✓ If someone told you that they had a remedy for poverty, out-of-wedlock births, crime, and a host of other social ills, how would you respond? Even a cynic would at least want to hear what this person had to say. The truth is that the remedy is not really such a mystery; a growing body of social-scientific evidence demonstrates that the root cause of poverty, crime, and many of the problems attendant thereto are linked undeniably to the presence or absence of marriage.

Disrupted families

For more information about the effects of divorce on children read Robert Hughes, Jr.'s article "The Effects of Divorce on Children" at www.hec.ohio-state.edu/famlife/divorce/effects.htm.

Children in families disrupted by divorce and out-of-wedlock birth do worse than children in intact families on several measures of well-being. Broken families earn less and experience lower levels of educational achievement. There is a direct statistical link between single parenthood and virtually every major type of crime. And while the public is generally aware of the correlation between these problems and the breakdown of the family unit, most are probably unaware of the breadth of the supporting evidence.

The following is a brief overview of the research demonstrating the links between broken families and poverty, crime, and children's well-being:

Poverty

Using bullet points is a constructive way of clarifying your argument.

- Fatherless children are six times more likely to live in poverty than children living with both parents. (U.S. Department of Health and Human Services, National Center for Health Statistics, Survey on Child Health, Washington, D.C., 1997).
- Almost half of American families experience poverty following a divorce. (Julia Heath, "Determinants of Spells of Poverty Following Divorce," Review of Social Economy, Vol. 49 (1992), pp. 305–315).
- Seventy-five percent of all women who apply for welfare benefits do so because of a disrupted marriage or a disrupted relationship in which they live with a male outside of marriage. (Organization for Economic Cooperation and Development, Factors Affecting the Labor Force Participation

of Lone Mothers in the United States, prepared by the Panel on Evaluation Factors Affecting the Labor Force Participation of Lone Mothers, Paris, 1989).

- The vast majority of children who live with a single parent are in households in the bottom 20 percent of earnings. Specifically, about 74 percent of families with children in the lowest income quarter are headed by single parents. Conversely, 95 percent of families with children in the highest quarter of income are headed by married parents. (Bureau of the Census, Current Population Survey, 1997).

- Over 12.5 million children in 1994 lived in single-parent families that earned less than $15,000 per year. Only 3 million such children lived with families that had annual incomes greater than $30,000. (Bureau of the Census, Current Population Survey, 1994).

According to the Census Bureau, in 1999 the number of single-mother families with children under 18 remained constant at 9.8 million.

Crime

- According to the U.S. Department of Health and Human Services, 70 percent of all juveniles in long-term correctional facilities did not live with their father growing up. In fact, a case study in Wisconsin revealed that nearly 88 percent of juvenile delinquents in state custody came from broken homes.

- A 1996 survey relating to the family background of jail inmates revealed that 60.3 percent grew up in broken homes. Furthermore, 46 percent indicated that a family member had been incarcerated. (Bureau of Justice Statistics Special Report, "Profile of Jail Inmates 1996," 1998).

- There is a strong correlation with the number of single parent families and the crime rate in cities with a population of over 100,000. (From the Journal of Legal Studies).

- According to a study conducted by the University of Pennsylvania, young men who grow up in homes without fathers are twice as likely to end up in jail as those who come from traditional two-parent families.

Eighty-four percent of children who live with one parent live with their mother. For more information see www.singleparent central.com/ factstat2.htm.

Do you think it is important for fathers to be present at home while their children are growing up?

Children's well-being

- According to a study published in Psychological Reports, children of broken families experience significantly lower self-esteem and poorer self-concepts than children of intact families. The former also report more depression.

- The U.S. Department of Health and Human Services reported that children of never-married mothers are more than twice as likely to have been treated for an emotional or behavioral problem.

37

- Children whose parents separate are significantly more likely to experience conduct and mood disorders, engage in early sexual activity and abuse drugs. This effect is especially strong for children whose parents separated when they were five years old or younger. (David M. Ferguson, John Horwood, and Michael T. Lynsky, "Parental Separation, Adolescent Psychopathology, and Problem Behaviors," Journal of the American Academy of Child Adolescent Psychiatry, 33, 1994).

U.S. and UK studies show that daughters of divorced parents are more likely to engage in early sexual intercourse outside marriage.

Nebraska statistics

Nebraska is not exempt from these problems. During the 1990's, Nebraska has averaged 6,351 divorces per year. Since 1980, the percentage of out-of-wedlock births has increased every year, except for a slight dip in 1995. In 1998, over 26 percent of births were to out-of-wedlock mothers. Statistics reveal that the average income of Nebraska women heading their families is $14,000.

Anti-family government policies

As healthy, intact families are replaced by living situations that lead to crime, abuse and a myriad of other problems, the burden on society will also become greater, and society itself will be less equipped to cope with it. Unfortunately, anti-family government policies have played a role in creating the current problem. Examples of such policies include the proliferation of no-fault divorce laws; welfare policies which provide disincentives for marriage; and family discriminatory tax policies (i.e. the marriage penalty, federal estate taxes, the earned income tax credit).

A "no-fault divorce" is one in which neither party is judged to be at fault; the key factor is that there is no real prospect of reconciliation.

Support for marriage

However, federal, state and local governments can play important roles in rebuilding the family to ensure that children escape the inherent problems associated with the disruption of marriage and out-of-wedlock births. One of the most effective things the State can do is adopt general policies and positions favoring marriage and the stability of two-parent homes. For instance, the State could encourage a public service ad campaign espousing the benefits of marriage. Given the high social costs associated with divorce and out-of-wedlock births, dollars expended on such a campaign would be money well-spent.

Other possible actions could include changes in no-fault divorce laws, better enforcement of child support laws, and revamping school curricula to ensure that the benefits of marriage and costs of divorce are fairly covered. In the

More than a third of schools now teach pupils abstinence from sexual intercourse and have stopped giving lessons on contraception.

private sector, businesses should be encouraged to become "pro-parenting" by doing such things as allowing flex time so that at least one parent can be home when the kids arrive after school. Churches and communities can also play vital roles by providing more parent surrogates for the parentless. Where parents are missing or unwilling to uphold their responsibilities, mentoring programs should be supported. Research has also shown that church involvement drastically reduces the likelihood of children from broken homes falling into the dangerous behaviors that beset many of their peers. Churches can further help by instituting pre-marital counseling and taking a strong stand against divorce and infidelity. It will take an integrated approach such as this to reverse the devastating effects of a culture that has devalued marriage.

The Charitable Choice provision of the welfare reform law enacted in 1996 gives the church access to federal funds like other social service providers. Visit www.crown.org/ SingleParents to find out how faith-based programs are meeting the needs of poor single-parent families.

ROSIE'S STORY
Rebecca Raphael

Rosie O'Donnell
is an actor,
comedian, and talk
show hostess. She
was born in 1962 in
Commack, New
York. She is a
lesbian and has
adopted children
with her partner.

X "I don't think America knows what a gay parent looks like: I am the gay parent," the entertainer tells ABCNEWS' Diane Sawyer in her first in-depth interview about her sexuality.

O'Donnell has three adopted children—Parker, 6, Chelsea, 4, and Blake, 2—and says she is in "a committed, long-term life relationship" with her partner of about four years, Kelli Carpenter. She talked about her experiences as a gay parent publicly for the first time with Sawyer, hoping to bring attention to the issue of gay adoption and a Florida law that prevents gay couples from adopting.

"I totally think I'm gay"

There's no earth-shattering coming-out story, O'Donnell says, just a realization that dawned on her in a private moment.

"When all my friends in high school, my girlfriends, were going out to bars and picking up men and fooling around on the beach," she says, "I would get Diet Coke and I was the designated driver. So it was never like a priority for me. I never thought about it."

When she was 18, she thought about it. "I remember driving my car when I got my permit," she says. "I was alone and I was like, 'I totally think I'm gay.' Like I says it out loud in the car."

She first fell in love with a woman a couple of years later; but she also had male lovers. "It took me a while to understand and to figure out all the things that made me me, where I was most comfortable, who I was, and how I was going to define my life," she says. "And I found the coat that fit me."

Her sexuality never has been and is not now "a big deal" for her, she says. "Part of the reason why I've never said that I was gay until now was because I didn't want that adjective assigned to my name for all of eternity. You know, gay Rosie O'Donnell."

O'Donnell, who lost her mother when she was 10 and describes her father as "not very available," says being gay was not that big of an obstacle in her generally difficult childhood. Still, she believes that being gay is incredibly challenging.

Do you think that
O'Donnell's own
upbringing gives
her more or less
understanding of
what a child needs
from its family?

"I don't think you choose whether or not you're gay," she says. "Who would choose it? It's a very difficult life. You get socially ostracized. You worry all the time whether or not you're in physical danger if you show affection to your partner. You're worried that you're an outcast with your friends and with society in general."

Florida case strikes a chord
Though there has been speculation that she chose to discuss her sexuality only because her talk show will come to an end this May, the actress/comedian says that is not so.

"I wanted there to be a reason" to talk about her sexuality, she says. And when she learned about a Florida gay parenting case, she found that reason and has made it her cause.

Steve Lofton and Roger Croteau are raising five HIV-positive children, three of whom are foster kids. The couple were able to adopt the other two in Oregon. The family was thrown into disarray when the state of Florida told them they had to give up one of their foster children, Bert, whom they have raised for 10 years. Lofton and Croteau would like to adopt Bert, but under Florida law they can't, because they are gay.

When O'Donnell read about the Lofton-Croteau case, she thought about her adopted son Parker: "My Lord, if somebody came to me now and said … 'We're going to take him now because you're gay,' my world would collapse. I'm lucky to have adopted my children, not in the state that I live, Florida. I'm lucky, because otherwise I would be in danger of losing my children."

The right to parent
O'Donnell says her own experiences as a mother make her certain that gay people should have the right to be parents.

"I know I'm a really good mother. I know it. I'm a really good mother. And I have every right to parent this child," she said. "It takes a lot to become a foster parent … You have to really want to save a child who others have deemed unsaveable. And for the state of Florida to tell anyone who's willing, capable, and able to do that, that they're unworthy, is wrong."

Asked about President Bush's statement—as well as the staunch belief of many—that children ought to be adopted only by a man and a woman who are married, O'Donnell says: "… President Bush is wrong about that…. [I]f he'd like, he and his wife are invited to come spend a weekend at my house with my children…. I'm sure his mind would change."

Being gay, she says, does not make someone a bad parent. And while the children of gay parents may face some ridicule

Visit www.lethimstay.com for more information on the Lofton-Croteau gay parenting case.

See the commentary box on the Florida ban on gay adoption on page 42.

For a transcript of President George W. Bush's (2001–) statement on gay adoptions visit www.gayvote.com/gayvote/candidates/record.html?record=1518.

COMMENTARY: Florida ban on gay adoption

Twenty-five years ago former beauty queen Anita Bryant led a successful campaign to abolish a Miami law banning discrimination against gay people. It was in the climate of homophobia created by Bryant's antigay crusade that in 1977 Florida legislators voted to ban gay adoption. Elaine Bloom, a former member of the House from Miami and one of those who had voted in favor of the ban, is now one of many people making efforts to get the law changed. "We expressed our shame at having been part of the people who voted in 1977," she says, admitting that the law was passed at a time when people knew little about gay parenting.

While there is much support for a change in the law, there are some Floridians who would stand in the way. Republican Randy Ball, a state legislator from Cape Canaveral and ex-marine, defended the gay adoption ban on *Primetime* and wrote letters to a number of newspapers stating his belief that homosexuals lead "unstable lives, as a rule."

The decision to change the law was triggered by gay parent and entertainer Rosie O'Donnell's public stand on the matter and her interview on *Primetime*. Further publicity included placing full-page advertisements in three Florida newspapers pressing for a change in the law.

O'Donnell used her own publicity to highlight the case of the Lofton-Croteau family. Steven Lofton and Roger Croteau, two gay men, are successfully parenting five HIV-positive children. They were able to adopt two of the children before coming to live in Florida, but the other three are Florida foster children. One of them, Bert, has been with the couple since he was nine weeks old and is now almost 11, but is due to be adopted by a heterosexual family. This situation has arisen because, as a gay couple in Florida, Steven and Roger cannot adopt Bert.

The Lofton-Croteaus are one of three families being represented by the American Civil Liberties Union (ACLU) in a landmark case challenging Florida's gay adoption ban. The ACLU's appeal is supported by the fact that the huge number of children currently in foster care could be adopted immediately if qualified but gay parents were allowed to come forward.

The ACLU's case is also backed by the American Academy of Pediatrics (AAP), alongside mainstream health and child welfare groups who support second-parent adoption by lesbian and gay parents' same-sex partners. The views of these groups are guided by a desire to see children get what they really need—love, guidance, stability, and security—and strengthened by the knowledge that the 568,000 children in foster care and the 117,000 children waiting to be adopted would fare far better in a loving, stable home environment whether heterosexual or gay.

On the other side Sandy Rios, president of Concerned Women for America, says the AAP has "ignored the mountain of research showing that children do best in mother-father, married households."

from their peers, O'Donnell thinks they can get past that.

"I do think the kids will get teased, and you know, in some capacity that's very sad, and eventually I think that will stop. … I'm not asking that people accept homosexuality. I'm not asking that they believe like I do that it's inborn. I'm not asking that. All I'm saying is don't let these children suffer without a family because of your bias."

For further information on lesbian and gay rights visit www.aclu.org.

The foster care system

O'Donnell is trying to keep the Lofton-Croteau family together, but she's also hoping to shed light on the hundreds of thousands of children who are lost in America's foster care system.

"I was stunned into action. I mean I never knew that there were half a million kids in foster care in America," says O'Donnell. "There are over 350,000 children with nowhere to go—children who are most likely aged out of the system, and go either directly on welfare or directly to jail. It stunned me as an adoptive parent."

With so many children aching for a family, she says, "I don't think that restricting the pool of adoptive parents is beneficial."

Most states do not specifically prohibit gay people from adopting children. Florida is the toughest of only three that do prohibit the practice because it prohibits adoptions by gay individuals as well as by gay couples.

O'Donnell dismisses claims that children adopted by gay parents are more likely to be gay. As for her own children, she says she hopes they will be straight. "I do. I think life is easier if you're straight. I hope that they are genuinely happy, whatever they are. That if they're gay, they know they're gay and they live a happy life. But if I were to pick, would I rather have my children have to go through the struggles of being gay in America, or being heterosexual? I would say heterosexual."

After emphasizing how much easier it is to be straight than gay, she says she wouldn't change her own sexuality. "I think if I could take a pill to make myself straight, I wouldn't do it, because I am who I am, and I've come to this point in my life and I'm very happy."

Summary

Is marriage essential to the family unit? Current statistics would indicate otherwise, but it is not just a case of figures. How is the family fairing in a country with declining marriage rates, increasing rates of cohabitation and single parenthood, and high divorce rates?

The first article, "The Importance of Marriage," presents a strong case for marriage being essential to the family unit. The author argues that the "root causes of poverty, crime, and many of the problems attendant thereto are linked undeniably to the presence or absence of marriage." Giving numerous statistics to support high poverty, crime, and child welfare rates among children raised outside of marriage, the author goes on to suggest how things could be improved. The article proposes that federal, state, and local government could play important roles in rebuilding the family and that changes in current law, such as the no-fault divorce legislation and child support laws, would also help reinforce the importance of marriage to society and the child.

In the second article Rebecca Raphael presents a positive case for gay parenting outside of marriage. She cites as her example Rosie O'Donnell, a gay parent with three adopted children, who believes that gay people should have the right to be parents. O'Donnell challenges President Bush's statement that children should be adopted only by a married man and woman. From her personal experience she believes that gay people can and do make good parents. O'Donnell goes on to say that with so many children in foster care in America, "I don't think that restricting the pool of adoptive parents is beneficial." The article concludes that it is better for children to be looked after in a loving, caring family unit than neglected in a foster home.

FURTHER INFORMATION:

Books:

Lasch, Christopher, *Haven in a Heartless World: The Family Besieged.* New York: W.W. Norton & Company, 1995.

Wilson, James Q., *The Marriage Problem: How Our Culture Has Weakened Families.* New York: HarperCollins, 2002.

Articles:

Rauch, Jonathan, "The Widening Marriage Gap." *National Journal,* May 19, 2001.

Useful websites:

www.unmarried.org/
Site of Alternatives to Marriage project.

http://marriage.rutgers.edu
Site of National Marriage Project.

The following debates in the Pro/Con series may also be of interest:

In this volume:

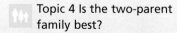

Topic 4 Is the two-parent family best?

Topic 5 Do gay couples make good parents?

IS MARRIAGE ESSENTIAL TO THE FAMILY UNIT?

YES: Scientific studies show that children from intact marriages are far more emotionally stable than those that are not

YES: By entering into this legal contract, couples show that their intention is to stay together

STABILITY
Does marriage create a more stable home in which to rear children?

COMMITMENT
Do married couples show greater commitment to themselves and to their families?

NO: The key factor in creating a stable home for children is the relationship between the parent or parents and their children

NO: The increase in divorce rates shows that increasing numbers of married couples do not remain committed to each other or their families

IS MARRIAGE ESSENTIAL TO THE FAMILY UNIT?
KEY POINTS

YES: It is outdated to expect relationships to last forever. The divorce rates show that marriage is not important to the family.

YES: Marriage is a legally binding contract that protects the emotional and financial rights of both parties

DIVORCE
Surely the increase in divorce rates indicates the insignificance of marriage to the family?

LEGAL RIGHTS
Does marriage provide the family with greater legal protection?

NO: The statistics just show how easy it is to get a divorce. Since one in three marriages is a remarriage, people still think marriage is important to the family unit.

NO: Cohabitation is far more practical and avoids lengthy legal battles over children, finances, and other matters

TEAM DEBATE

"Those who cannot understand how to put their thoughts on ice should not enter into the heat of debate."
—FRIEDRICH NIETZSCHE (1844–1900), GERMAN PHILOSOPHER

If we are to live in a democratic society, we must be able to discuss issues. This requires the ability to learn and inform ourselves by listening to alternative points of view. Issues can often be complex, and a good debate should involve in-depth research and an informative approach. There are many times in our lives when we will need to work with other people to present and discuss an issue or idea. This may be at school, at college, or in the workplace. Debating is a skill that is required even in daily conversation.

Team debate

A debate is a formal discussion that takes place between two teams. The affirmative team and the negative team take turns presenting opposing views on an agreed statement. Each team is awarded marks by the adjudicator or judged by the audience. A timekeeper ensures that each speaker uses the allocated time. The chairperson organizes and controls the debate.

Preparation

Debate is a team event, and so you must be able to work as a group. Group decisions should be unanimous in order to avoid later conflict. The skills you learn from working with other people, such as communication, listening, and empathizing, are invaluable. The following points will give you some clear guidelines:

- Choose the leader of your debating team. He or she should be strong and confident. Select someone who will encourage the group to work together.
- Choose the order of your speakers. Try to use each individual's strengths.
- Look carefully at the moot (or statement). Discuss and research it with your team. Outline a research plan to make sure that everyone understands their individual focus point.
- Decide on how your team will approach the debate. What are the key points you wish to raise? Have you got evidence to support them?
- Discuss possible arguments that the opposing team might make. This will assist in the development of your team's argument. You must be prepared for alternative opinions.
- Write your debate speeches. Work together to avoid repetition and to ensure all issues and facts are covered (see *Argumentation Skills,* pages 60–61, in the *Economics* volume).
- Make sure you have a clear team approach. Does the argument come across clearly?
- Most importantly, work together. Listen to each other's opinions and ideas.

GENERAL DEBATING TIPS

The following factors should always be taken into consideration when entering into a debate:

Evidence   Be sure of your facts, since evidence may be disputed. You should be able to cite your source. When researching, it is best to check with more than one source to ensure that information is unbiased. Evidence should be objective and unemotional.

Clarity   Avoid generalizations. Use terms that are objective to prevent the opposing side from using any subjective language to their advantage. For example, terms such as "liberals" may easily be misconstrued—always clarify your definitions.

Opposition   Your argument will be stronger if you take the time to fully investigate its refutation (examination and rebuttal of the opposing argument). Practice your argument with your team, peers, and family to help you examine different opinions.

Teamwork   Work as a team to construct your argument. The whole team must work together to create a cohesive and structured case for debate.

CONTENT AND PRESENTATION

You may be judged on your debating skills. If you are taking part in an official debate, study the grading sheet to understand how points are awarded. The following advice should also be useful.

Content
- **Introduction**: Clearly outline your argument. Use voice, body language, and eye contact to engage the audience.
- **Ideas**: Should be of good quality and show development.
- **Refutation**: Present a strong attack on the opposing argument.
- **Peroration**: Reiterate main points in concluding remarks or summary.

Presentation
- **Voice**: Vary the pace and pitch to engage the audience.
- **Body language**: Present yourself as confident. Avoid slouching or excessive movement.
- **Personality**: Win over your audience. Don't hesitate to use humor when it is appropriate.
- **Eye contact**: Appeal to your audience; look at them each individually.

PARENTS AND PARENTING

INTRODUCTION

In 1992 former Vice President Dan Quayle criticized the award-winning TV show *Murphy Brown* for advocating single motherhood. While Quayle's comments caused much heated debate, they also served to highlight that the perceived norm of two married heterosexual parents living together in the same household is outdated. This section examines issues in parenting.

In 2000 the U.S. Census Bureau reported that more than a quarter of children under 18 lived with one parent. More than four-fifths of them lived with their mother, who in many cases was either separated or divorced from her husband. However, a growing number were women who were simply opting to bring up their children alone. Similarly, the numbers of gay and single people fostering and adopting children has also risen, as has the number of transracial adoptions,

While many people applaud these developments in parenting, some critics claim that the changes have contributed to the rising rates of juvenile crime and teenage delinquency in the United States. They argue that parents are failing to take responsibility for the actions of their children— whether it be through neglect or simply lack of time.

Two-parent families

Those same critics claim that two parents are the best option for children.

Topic 4 examines this subject in greater detail, looking at whether two parents really do provide a better and more stable environment. Jacqueline Kirby in the "yes" article asserts that for the first time in history children are more likely to live with a single parent for reasons other than death. She claims that single-mother families are more likely to live in poverty. Kirby argues that this could be prevented by encouraging marriage and promoting the two-parent family through education, among other things.

In the "no" article authors Cake, Hanson, and Cormell examine single-parent adoptions. They argue that single parents want to have children to share their own happy experience of childhood with them. They also claim that single parents can focus all their attention on bringing up a child. They assert that having two parents is not necessarily a better option.

Gay and transracial parenting

While advocates of the single-parent family tend to support adoption by single people because it provides unwanted children with a chance for a better future, the question of who makes a good parent is still controversial.

Gay parenting has received a lot of media attention in recent years mainly via a series of high-profile court cases. Recent studies show that around 14 million children live with a gay parent. Topic 5 asks if gay parents are good parents. The "yes" article is an extract from an American Civil Liberties Union (ACLU) factsheet on gay parenting, adoption, and fostercare. It deals with the myths and realities surrounding the subject. The ACLU argues that there is no statistical evidence to show that gay parents are unfit. Timothy J. Dailey, however, disagrees. He asserts that research on homosexual parenting is poor and that in reality the gay lifestyle is harmful to children, who actually require both a mother and a father.

However, recent research has shown that there are around 500,000 children

Black Social Workers, which is strongly opposed to transracial adoption, and argues that there is more to bringing up a child than just love and money. Whatever standpoint one takes on these issues, parenting has become a key issue in the United States, and many people are asking if some of the current problems in society are actually the fault of parental neglect.

Parental responsibility?

To many critics of current family life absentee fathers are a major problem. There are, however, a growing number of men who want to have more parental rights. But is that necessarily a

---

"Oh what a tangled web parents weave,
When they think their children are naive."
—OGDEN NASH (1902–1971), POET

---

living in fostercare and 100,000 of them are waiting to be adopted. Thus, should sex or race prevent children from having a loving, stable home?

Gay parenting is not the only contentious issue when it comes to adoption though. In 1998 around 15 percent of the 6,000 adoptions of fostercare children were transracial ones, but many critics question whether parents are able to bring up children of other races with an understanding of their own culture.

Topic 6 deals with this issue. In the "yes" article Elizabeth Bartholet draws on her own experience to argue that the relationship between parent and child transcends racial difference. Clark Kaufman, on the other hand, looks at the views of the National Association of

good thing? In the "yes" article of Topic 7 Jayne Keedle claims that we live in a society that favors mothers, and that is unfair since many fathers want more access to their children; she asserts that fathers matter too. Beth Owen, however, disagrees, stating that men do not deserve more parental rights since many of society's ills are the result of "bad" fathers.

Raffique Shah goes further in Topic 8, claiming that legislation should be introduced to make delinquent parents accountable since they invariably cause delinquent children.

However, an extract from an interview with the Oklahoma bomber's father shows that sometimes, even with loving parents, certain people simply commit crimes.

Topic 4

IS THE TWO-PARENT FAMILY BEST?

YES
FROM "SINGLE-PARENT FAMILIES IN POVERTY"
SINGLE PARENTS LIVING IN POVERTY, VOLUME 1, ISSUE 1, SPRING 1995
JACQUELINE KIRBY

NO
FROM "SINGLE PARENT ADOPTIONS: WHY NOT"?
HTTP://ADOPTION.ABOUT.COM/LIBRARY/WRITES/UC120801A.HTM
CAKE, HANSON, AND CORMELL

INTRODUCTION

According to the Census Bureau's annual report on families and living arrangements in 2000, about 27 percent of all children under the age of 18 lived with one parent. The majority of them—about 84 percent—resided with their mother. Recent research shows that the number of children living with one parent will increase during the 21st century. But what effect does being part of a one-parent family have on the children concerned? Is living with two parents better for a child?

The writer Barbara Dafoe Whitehead claims that "divorce and out-of-wedlock childbirth are transforming the lives of American children." Whitehead argues in her book *The Divorce Culture* that the concept of divorce has changed from that of last resort to one of entitlement, and that as a result, children are being increasingly neglected.

A survey carried out by the National Center for Health Statistics (NCHS) asserted that children living in two-parent families are two to three times less likely to suffer from behavioral problems. They are also less likely to drop out of school, to have teenage pregnancies, or to commit crimes. The NCHS similarly found that children with two parents still living together were less likely to suffer sexual abuse, although other studies have shown that families with two parents, especially since 1945, have an equally high incidence of alcholism and abuse.

Yet the census figures still illustrate that more than a quarter of children today live in single-parent families. That is the result of a number of factors, such as fewer people choosing to marry, more people refusing to stay in relationships that are not working, more women deciding to bring up children by themselves, and more single people being allowed to adopt or foster children.

If single-parent families are a fact of U.S. society, is there any point in trying to turn back the clock and promote the two-parent family as an ideal? As one woman wrote in a letter published in *The New York Times*, "Let's stop moralizing or blaming single parents … and give them the respect they have earned and the support they deserve."

Sara McLanahan and Irwin Garfinkel argued in their 1986 book *Single Mothers and Their Children* that half of single mothers lived below the poverty line and that divorce always brings a decline in the standard of living for the mother and child. Similarly, they found that single-mother families tended to suffer from welfare dependency, which from the evidence they surveyed seemed to pass from generation to generation. Other research shows that relationships between children and their mothers weaken after divorce, and mother-daughter relationships deteriorate during adolescence. But critics argue this has a lot to do with the way that single-parent families are perceived in U.S. society.

> *"Your family, my family—which is composed of an immediate family of a wife and three children, a larger family with grandparents and aunts and uncles."*
> —DAN QUAYLE, FORMER VICE PRESIDENT

The media continue to promote the image of the two-parent family as the best option. Since the 1950s television shows such as *I Love Lucy* and *Father Knows Best* have presented two parents living happily with with their

children as the norm. There are now more television shows and films showing single-parent families. However, in 1992 then Vice President Dan Quayle criticized the television show *Murphy Brown* for advocating single motherhood. This prompted the show's creator, Diane English, to say, "To all you mothers out there who are raising your children alone either by choice or necessity, don't let anyone tell you you're not a family."

Despite signs that the two-parent family is not always ideal, the government continues to promote it. The 1996 Welfare Reform Bill required every state to develop policies to reduce out-of-wedlock births. Subsequently, in September 2001 the District of Columbia, Alabama, and Michigan were each awarded bonuses of $25 million for achieving the largest decreases in this area. Health and Human Services Secretary Tommy G. Thompson said, "By emphasizing the importance of marriage and family, we can change the culture of poverty into one of responsibility and success." President George W. Bush's administration has also allocated millions of dollars to abstinence education to help reduce the high rate of teenage pregnancy.

Critics argue that such policies simply serve to underline that single parenthood is something to be ashamed of. They assert that this standpoint is unrealistic in a climate in which more single people are fostering and adopting children. Furthermore, they state that prevailing problems have more to do with lack of love, respect, and morality in most families today, whether they have two parents or one. The two articles that follow examine the argument.

SINGLE-PARENT FAMILIES IN POVERTY
Jacqueline Kirby

This article was written in 1995. Go to www.census.gov/ population/www/ socdemo/hh- fam.html for latest figures on families and living arrangements.

Why might so many children live with their mothers rather than their fathers?

One of the most striking changes in family structure over the last twenty years has been the increase in single-parent families. In 1970, the number of single-parent families with children under the age of 18 was 3.8 million. By 1990, the number had more than doubled to 9.7 million. For the first time in history, children are more likely to reside in a single-parent family for reasons other than the death of a parent. One in four children are born to an unmarried mother, many of whom are teenagers. Another 40 percent of children under 18 will experience parental breakup.

Ninety percent of single-parent families are headed by females. Not surprisingly, single mothers with dependent children have the highest rate of poverty across all demographic groups…. Approximately 60 percent of U.S. children living in mother-only families are impoverished, compared with only 11 percent of two-parent families. The rate of poverty is even higher in African-American single-parent families, in which two out of every three children are poor.

Effects on children

Past research has indicated that children from single-parent families are more likely to experience less healthy lives, on the average, than children from intact families. For instance, children growing up with only one parent are more likely to drop out of school, bear children out of wedlock, and have trouble keeping jobs as young adults. Other consequences include risks to psychological development, social behavior, and sex-role identification.

In a study to determine cause and effect a "confounding variable" is a factor that the researcher does not or cannot take into account but that can still affect the results.

However, recent reviews criticize the methodology of many of these studies which support the "deviant" model of single-family structures. Confounding variables, such as income and social class, explain a large portion of the negative findings. When income is considered, substantially fewer differences arise between the intellectual development, academic achievement, and behavior of children in single-parent and two-parent families. Lack of income has been identified as the single most important factor in accounting for the differences in children from various family forms….

Poverty

Mother-only families are more likely to be poor because of the lower earning capacity of women, inadequate public assistance and childcare subsidies, and lack of enforced child support from nonresidential fathers. The median annual income for female-headed households with children under six years old is roughly one-fourth that of two-parent families. However, the number of children per family unit is generally comparable, approximately two per household.

For further debate on child support and its enforcement see Topic 7 Should fathers have more parental rights?

Childcare costs

One of the major expenditures of single parents is childcare. On average, a poor mother spends 32 percent of her total weekly income on childcare. This percentage nearly doubles when more than one child needs care. For this reason, 65 percent of single parents are turning to informal, unpaid arrangements—such as extended family or neighbors—as alternatives to formal day care (Schmottroth, 1994). Although this form of childcare may allow the single parent's limited income to be distributed across a greater set of needs (i.e., housing, clothing, food), quality of care may be sacrificed.

Poor, single, working parents often are forced to choose between quality and flexibility of childcare arrangements. Many jobs offering adequate pay require long and/or irregular hours. For many single parents, this may mean using less well-trained or experienced childcare providers who are working long hours or supervising too many children.

Approximately 53 percent of single mothers are not in the work force because they are unable to find affordable, quality, childcare. The majority of these mothers have no high school diploma, leaving them with few job opportunities or jobs that pay only the minimum wage. Parents with two or more children often have little money left after paying taxes and childcare. As a result, single parents are forced to stay home and apply for public assistance to ensure adequate housing, food, and medical coverage for their children.

In October 2002 the federal minimum wage was $5.15 per hour, having last been raised by Congress on September 1, 1997. Go to www.dol.gov/dol/esa/public/minwage/main.htm for more information about the minimum wage.

African-American single mothers and their children may experience the most adverse consequences of unemployment because their earnings constitute a greater percentage of their total family income. The reasons cited for this disparity are that African-American mothers are less likely to [be] awarded child support payments, to receive child support payments, or to have a second wage earner living in the household…. Long-term unemployment markedly increases the likelihood of poverty, receipt of public assistance, negative life changes, and exposure to public assistance, negative life changes, and exposure to chronic, stressful conditions, such as inadequate housing and poor neighborhoods.

Poverty's effects on parenting

Income loss appears to affect the well-being of children indirectly through negative impact on family relations and parenting. Single parents experience a variety of stressors related to poverty (i.e., financial, emotional, social). The link between economic stress and mental health has been documented in various studies. Single mothers must obtain sufficient money to cover the most basic needs, such as food, shelter, and clothing.

Financial strain is one of the strongest predictors of depression in single parents. Higher levels of depression is predictive of more punitive disciplinary practices and decreased parental nurturance, support, and satisfaction with the parenting role….The chronic strains of poverty combined with task overload significantly increases vulnerability to new life stressors. Poor single mothers often experience a cycle of hopelessness and despair which is detrimental to both themselves and their children.

"Task overload" means not having enough time in a day to complete one's workload or having too many tasks to take care of in a short amount of time.

Overcoming difficult circumstances

Despite the seemingly insurmountable challenges facing poor single parents, many families have increasingly demonstrated themselves to be viable, well-adjusted, alternative family forms…. Many are able to function well and to promote education, resourcefulness, and responsibility in their children. Successful single parent families have adopted more adaptive functioning styles including:

1) more available personal resources, which enhances their coping effectiveness;

2) better family organization, which balances household responsibilities and decreases task overload;

3) a positive family concept, which values loyalty, home-centeredness, consideration, communication, and closeness;

4) an ability to highlight positive events and place less emphasis on negative aspects of stressful events; and

5) possessing less stress-producing, supportive social networks.

For example, adaptive mothers demonstrated strong personal authority by controlling their schedules to allow more time for relaxing activities (i.e., dating, going to the movies, talking with friends, etc.). Adaptive families possessed a sense of control over their own destiny and perceived themselves as functioning families had less frequent contact with relatives and experienced more reciprocity within these support systems than did the less adaptive families.

Implications for family life educators

While encouraging marriage is important, recognizing that women are increasingly raising children alone and are at a disproportionate risk for poverty is equally important. For many, especially those in abusive relationships, marriage or remarriage is not a viable solution. Policies are needed which will work to ensure the future health and well-being of single parents and their children.

Many opportunities exist for Family Life Educators to address these issues through proactive programming. The University of Wisconsin's Center for Families Studies (1993) outlines various ways to:

Using numbered points enables the author to present information clearly and concisely. Bullet points or subheadings can do a similar job.

1) promote strong, stable, two-parent families and improve the quality of marriage through premarital education programs which focus on self-assessment and teaching skills for strengthening relationships (i.e., effective communication);

2) provide parenting education in elementary schools, colleges, churches, and court-mandated classes for divorcing parents;

3) advocate child support enforcement, children's allowances, welfare reform, and quality childcare;

4) encourage job training and financial management education for teenagers and young adults;

5) provide educational programming to employers about workplace reforms which allow single parents to balance the competing demands of work and family;

6) educate and train local leaders to positively influence family-related legislation.

SINGLE PARENT ADOPTIONS: WHY NOT?
Cake, Hanson, and Cormell

NO

The authors begin with government statistics, which give their argument more credibility.

According to the National Council For Adoption (NCFA), as of 1997 there were half a million children in substitute care. About 22 percent of those, over 100,000 children, will be in need of a permanent home with a family. Adoption offers a wonderful opportunity for a child in need of a family. This is the focus of the adoption philosophy.

Why parents adopt

For parentless children, adoption provides the nurturing, love, and security that all children deserve. More than just providing a loving and safe environment like fostering children, adoption is a lifetime commitment to the health and welfare of another human being. In order to best secure families that will provide the best environment for a child, adoption agencies have established a set of qualifications for adoptive parents. The criteria are based on various aspects of the prospective adopting parents: age, fertility status, previous children, financial status, employment, religion, background, and marital status. All of these are important issues to consider when placing a child in a new family, however, marital status seems to be the primary focus of some debate. Concerns over single parent adoptions should be laid to rest by the many benefits singles have to offer children in need of a home.

Do you agree that these are important issues with regard to adoption? Are there any others you would like to see included?

Nurture vs. nature

Single parents adopt for many of the same reasons as married couples. Single parents have the urge to nurture and raise a child. They seek to have a family unit and share their life with another, just as married couples do.

According to an article from the National Adoption Information Clearinghouse, "Because many women have pursued careers and put off marriage and having children until they are older, they find that they have reached their thirties, without a husband, but with a compelling desire for a child." The number one reason single parents want to adopt is the fact that their own childhood was fulfilling and happy and they are ready to share that experience. Single parents approach adoption with the same commitment and devotion as a married couple.

The National Adoption Information Clearinghouse "is a national resource for information on all aspects of adoption for professionals, policy makers, and the general public."

COMMENTARY: Adoption in the United States

Laws on adoption in the United States are only about 150 years old. They were gradually introduced by the various state legislatures between 1851, when Massachusetts became the first state to act, and 1929. Until the 1850s children whose parents could not care for them could be adopted informally, but without firm expectations, or were placed as apprentices or domestic servants. With the enactment of adoption legislation, however, prospective adoptive parents could apply to a judge, who by approving their case granted their adopted child the same rights as any natural, legitimate offspring.

"Closed" and "open" adoptions

Formal adoptions remained fairly rare, however, until the end of World War I (1914–1918), when a boom took place. The trend at the time was toward secrecy in such matters, and by the 1930s a system of so-called "closed" adoptions had been put in place. Under this system the identity of the birth parents was kept secret from the adoptive parents and the child. With many adoptions being the result of illegitimate births, this situation was thought to protect (a) the child from the disgrace of having been born out of wedlock; (b) the birth parents from the stigma of having had an illegitimate child; and (c) the adoptive parents from the shame of raising a child born out of wedlock. Since the 1970s, however, changes in customs and attitudes have permitted the system of "open" adoption under which the birth and adoptive parents know each other's identities, and the former can remain in contact with the child.

Modern adoption practice

In a "traditional" adoption the child is placed with a married couple, but since about 1970 single-parent adoptions have been possible. Today all the states allow single-parent adoptions by heterosexual individuals, and most states permit adoptions by gay or lesbian individuals. In the case of unmarried couples wishing to adopt, the situation is different. Most states will not permit a couple, whether heterosexual or homosexual, to adopt unless they are legally married. There have been exceptions, though, and an alternative is for one partner to adopt a child and for the other to apply for a "second-parent adoption" for the child at a later date.

Although most adoptions take place within the same race, according to 1993 estimates (the latest available) 8 percent of adoptions are transracial, that is, parents adopting a child of another race. Included in the 1993 estimate were transracial adoptions from outside the United States, so-called "international" or "intercountry" adoption. This option has been available to prospective adoptive parents since the 1950s but burgeoned during the 1990s. In 1992, 6,472 international adoptees arrived in the United States; by 1999 the annual figure had risen to 16,396.

One argument against single parent adoptions is that it deprives children of a traditional two-parent family. Missing a father or a mother would result in emotional and physical problems for the children. One example, a study recently published in the *Journal of Personality and Social Psychology,* was performed by Vanderbilt University. [It claimed]… that daughters without fathers experience puberty earlier than girls with close, supportive relationships with two parents (Fox). Supporters of single parent adoption believe that an unstable or broken home can cause more damage to a child than the lack of an additional parent.

A stable home

With the high divorce rate in this country, single parent adoption provides a much more solid environment: a home free from the issues of an unstable, broken home and its effects on the child. Single parents are usually of higher education and have higher incomes in comparison to the country's average. They have concentrated on their careers and have established a stable home that would benefit a child. Divorced parents are dealing with emotional and financial stress, which can negatively affect a child. A *New York Times* article reports that out of one-fifth of the nation's 51.1 million Caucasian children, over half of the 9.8 million African-American children, and almost one-third of the 7 million Hispanic children live with one parent due to divorce and unwed mothers. With these types of statistics, there is no reason to discriminate against a single person for adopting a child when she/he is quite capable of providing a stable and nurturing environment.

"The adoption picture has ... changed" and there is a great shortage of adoptive parents for older children and those with disabilities. Single parents can help to fill this shortage. The majority of couples looking to adopt want a healthy Caucasian baby. However, "the number of healthy Caucasian infants available for adoption has decreased dramatically due to birth control, legalized abortion, and the decision of unwed mothers to keep their babies". Many single adults may have a career that allows time for an older child and choose not to have the physical demands of caring for an infant. Raising a child from infancy may not appeal to a career oriented person, but a school-aged child or teenager may be more appealing. A single parent may also have an expertise or a passion that would benefit a child with disabilities. A single parent does not have a spouse to split their time with and can devote their sole attention to a disabled child. In

Why do you think single parents have usually reached higher education and a higher income than the national average?

In this sense "Caucasian" means "of or relating to the white race of mankind as classified according to physical features." The term was originally used by 18th- and 19th-century anthropologists to describe the peoples of Europe, northern Africa, and parts of south and western Asia.

Does this seem like a good idea to you? Should people be able to create families without going through the process of having and caring for young infants?

addition, many single parents choosing to adopt are financially stable and can deal with the added costs of disabilities. It is a shame to watch older, disabled, or children of other ethnicities left behind when they could have the secure environment and sole-love of a single parent.

The sole beneficiary of love and attention

A single parent can provide a loving and nurturing home for a child. Adoptive singles use family and friends for extended support. As our former first lady, Hillary Clinton, said, "It takes a village to raise a child." They give the child their sole attention and all of their love. Financially, they have planned for the future and the majority of single adoptive parents are settled in their careers. With a large percentage of the population's children living in a broken home, single parents can provide the emotional, financial and physical support without the damage of divorce. If a single parent has met all other qualifications other than marriage, then there is not a valid reason to deny adoption and many reasons to approve.

The marital issue in regards to adoption will continue to be debated. One must consider that there is such a vast difference in lifestyles between now and just fifty years ago. There is a struggle to maintain morals and ways of the past yet make way for a new era and modern way of thinking. Adoption is a wonderful opportunity for a child to have the family she/he so desperately needs. One must keep in mind the main goal is to place a child by considering what is in the child's best interest and to place other assumptions aside.

The African proverb "It takes a village to raise a child" was used by Hillary Rodham Clinton as the title for a book published in 1996 and was also the theme of a speech by her in the same year. Her views triggered a political debate on children and the family. To find out more, go to www.libertynet.org/~edcivic/village.html.

Summary

In "Single-Parent Families in Poverty" Jacqueline Kirby asserts that recent research has pinpointed a shortage of income in single-parent families as being largely to blame for any unwanted behaviors or lack of development in these families' children. The author explains that poverty is endemic in single-parent families. In 90 percent of single-parent families the parent is the mother, and she often faces great difficulties in earning enough to support herself and her children, especially when she has to pay for child care while she is at work. The upshot of this economic stress can be a downward spiral of depression and despair. On a positive note, though, Kirby points out that many one-parent families adapt to their situation and show resilience, resourcefulness, and mutual support.

In "Single Parent Adoptions: Why Not?" the authors argue that there are tens of thousands of children in need of a family and that "adoption offers a wonderful opportunity." They contend that single people adopt for similar reasons as those that motivate couples but that the main impetus often stems from single parents' own happy childhoods and the wish to pass on these experiences. The authors argue that single people can provide a more stable environment for a child than the broken home of a divorced couple. They go on to suggest that in a changing adoption landscape, in which "the number of healthy Caucasian infants available for adoption has decreased dramatically," single parents may come into their own. Single parents may be suited to adopting older children and may also have the love to spare and the financial means to take care of a disabled child. The authors state, "One must keep in mind the main goal is to place a child by considering what is in the child's best interest and to place other assumptions aside."

FURTHER INFORMATION:

Books:

Edin, Kathryn, *Making Ends Meet: How Single Mothers Survive Welfare and Low-Wage Work*. New York: Russell Sage Foundation, 1997.

Lasch, Christopher, *Haven in a Heartless World: The Family Besieged*. New York: W. W. Norton, 1995 (reprinted).

Articles:

Dafoe Whitehead, Barbara, "Dan Quayle Was Right." *The Atlantic Monthly*, April 1993.

Useful websites:

www.calib.com/naic/

National Adoption Information Clearinghouse site.

The following debates in the Pro/Con series may also be of interest:

In this volume:

Topic 1 Does society support family values?

Topic 3 Is marriage essential to the family unit?

Part 2: Parents and parenting

Part 4: The family and society

IS THE TWO-PARENT FAMILY BEST?

YES: *There is still a stigma attached to being a single-parent family. Children may be teased and treated differently by their peers as a result.*

YES: *Children need proper role models, and having a "mother" and "father" around helps them develop appropriate social, moral, and cultural skills*

SOCIETY
Are single-parent families treated differently by society?

SUPPORT
Does the traditional family setup provide better support to children?

NO: *Single-parent families are more common than they were and have a strong support system*

NO: *Not necessarily. An unstable two-parent home can cause more damage to a child than a stable home with a single parent.*

IS THE TWO-PARENT FAMILY BEST?
KEY POINTS

YES: *Single parents are often living in poverty, the main cause of difference in the quality of a child's upbringing*

YES: *Children learn their behaviors from their parents and are less likely to turn to crime if brought up in a stable home environment. Also, single parents are less likely to be able to spend time with their children and monitor who they are associating with and what they are doing.*

FAMILY INCOME
Can a two-parent family afford children more easily?

BEHAVIOR
Are children from two-parent families less likely to commit crime?

NO: *Many single parents enjoy a higher-than-average income; it is the income, not the number of parents, that is the important factor in a child's development*

NO: *There have been numerous "celebrity" cases of people from stable, often affluent upbringings committing horrendous crimes*

Topic 5

DO GAY COUPLES MAKE GOOD PARENTS?

YES

FROM "OVERVIEW OF LESBIAN AND GAY PARENTING, ADOPTION AND FOSTER CARE"
ACLU FACT SHEET, APRIL 6, 1999
AMERICAN CIVIL LIBERTIES UNION

NO

FROM "HOMOSEXUAL PARENTING: PLACING CHILDREN AT RISK"
FAMILY RESEARCH COUNCIL
TIMOTHY J. DAILEY

INTRODUCTION

The issue of whether gay and lesbian people should be allowed to foster or adopt children has been a contentious one for many years.

While the gay community argues that it is a fundamental human right to both have and raise a family and to be treated equally under the eyes of the law, many antigay groups assert that gay adoption or foster care is not in the best interest of the child, and that the heterosexual two-parent model is still the best kind of family unit.

According to the American Civil Liberties Union (ACLU), however, there are an estimated 500,000 children in foster care nationwide, and 100,000 of these children are awaiting adoption. In 1997 there were qualified adoptive parents available for only 20 percent of these fostered children. Similarly, according to the Child Welfare League of America, in 1996 only 1 child in every 5 available for adoption was actually placed with suitable parents.

So, if the number of children in foster homes and orphanages currently exceeds the number of people who are willing to adopt them, should adoption laws be changed to allow prospective parents to adopt who do not fit into the traditionally accepted mold? Do gay parents really make such bad parents? Are heterosexual parents so much better?

In the last 50 years or so changes in society have given rise to new definitions of what constitutes a family. In most of the Western world the orthodox family, consisting of a mother, a father, and dependent children, is no longer the norm. Most families in the United States today are made up of unmarried male and female partners and their children, single-parent families, extended families, culturally or religiously mixed families, and families parented by a gay parent or parents.

Recent research suggests that around 14 million children live with at least one gay parent across the nation. But is that about to change?

Florida prohibits gay people, both couples and individuals, from adopting, although they can serve as foster parents. Mississippi and Utah also have legislation in place to prevent same-sex parent adoption. Similarly, Arkansas, Idaho, Indiana, Oklahoma, Texas, and Utah are also considering bans on same-sex adoption and foster care.

But why is there so much resistance? In the last 25 years the gay and lesbian community has fought to reverse a series of what they argue are outdated and prejudicial laws that hamper their ability to adopt or foster children.

> *"People need to be judged on their individual fitness as to whether or not they can be adoptive parents."*
> —MATT COLES, NATIONAL DIRECTOR, ACLU'S LESBIAN AND GAY RIGHTS PROJECT

In 1981 Florida passed a law that prohibited gay and lesbian adoption. It was enacted following Baptist singer Anita Bryant's "Save our Children" campaign, originally launched in 1977.

Bryant objected to a Florida ordinance that made it illegal to discriminate against people on grounds of sexual orientation. She argued, "What these people really want ... is the legal right to propose to our children that there is an acceptable alternate way of life. ...

I will lead such a crusade to stop it as this country has not seen before." Her actions led to the ordinance's repeal and the passing of the 1981 act, but it also arguably resulted in far stronger support for the gay rights movement.

Various civil rights groups and individuals have challenged the law. The ACLU, in a highly publicized campaign, is backing five gay men who argue that Florida law discriminates against homosexuals since almost anyone else in the state can apply to adopt, even people who are single or have a history of substance abuse or violence. The campaign has received much public support, including from talkshow host Rosie O'Donnell (see Topic 3, pages 40-43).

Supporters of gay adoption and fostering argue that there is no credible research to show that children raised in a same-sex parent environment suffer. They refute the argument that children will be more likely to be abused or abuse. They further assert that a child brought up within this nontraditional framework would be less likely to have prejudices and would be more accepting of other people, regardless of sexual orientation, race, class, or gender.

Opponents, such as Ken Connor, president of the Family Research Council, argue that children should be brought up by a man and a woman. Connor asserts that adoption by gay people "trivializes the contribution that each gender ... makes to the development of children.... These roles are important to the healthy growth and development [and] maturation of a child." Connor's view is supported by many people in the United States.

The following two articles examine the pros and cons of whether gay parents can be good parents.

OVERVIEW OF LESBIAN AND GAY PARENTING, ADOPTION AND FOSTER CARE
American Civil Liberties Union

By stating the main premise of its argument at the very beginning, the ACLU makes its position very clear.

YES

☑ ...Recognizing that lesbians and gay men can be good parents, the vast majority of states no longer deny custody or visitation to a person based on sexual orientation. State agencies and courts now apply a "best interest of the child" standard to decide these cases. Under this approach, a person's sexual orientation cannot be the basis for ending or limiting parent-child relationships unless it is demonstrated that it causes harm to a child—a claim that has been routinely disproved by social science research. Using this standard, more than 22 states to date have allowed lesbians and gay men to adopt children either through state-run or private adoption agencies.

Nonetheless, a few states—relying on myths and stereotypes—have used a parent's sexual orientation to deny custody, adoption, visitation and foster care. For instance, two states (Florida and New Hampshire) have laws that expressly bar lesbians and gay men from ever adopting children. In a notorious 1993 decision, a court in Virginia took away Sharon Bottoms' 2-year-old son simply because of her sexual orientation, and transferred custody to the boy's maternal grandmother. And Arkansas has just adopted a policy prohibiting lesbians, gay men, and those who live with them, from serving as foster parents.

Do you think that being gay is a good reason for parting a child from its mother? Does sexual orientation make a parent less able to bring up a child?

Research overview of lesbian and gay parenting

All of the research to date has reached the same unequivocal conclusion about gay parenting: the children of lesbian and gay parents grow up as successfully as the children of heterosexual parents. In fact, not a single study has found the children of lesbian or gay parents to be disadvantaged because of their parents' sexual orientation.

Other key findings include:
* There is no evidence to suggest that lesbians and gay men are unfit to be parents.

- Home environments with lesbian and gay parents are as likely to successfully support a child's development as those with heterosexual parents.
- Good parenting is not influenced by sexual orientation. Rather, it is influenced most profoundly by a parent's ability to create a loving and nurturing home—an ability that does not depend on whether a parent is gay or straight.
- There is no evidence to suggest that the children of lesbian and gay parents are less intelligent, suffer from more problems, are less popular, or have lower self-esteem than children of heterosexual parents.
- The children of lesbian and gay parents grow up as happy, healthy and well-adjusted as the children of heterosexual parents. ...

Do you think that the ACLU's evidence would be more credible if it were supported by details from specific studies? Or would more details detract from the case being made?

A crisis in adoption and foster care

In the past two decades, child welfare agencies have changed their policies to make adoption and foster care possible for a much broader range of adults, including minority families, older individuals, families who already have children, single parents (male and female), individuals with physical disabilities, and families across a broad economic range. These changes have often been controversial at the outset. According to the CWLA, "at one time or another, the inclusion of each of these groups has caused controversy. Many well-intended individuals vigorously opposed including each new group as potential adopters and voiced concern that standards were being lowered in a way that could forever damage the field of adoption." As a result of the increased inclusiveness of modern adoption and foster care policies, thousands of children now have homes with qualified parents.

The Child Welfare League of America (CWLA) was founded in 1920. It is the oldest nonprofit organization in the United States whose aim is to protect children and promote and strengthen families.

Myths vs. facts

Myth: The only acceptable home for a child is one with a mother and father who are married to each other.
Fact: Children without homes do not have the option of choosing between a married mother and father or some other type of parent(s).... There simply are not enough married mothers and fathers who are interested in adoption and foster care. Last year only 20,000 of the 100,000 foster children in need of adoption were adopted, including children adopted by single people as well as married couples. Our adoption and foster care policies must deal with reality, or these children will never have stable and loving homes.

Go to http://hometown.aol.com/afresources/frc/foster.html to find links to foster care and adoption sites.

Making a statement and then using evidence to dispute it is a good tool with which to enforce a point.

When considering adoption or foster care, should it matter if the gay and lesbian people concerned are in stable relationships? Go to www.census.org, and find out how many single-parent families there are in the United States.

Myth: Children need a mother and a father to have proper male and female role models.

Fact: Children without homes have neither a mother nor a father as role models. And children get their role models from many places besides their parents. These include grandparents, aunts and uncles, teachers, friends, and neighbors. In a case-by-case evaluation, trained professionals can ensure that the child to be adopted or placed in foster care is moving into an environment with adequate role models of all types.

Myth: Gays and lesbians don't have stable relationships and don't know how to be good parents.

Fact: … [T]he majority of lesbians and gay men are in stable committed relationships. Of course some of these relationships have problems, as do some heterosexual relationships. The adoption and foster care screening process is very rigorous, including extensive home visits and interviews of prospective parents. It is designed to screen out those individuals who are not qualified to adopt or be foster parents, for whatever reason. All of the evidence shows that lesbians and gay men can and do make good parents. The American Psychological Association, in a recent report reviewing the research, observed that "not a single study has found children of gay or lesbian parents to be disadvantaged in any significant respect relative to children of heterosexual parents," and concluded that "home environments provided by gay and lesbian parents are as likely as those provided by heterosexual parents to support and enable children's psychosocial growth." That is why the Child Welfare League of America, the nation's oldest children's advocacy organization, and the North American Council on Adoptable Children say that gays and lesbians seeking to adopt should be evaluated just like other adoptive applicants.

Myth: Children raised by gay or lesbian parents are more likely to grow up gay themselves.

Fact: All of the available evidence demonstrates that the sexual orientation of parents has no impact on the sexual orientation of their children and that children of lesbian and gay parents are no more likely than any other child to grow up to be gay. There is some evidence that children of gays and lesbians are more tolerant of diversity, but this is certainly not a disadvantage. Of course, some children of lesbians and gay men will grow up to be gay, as will some children of heterosexual parents….

Myth: Children who are raised by lesbian or gay parents will be subjected to harassment and will be rejected by their peers.
Fact: Children make fun of other children for all kinds of reasons: for being too short or too tall, for being too thin or too fat, for being of a different race or religion or speaking a different language. Children show remarkable resiliency, especially if they are provided with a stable and loving home environment. Children in foster care can face tremendous abuse from their peers for being parentless. These children often internalize that abuse, and often feel unwanted....

Myth: Lesbians and gay men are more likely to molest children.
Fact: There is no connection between homosexuality and pedophilia. All of the legitimate scientific evidence shows that. Sexual orientation, whether heterosexual or homosexual, is an adult sexual attraction to others. Pedophilia, on the other hand, is an adult sexual attraction to children. Ninety percent of child abuse is committed by heterosexual men. In one study of 269 cases of child sexual abuse, only two offenders were gay or lesbian. Of the cases studied involving molestation of a boy by a man, 74 percent of the men were or had been in a heterosexual relationship with the boy's mother or another female relative. The study concluded that "a child's risk of being molested by his or her relative's heterosexual partner is over 100 times greater than by someone who might be identifiable as being homosexual, lesbian, or bisexual."

Myth: Children raised by lesbians and gay men will be brought up in an "immoral" environment.
Fact: There are all kinds of disagreements in this country about what is moral and what is immoral. Some people may think raising children without religion is immoral, yet atheists are allowed to adopt and be foster parents. Some people think drinking and gambling are immoral, but these things don't disqualify someone from being evaluated as an adoptive or foster parent.

If we eliminated all of the people who could possibly be considered "immoral," we would have almost no parents left to adopt and provide foster care. That can't be the right solution. What we can probably all agree on is that it is immoral to leave children without homes when there are qualified parents waiting to raise them. And that is what many gays and lesbians can do.

Can we really compare the harassment that children suffer from having same-sex parents to being teased about being "too thin or too fat"? Do you think a more factually based argument would work better?

According to the National Child Abuse and Neglect Data System, over 5 million children were referred to child protection agencies in 2000.

The author argues that views on what is moral or immoral differ greatly within the United States. Do you think that is true? What characteristics do you feel are important in deciding who should be able to adopt or foster a child?

HOMOSEXUAL PARENTING: PLACING CHILDREN AT RISK
Timothy J. Dailey

NO

X A number of studies in recent years have purported to show that children raised in gay and lesbian households fare no worse than those reared in traditional families. Yet much of that research fails to meet acceptable standards for psychological research; it is compromised by methodological flaws and driven by political agendas instead of an objective search for truth. In addition, openly lesbian researchers sometimes conduct research with an interest in portraying homosexual parenting in a positive light. The deficiencies of studies on homosexual parenting include reliance upon an inadequate sample size, lack of random sampling, lack of anonymity of research participants, and self-presentation bias.

> *Dailey begins his argument by discrediting recent studies on gay parenting.*

Methodology

The presence of methodological defects—a mark of substandard research—would be cause for rejection of research conducted in virtually any other subject area. The overlooking of such deficiencies in research papers on homosexual failures can be attributed to the "politically correct" determination within those in the social science professions to "prove" that homosexual households are no different than traditional families.

However, no amount of scholarly legerdemain contained in an accumulation of flawed studies can obscure the well-established and growing body of evidence showing that both mothers and fathers provide unique and irreplaceable contributions to the raising of children. Children raised in traditional families by a mother and father are happier, healthier, and more successful than children raised in non-traditional environments.

David Cramer, whose review of twenty studies on homosexual parenting appeared in the *Journal of Counseling and Development*, found the following: "The generalizability of the studies is limited. Few studies employed control groups and most had small samples. Almost all parents were Anglo-American, middle class, and well educated. Measures for assessing gender roles in young children tend to focus on social behavior and generally are not accurate psychological instruments. Therefore it is impossible to make large scale generalizations … that would be applicable to all children."

Since these words were penned in 1986, the number of studies on the subject of homosexual parenting has steadily grown. The fact that these studies continue to be flawed by the methodological errors warned about by Cramer has not inhibited the proponents of homosexual parenting from their sanguine assessment of the outcomes of children raised in homosexual households.

Silverstein and Auerbach, for example, see no essential difference between traditional mother–father families and homosexual-led families.… [T]hey suggest that "gay and lesbian parents can create a positive family context."

This conclusion is echoed in the official statement on homosexual parenting by the American Psychological Association's Public Interest Directorate, authored by openly lesbian activist Charlotte J. Patterson of the University of Virginia. "…Not a single study has found children of gay or lesbian parents to be disadvantaged in any significant respect relative to children of heterosexual parents."

> Go to
> www.apa.org/
> pi/parent.html
> to look at
> Patterson's findings.

Problems with homosexual parenting research

Upon closer examination, however, this conclusion is not as confident as it appears. In the next paragraph, Patterson qualifies her statement. Echoing Cramer's concern from a decade earlier, she writes: "It should be acknowledged that research on lesbian and gay parents and their children is still very new and relatively scarce.… Longitudinal studies that follow lesbian and gay families over time are badly needed." The years have passed since Patterson's admission of the inadequacy of homosexual parenting studies, and we still await definitive, objective research substantiating her claims.…

Research in this area has also been criticized for using poorly matched or no control groups in designs that call for such controls. … Other criticisms have been that most studies have involved relatively small samples [and] that there have been inadequacies in assessment procedures employed in some studies.…

One suspects that the lack of studies with proper design and controls is due to the political agendas driving the acceptance of homosexual parenting, which favor inadequate and superficial research yielding the desired results.

> The author argues
> that political
> agendas could be
> the reason behind
> the lack of properly
> controlled studies in
> this area. What
> other factors could
> have led to this
> situation?

In a study published in the *Journal of Divorce and Remarriage*, P. Belcastro et al. reviewed 14 studies on homosexual parenting according to accepted scientific standards. Their "most impressive finding" was that "all of the studies lacked external validity. The conclusion that there are no significant differences in children raised by lesbian mothers versus heterosexual mothers is not supported by the published research data base." Similarly, in their study of lesbian couples in Family Relations, L. Keopke et al. remark, "Conducting research in the gay community is fraught with methodological problems...."

Naming and quoting from reputable sources can enhance your argument.

The problems
Inadequate sample size. Studies examining the effects of homosexual parenting are weakened by inordinately small sample size....

Lack of random sampling. Researchers use random sampling to ensure that the study participants are representative of the population being studied (for example, homosexuals or lesbians). Findings from unrepresentative samples have no legitimate generalization to the larger population....

Lack of anonymity of research participants. Research procedures guaranteeing complete anonymity are necessary to prevent a source of bias as to who will consent to participate as a research subject, and ensure the truthfulness and candor of their answers.

Self-presentation bias. A lack of random sampling and the absence of controls guaranteeing anonymity allow subjects to present a misleading picture to the researcher that conforms to the subject's attitudes or opinions and suppresses evidence that does not conform to the image he or she desires to present....

While Dailey has previously quoted extensively from other sources to support his argument, he does not do that here. Why do you think that might be?

Harmful aspects of the homosexual lifestyle
Homosexual promiscuity. Studies indicate that the average male homosexual has hundreds of sex partners in his lifetime, a lifestyle that—is difficult for even "committed" homosexuals to break free of and which is not conducive to a healthy ... atmosphere for the raising of children....

Unhealthy aspects of 'monogamous' homosexual relationships. Even those homosexual relationships that are loosely termed "monogamous" do not necessarily result in healthier behavior....

Rate of intimate partner violence within marriage. A little-reported fact is that homosexual and lesbian relationships are far more violent than are traditional married households....

Reduced life span. Another factor contributing to the instability of male homosexual households, which raises the possibility of major disruption for children raised in such households, is the significantly reduced life expectancy of male homosexuals.

Sexual identity confusion. The claim that homosexual households do not "recruit" children into the homosexual lifestyle is refuted by the growing evidence that children raised in such households are more likely to engage in sexual experimentation and in homosexual behavior....

Go to www.google.com, and find out what the average life expectancy of male homosexuals is in comparison to male heterosexuals. Is the author right?

Children need a mom and dad

The importance of the traditional family has been increasingly verified by research showing that children from married two-parent households do better academically, financially, emotionally, and behaviorally. They delay sex longer, have better health, and receive more parental support. Homosexual or lesbian households are no substitute for a family: Children also need both a mother and a father....

According to the census figures, most children are not brought up in a family with both a mother and father present. Do you think that children really need a mother and a father to become well-balanced individuals?

Author and sociologist David Popenoe confirms that mothers and fathers fulfill different roles in their children's lives. In *Life without Father* Popenoe notes, "Through their play, as well as in their other child-rearing activities, fathers tend to stress competition, challenge, initiative, risk taking and independence. Mothers in their care-taking roles, in contrast, stress emotional security and personal safety.... "Both dimensions are critical for an efficient, balanced, and humane child-rearing regime."

The complementary aspects of parenting that mothers and fathers contribute to the rearing of children are rooted in the innate differences of the two sexes, and can no more be arbitrarily substituted than can the very nature of male and female. Accusations of sexism and homophobia notwithstanding, along with attempts to deny the importance of both mothers and fathers in the rearing of children, the oldest family structure of all turns out to be the best....

Summary

The issue of whether gay and lesbian parents make good parents is a controversial one; but as the numbers of children in foster care mount, it is becoming increasingly important to place children in loving, stable homes. The first argument, taken from an American Civil Liberties Union fact sheet, tries to dispel "myths" surrounding gay adoption. Among other things, the ACLU argues that there is no evidence to support the notion that gay parents make worse parents or that children suffer. Similarly, it asserts that gay people are capable of providing a stable, warm environment for a child to grow up in.

Timothy J. Dailey, on the other hand, argues that it is difficult to calculate the effects of gay parents on children since the studies so far have suffered from their methodology. Dailey asserts that research has shown that heterosexual parents are the best option for children. He states that children brought up by gay people are more likely to have sexual identity problems, have troubled upbringings, suffer incest or sexual abuse, and suffer as a result of their parents' sexual lifestyle.

The key map opposite sums up some of the main arguments in this debate. For further information see below.

FURTHER INFORMATION:

Books:

Moberly, Elizabeth R., *Psychogenesis: The Early Development of Gender Identity*, London: Routledge & Kegan Paul Limited, 1979.

Useful websites:

www.aclu.org

American Civil Liberties Union site features a lot of articles on gay and lesbian issues, including parenting.

http://www.apa.org/pi/parent.html

Article by Charlotte J. Patterson, which argues that having gay parents does not adversely affect children.

www.fostercare.net

Site giving advice and information on foster care in the United States.

www.census.org

Provides up-to-date information on family living conditions and summary reports.

http://www.firstthings.com/ftissues/ft9802/opinion/saltzman.html

Article by Russell E. Saltzman on adoption measures in the United States.

The following debates in the Pro/Con series may also be of interest:

In this volume:

Topic 1 Does society support family values?

Topic 3 Is marriage essential to the family unit?

Part 2: Parents and parenting, pages 48–49.

Topic 6 Should couples be able to adopt children of a different race?

Topic 8 Should parents be held responsible for the behavior of their children?

DO GAY COUPLES MAKE GOOD PARENTS?

YES: Some states still make it very difficult for gay people to adopt even when they have proved themselves to be good parents

YES: Most children would choose to be brought up by two parents in a socially accepted environment

SOCIETY
Does society discriminate against gay parents?

CHILDREN'S RIGHTS
Should the rights and views of the child be taken into consideration when deciding whether gay parents should adopt?

NO: More gay people are fostering and adopting children—the talkshow host Rosie O'Donnell is a famous example

DO GAY COUPLES MAKE GOOD PARENTS? KEY POINTS

NO: There are not enough heterosexual couples available to adopt the children in care. It is important for them to be placed in a caring, loving environment, and gay people can provide that as well as other people.

YES: Evidence shows that two heterosexual parents are the best option for children, and in any other environment they suffer

YES: Children brought up in a gay environment are more likely to be confused about sexual identity, are more likely to be abused, and are more likely to be socially challenged

MYTHS VS. REALITY
Is it true that children brought up by gay parents suffer?

NO: Children are teased about all sorts of things, from the way they dress to the car their parents drive; being teased about a parent's sexual orientation is not that different

NO: Since these children are very much wanted, they are more likely to be stable, happy, unprejudiced people

Topic 6
SHOULD COUPLES BE ALLOWED TO ADOPT CHILDREN OF A DIFFERENT RACE?

YES

FROM "ADOPTION AND RACE"
WWW.PACTADOPT.ORG
ELIZABETH BARTHOLET

NO

"TRANSRACIAL ADOPTIONS ENCOUNTER OPPOSITION"
THE DESMOINES REGISTER, NOVEMBER 13, 2000
CLARK KAUFFMAN

INTRODUCTION

In 1998 about 15 percent of the 36,000 adoptions of foster children were transracial or transcultural. But the subject of transracial adoption, or the joining of racially different parents and children in adoptive families, has been controversial for many years. The subject raises many issues concerning the family, the welfare of children, and the law. Above all, perhaps, it raises questions about race and racism. Can parents really bring up children of other races with an understanding of their true cultural heritage? Can parents even understand what life is like for people of other races in America? And can such parents deal with the racist attitudes that their transracial relationship may cause?

While critics argue that children of transracial adoption invariably suffer cultural and social feelings of inferiority and inadequacy, advocates believe the pros far outweigh the cons and that, with adequate support and education,

neither the child nor the parents in transracial adoptions need suffer.

In a 1995 report for the Heritage Foundation William H.G. FitzGerald and Patrick F. Hagan argued that two forms of racial discrimination affect transracial adoption—that against adoptive parents and that against the children waiting to be adopted. More black children are available for adoption than other races, despite the fact that statistically blacks adopt at a faster rate than whites. The report asserts that although all efforts should be made to place black children with black parents, blocking transracial adoptions discriminates against many needy children. This attitude is backed by transracial adoption specialist Professor Rita Simon, who states that all studies have shown that "transracial adoptions serve the children's best interests." Yet if that is the case, why is there still so much opposition to transracial adoption? Surely any family is better than no family at all?

The National Association of Black Social Workers (NABSW) has publicly declared its opposition to transracial adoption—specifically to the adoption of black children by white parents, declaring that the "preservation of the African-American family" formed the basis of their announcement. Their view is supported by other groups that argue that white people do not have the cultural skills necessary to teach a child of another race about his or her particular culture. Testimonies of some transracial adoptees support this view. For example, black 25-year-old Rachel Noerdlinger, who was adopted as a child by white parents, says, "Although love should be enough … [it] does not replace the importance of knowing your own ethnicity and culture."

> *"[It is] an abominable notion that race must be the dominant factor in deciding who can deliver loving care and protection to a child.*
>
> —CARL T. ROWAN,
>
> BLACK JOURNALIST

According to the National Adoption Information Clearinghouse (NAIC), however, research shows transracial adoption is a viable means of providing stable homes for waiting children. The NAIC states that 12 studies support the viewpoint that about 75 percent of all preadolescent children adjust well to their adoptive homes.

Changes in adoption laws reflect these opposing views. In October 1994

Senator Howard Metzenbaum introduced the Multiethnic Placement Act, which prohibited an adoption or foster agency that was getting federal assistance from delaying or denying the placement of a child on the basis of race, color, or the national origin of either the parents or the child involved. However, the Clinton administration supported race matching and altered the legislation so that lack of race matching could be used to delay or deny a placement. The Bunning Amendment subsequently repealed the act, but opposition to transracial adoption is still substantial.

Most government and private adoption agencies agree that parents and children involved in transracial adoptions need support and education. Pat Eldridge of the Lutheran social service says, "It is important for the parents to realize that they are not just adopting a baby, they are adding a person to the family. This child is going to grow up, start dating, marry someday, and they are going to be an interracial family from this point on." Eldridge runs workshops asking parents to question racism in their communities. There are also numerous resources for transracial families on the Internet. Is this type of support and education enough?

The following articles look at the debate further. In the first Elizabeth Bartholet of Harvard Law School uses her own experience as the mother of a transracially adopted child to argue that race should not be a barrier to love and commitment and that the relationship actually transcends racial differences. Clark Kauffman, on the other hand, suggests that love is not enough and that only those who have lived and experienced a culture firsthand can pass on heritage and culture to a child.

ADOPTION AND RACE
Elizabeth Bartholet

YES

One day when Christopher is three and a half, he says to me across the kitchen table at dinner, "I wish you looked like me." I respond, wanting not to understand him, "What do you mean?" And he says, "I wish you were the same color." I try to reassure him, telling him that it makes no difference to me that he and I look different—in fact, I like it that way. But my comments seem not to the point. He repeats that he wishes I looked like him, and his voice and eyes reveal his pain.

The author begins her article with a moving personal story. This can be an effective way in which to engage the reader's sympathy.

I am left to puzzle at the meaning of this pain. Is it one of a thousand pains that a child will experience as he discovers differences between himself and others—in this case, a difference between himself and his school friends, with their same-race parents? Is it, as the opponents would have us believe, part of a permanent anguish caused by the sense that he does not truly belong in the place where he should most surely belong—his family? Or is it simply a signal that living as part of a multiracial, multiethnic, multicultural family will force us to confront racial and other differences on a regular basis?

This child is as much inside my skin as any child could be. It feels entirely right that he should be there. Yet the powers that be in today's adoption world proclaim with near unanimity that race-mixing in the context of adoption should be avoided if at all possible, at least where black- or brown-skinned American children are involved.

Ideology

Bartholet gets to the heart of the question: whether different-race families can be "natural." What do you think? Does race really matter?

Racial matching policies represent a coming together of powerful and related ideologies—old-fashioned White racism, modern-day Black nationalism, and what I call "biologism," the idea that what is "natural" in the context of the biologic family is what is normal and desirable in the context of adoption. Biologic families usually have same-race parents and children. The laws and policies surrounding adoption in this country have generally structured adoption in imitation of biology and reflect widespread and powerful feelings that parent-child relationships will work best between biological "likes" and related fears that parents will

COMMENTARY: The Multiethnic Placement Act

The Multiethnic Placement Act (MEPA) was introduced by Senator Howard Metzenbaum (Democrat, Ohio) on July 14, 1993, and passed by the Senate on March 25, 1994. Representative Alan Wheat (Democrat, Missouri) then introduced identical legislation in the House of Representatives, and MEPA was signed into law as part of the Improving America's Schools Act in October 1994. At the time of MEPA's introduction almost 500,000 children were in foster care in the United States (an increase of 63 percent since 1984), tens of thousands were awaiting adoption, and the average length of time a child had to wait to be adopted was 2 years, 8 months. In response to these findings the purpose of MEPA was to prohibit the use of either a child's or prospective parent's race, color, or national origin to delay or deny a child's placement, and to expand the number of racially and ethnically diverse foster and adoptive parents. The act does, however, allow race, color, and national origin to be a factor in placing a child with a family if it is considered relevant to the child's best interests. In 1995 the Department of Health and Human Services (HHS) issued a detailed guide to assist states and agencies in how to implement MEPA.

In 1996 MEPA was amended by provisions for the removal of barriers to Interethnic Adoption (IEP), which was included in the Small Business Job Protection Act, to remove potentially misleading language and clarify the objectives. In its own words MEPA–IEP set out its purpose to "reduce the length of time that children wait to be adopted; facilitate the diligent recruitment and retention of foster and adoptive families; and eliminate discrimination on the basis of race, color, or national origin of either the prospective parent or the child." The IEP amendment also strengthened enforcement procedures by allowing the state to withhold adoption assistance funds from any adoption agency that did not comply with its directives and by giving the individual the right to challenge in the federal courts the state or other entity alleged to be in violation of the act.

However, MEPA–IEP has met with criticism from both sides. Organizations such as the National Association of Black Social Workers believe that the act does not give enough consideration to the importance of race and culture in adoption. On the other hand, groups such as the American Civil Liberties Union believe MEPA–IEP does not go far enough in removing all the obstacles to transracial adoption. Howard Metzenbaum, who sponsored MEPA, has also accused the HHS, the government department responsible for implementing MEPA–IEP, of being lax in enforcing it. He protests, "The social workers continue to discriminate, while the kids remain in foster homes and in public institutions. The problem lies at the doorstep of HHS.... To HHS I say ... [y]ou should be ashamed ... because it's those little kids out there, those black kids, who are not getting the benefit of the legislation that you and I authored."

not be able truly to love and nurture biological "unlikes." These feelings and fears have much in common with concerns among both Blacks and Whites in our society about the dangers involved in crossing racial boundaries. It is thus understandable that there is so much support for racial matching in the adoption context.

But the question is whether we should be so reluctant to cross boundaries of racial "otherness" in adoption—whether today's powerful racial-matching policies make sense from the viewpoint of either the children involved or the larger society. It is a question of growing practical importance. Children of color are pouring into the already overburdened foster care system. In the five-year period from 1986 to 1991, the number of children in foster care rose by 50 percent. There is increasing talk of bringing back the orphanages of the nineteenth and early twentieth centuries. Current policies stand in the way of placing the children in need of homes with available adoptive families.

Do you agree that the question is practical rather than moral?

One of the best-known images of the type of 19th-century orphanage the author is referring to appears in Charles Dickens' novel Oliver Twist.

Racial matching and evidence

The major argument made in support of racial matching is that transracial adoption would hurt children. Many claims have been made as to how and why Black children would suffer if denied a same-race upbringing. However, there is virtually no evidence in the entire body of empirical research on transracial adoption that it has a harmful effect on children. By contrast, there is extensive, unrefuted, and overwhelmingly powerful evidence that delays in permanent placement do devastating damage to children.

Picking up on weak points of evidence in opposing arguments is a good way to make a case in debates.

These studies of transracial adoption were conducted by a diverse group of researchers that included Blacks and Whites, critics and supporters. The research shows that transracial adoption works well from the viewpoint of the children and the adoptive families involved. The children are doing well in terms of achievement, adjustment, and self-esteem, and they compare well with children raised in same-race families. They seem fully integrated in their families and communities yet have developed strong senses of racial identity. The studies provide no basis for concluding that placing Black children with White rather than Black families has any negative impact on the children's welfare.

The research does indicate some interesting differences in transracially-adopted people's attitudes about race and race relations, which critics of transracial adoption cite as evidence that supports their position. But this evidence is positively heart-warming for those who believe that Blacks and Whites should learn to live compatibly in one world, with respect and concern for each other and with appreciation of their racial and cultural differences as well as their common humanity. The studies reveal that Blacks adopted by Whites appear more positive than Blacks raised by Blacks about relationships with Whites, more comfortable in those relationships, and more interested in a racially integrated lifestyle. They think race is not the most important factor in defining who they are or who their friends should be.

If there were more transracial adoptions, would society be more racially integrated?

Conclusions

These findings are taken as evidence of inappropriate racial attitudes by the critics of transracial adoption. But studies of transracial adoptive families have given voice to the positive implications seen in this evidence. Noting that transracially-adopted people perceive "their world as essentially pluralistic and multicolored," one report concludes that they represent "a different and special cohort, one socialized in two worlds and therefore perhaps better prepared to operate in both. The hope is that having had this unique racial experience, they will have gained a greater sense of security about who they are and will be better able to negotiate in the worlds of both their biological inheritance and their socialization."

"Pluralistic" in this context means a state of society in which people participate in diverse ethnic, racial, religious, and social groups while maintaining their own traditional cultures.

These conclusions challenge many of the critics' claims. Many of these adopted people have essentially as strong a sense of Black identity and racial pride as other African American children.

White families do vary as to how much they help their Black children feel part of the Black community and proud of their Black heritage, but there is no evidence that Black parents do a better job than White parents of raising Black children with a sense of pride in their racial background. Nor is there any evidence that any differences that do exist in racial attitudes have any negative implications for the well-being of those raised transracially.

Do you think the situation might be different for a white child brought up by black parents? Could black parents give that child pride in its racial background?

In the context of a society that is struggling with the issue of how to deal with racial hostilities, the studies of transracial adoptive families are extraordinarily interesting. They show parents and children, brothers and sisters, relating to one another as if race were no barrier to love and commitment. They show the Black and the White growing up with the sense that race should not be a barrier in their relationships with people in the larger social context. In a society torn by racial conflict, these studies show human beings transcending racial difference.

TRANSRACIAL ADOPTIONS ENCOUNTEER OPPOSITION
Clark Kauffman

"Genocide" is the deliberate and systematic destruction of a racial, political, or cultural group. The suggestion here is that whites who adopt black children destroy their children's relationship with their cultural heritage. Do you agree?

NO

Are hugs color-sensitive?

Amy Russell is white. Her nine adopted children are black. She has some definite opinions as to whether white couples who adopt black children are committing "cultural genocide" as some adoption experts claim. "These are my children, and I love them," says the Mount Vernon mother. "And I'm not convinced that brown arms feel any different from white arms when you need a hug."

Rudolph Smith, president of the National Association of Black Social Workers, isn't one to question a mother's love for her children, but his organization strongly opposes the adoption of black children by white couples.

Preservation of culture

"We believe in the preservation of the African-American family," Smith says. "And to that extent, we oppose our black children being adopted into any other culture or being raised by any other folks other than African-Americans. There's a lot more to raising a child than simply loving a child and providing a roof and some meals."

Smith is not alone. Federal law prohibits consideration of race in adoptions handled by public agencies, but the North American Council on Adoptable Children and the Child Welfare League of America agree with the black social workers association that agencies should make aggressive efforts to place children with parents of the same race.

For the full report from the North American Council on Adoptable Children (NACAC) see the article "Barriers to Same Race Replacement" written by Tom Gilles and Joe Droll, executive director of NACAC, at www.nysccc.org/T-Rarts/Barriers.html.

Their position stems not from a belief that whites are inferior as parents, but that white parents are incapable of instilling in black children a sense of black heritage and culture. "The only way one can instill that in an African-American child is to have some first-hand experience, some knowledge of what it is to be black in America," Smith says. "These are issues that can't be appreciated, taught or understood by someone who hasn't lived the experience."

The debate

The debate over who should be allowed to adopt black children comes at a time when minority children make up 67 percent of all children in the public foster-care system.

Should couples be allowed to adopt children of a different race?

Nicole Kidman and Tom Cruise were one of a number of celebrity couples who adopted children from a different race and culture.

For more information about the National Council for Adoption (NCFA) see their website at www.ncfa-usa.org/.

On average, a black child waits over four years for a permanent home.

William Pierce of the National Council for Adoption calls the argument that whites can't effectively raise black children "racist claptrap" that has undermined the law prohibiting public agencies—but not privately financed agencies—from considering race when placing children with adoptive parents.

COMMENTARY: Transracial and transcultural adoption trends

Transracial and transcultural adoption in the United States originated in the 1940s as a result of World War II (1939–45), when many European children were orphaned, abandoned, or separated from their parents. Many U.S. families, moved by their plight, wanted to take these children in, and the first transcultural adoptions were organized.

Korean children

The trend really took off, however, after the Korean War (1950–1953), which started the largest wave of transracial adoptions that has ever taken place in the world. For the next three decades around 150,000 Korean children were adopted by U.S. families. Until 1991 there were more transracial adoptions of Korean children than any other group; in that year only 1,817 Korean children were adopted, compared to 2,552 Romanian children. By 1999 South Korean adoptions (2,008) came in third, after Russia (4,348) and China (4,101).

Vietnamese children

Another wave of transracial, transcultural adoption followed U.S. military involvement in Vietnam (1962–1973). In 1975 a series of rescue operations known as "Operation Baby Lift" brought 2,000 Vietnamese and mixed-race children (many fathered by American soldiers) to the United States.

Closer to home

In the mid-1980s another transcultural adoption trend began, with children from poverty-ridden areas in Central America and South America, including war-torn El Salvador, being adopted by white U.S. families. Within the United States 90 percent of adopted Native American children were placed with white parents prior to 1978. By 1997 that figure had fallen to 20 percent. Since the 1970s the adoption of black children by white parents in the United States has increased due to the large numbers in foster care—in 1995, 45 percent of children in foster care were of African American origin.

Howard Metzenbaum

Former U.S. Sen. Howard Metzenbaum is the man who sponsored the law to eliminate race preference in adoptions. Today, Metzenbaum says his law has failed because the Clinton administration and Health and Human Services Secretary Donna Shalala have refused to enforce it.

"I have written them, I have beseeched them, I have needled them and I have criticized them publicly, but frankly I think the minority team over at HHS, in my opinion, has the secretary scared," he says. "It's an absolute travesty. You can have the best laws in the world, and if they're not enforced, they're not worth a tinker's damn."

Pierce says the Clinton administration is afraid to anger those who oppose transracial adoption. "You've got people who are running scared, afraid of being accused of racism," he says. "But this is not all blacks on one side of the issue and all whites on the other side. It's some blacks and some whites on one side, and some blacks and some whites on the other side."

Metzenbaum agrees, noting that his legislation was supported by Jesse Jackson and other prominent black leaders. Those leaders, however, are not the people charged with implementing the law. That job falls to front-line social workers who must match prospective parents with children in need of a home. According to the Government Accounting Office, the "long-standing social work practices and beliefs of some caseworkers" represent the biggest obstacle to colorblind adoption in America today.

Dr. Donna Shalala (1941–), secretary of health and human services under the Clinton administration (1993–2000), was the longest-serving secretary of health and human services in history. Her major policy initiatives included revision of health-care financing, expansion of the Head Start program for preschool children, universal child immunization, expansion of AIDS research, and welfare reform.

Summary

Why is transracial or transcultural adoption such a topical issue, particularly with the high number of children in foster care? Harvard professor Elizabeth Bartholet examines her own experience in "Adoption and Race." Bartholet argues that "This child is as much inside my skin as any child could be. It feels entirely right that he should be there. Yet the powers that be in today's adoption world proclaim with near unanimity that race-mixing in the context of adoption should be avoided if at all possible, at least where black- or brown-skinned American children are involved." Bartholet asserts that huge numbers of black children are pouring into an overburdened foster care system, and that while critics of transracial adoption argue that it hurts the child, in reality studies show that delays in placement do more harm. The author further argues that in a world in which racial hostility and tensions are rife, transracial adoption shows people living together irrespective of color, "human beings transcending racial difference."

Conversely, the article by Clark Kauffman, "Transracial Adoptions Encounter Opposition," looks at the views of the National Association of Black Social Workers (NABSW), which strongly opposes the adoption of black children by white people. The NABSW argues that there is more to raising a child than just loving it and putting food on the table. The author asserts that the NABSW is not alone; it is supported by other adoption agencies that believe that children should be placed in same-race families.

FURTHER INFORMATION:

Books:

Patton, Sandra, *Transracial Adoption in Contemporary America*. New York: New York University Press, 2000.

Steinberg, Gail, and Beth Hall, *Inside Transracial Adoption*. Indianapolis, IN: Perspective Press, 2000.

Fogg-Davis, Hawley, *The Ethics of Transracial Adoption*, Ithaca, NY: Cornell University Press, 2002.

Articles:

Hamlin, Jennifer "International Adoption Raises Culture Questions," *Adoptive Families*, Sept/Oct 1999.

Useful websites:

www.racerelations.about.com/library/weekly/aa121700a.htm
"Adopting by Color" on the *About* website.
www.abanet.org/publiced/focus.f96adop.html
"Thinking and Teaching about Transracial Adoption" by

Twila L. Perry for the "Focus on Law Studies" section of the American Bar Association website.

www.heritage.org/library/categories/healthwel/bg1045.html
Report for the Heritage Foundation, "Why Serious Welfare Reform Must Include Serious Adoption Reform" by Patrick F. Fagan and William H.G. Fitzgerald.

www.nysccc.org/T-Rarts/Noerdlinger.html
"A Last Resort: The Identity My White Parents Couldn't Give Me" by Rachel Noerdlinger.

The following debates in the Pro/Con series may also be of interest:

In this volume:

 Topic 2 Is the family the source of prejudice?

SHOULD COUPLES BE ALLOWED TO ADOPT CHILDREN OF A DIFFERENT RACE?

YES: There are so many children in foster care who deserve a loving, stable family to grow up in regardless of race issues

YES: Parents in transcultural adoptions can learn about a child's culture and teach its values along the way with support groups commited to helping them.

NECESSITY
Should race be less a factor when so many children in foster care need permanent adoption placements?

RACE AND CULTURE
Can parents of a different race or culture properly instill in an adopted child his or her own cultural values and pride?

NO: Love needs to be allied to a child's sense of racial and cultural identity

NO: Parents are incapable of teaching their adopted child about a culture they have never experienced. No amount of effort from support groups can make up for this.

YES: Laws like the Multiethnic Placement Act were created for the benefit of children waiting to be adopted. The laws should be clarified and enforced so that children can be placed without the delay or discrimination that deprives them of a loving home.

SHOULD COUPLES BE ABLE TO ADOPT CHILDREN OF A DIFFERENT RACE?

KEY POINTS

YES: Different races living together in loving family units will lead to a greater tolerance of other races within society

LAW ENFORCEMENT
Should the government create definitive laws in support of transracial adoption and make more effort to enforce them?

RACIAL TOLERANCE
Can transracial adoption lead to greater racial tolerance?

NO: Such laws and their enforcement will place many children in inappropriate families, and this will not be of ultimate benefit to the child

NO: It will eventually lead to the destruction of the cultures of the adopted children, which will be usurped by the cultures of the parents

85

Topic 7

SHOULD FATHERS HAVE MORE PARENTAL RIGHTS?

YES

FROM "FATHERS MATTER"

THE HARTFORD ADVOCATE

JAYNE KEEDLE

NO

FROM "THE WOMEN'S VOTE, A NEWSLETTER: COVERING ISSUES RELEVANT TO WOMEN"

THE COMMITTEE FOR MOTHER AND CHILD RIGHTS, INC., FEBRUARY 1996

BETH OWEN

INTRODUCTION

The question of parental rights often becomes an issue after the breakdown of a relationship, be it a divorce or, increasingly, when two people split up who have children but are not married. Usually the parents each move to a separate residence, and the question arises whether the mother or the father should have custody of (ultimate responsibility for) the children. If it is agreed between the parents, their lawyers, or in a court that the mother should have custody, the children will live with her; if the father gains custody, the reverse is the case. Increasingly, parents agree on or are awarded "joint custody." While this may mean that the children spend a roughly equal amount of time living with each parent, the reality of the situation is more often one of "joint legal custody." In this case both parents share legal responsibility for the children, but the latter still spend the majority of their time either with the mother or with the father.

Historically, the question of which parent should have legal and custodial responsibility for the children after a marital breakup began at least in ancient Rome more than 2,000 years ago. Then husbands and fathers had complete control over their wives and children. A mother did not gain custody of her children even in the event of the father's death.

Today certain cultures still habitually award custody to the male parent should a couple divorce. For example, in Pakistan and parts of the Middle East the courts interpret Islamic (Shariah) law in such a way that the father nearly always gains custody of children over a certain age—usually age seven in the case of boys, nine in the case of girls. However, the following debate concentrates on the situation in the West, specifically in the United States.

The patriarchal attitude of ancient Rome continued under English law and was later carried over into early

American law. As a result, throughout the 17th and 18th centuries the father almost always gained custody in cases of divorce.

The Industrial Revolution and the increased urbanization that took place during the 19th century led to a number of sociological changes in the United States.

As farming ceased to be the main source of income for families, men were often forced to leave home to work in the cities. Their role became that of the wage earner, while their wives remained in the home caring for the children. At the same time, society began to take an almost reverential view of motherhood. By the 1920s these changes had become firmly rooted in the legal system.

From this time on, mothers were normally granted sole legal custody of their children after a divorce.

"… the most important thing is that his father was adjudged by people who made an honest effort to determine that he was a good father…."

—BILL CLINTON, 42ND PRESIDENT, ON THE DECISION TO RETURN ELIAN GONZALEZ TO HIS FATHER IN CUBA

The feminist movement of the late 1960s and early 1970s helped bring about another major change in society. As women began to gain equal rights with men—rights to equal pay for doing the same work as men and so on—so men began to lobby for equal rights to custody and responsibility for their children.

In 1970 the Uniform Marriage and Divorce Act was passed. Instead of basing the right to custody on gender, the act encouraged courts to consider what was in the "best interests" of the children in question. Most states adopted this law, and legal systems began to apply the notion of joint custody. Nonetheless, the statistics for 1990 showed that mothers still gained sole custody of their children in 72 percent of cases. This figure has changed little of late.

People who argue that fathers are marginalized by society and the legal process when it comes to parental rights point to statistics indicating that children raised by their mothers alone are more likely to show behavioral disorders, drop out of school, or end up in prison. Writers like Jayne Keedle in the "yes" article point to a "mother knows best" female bias in welfare agencies, schools, and government, and to the adversarial nature of the courts that results in many men abandoning their rights and responsibilities as fathers.

Other people contend that fathers are awarded sole or joint custody more often than is in the interests of their children. These people further maintain that men win custody of their children in most instances in which they choose to contest the case in court. Those who claim that fathers have enough, or even too many, rights as parents, as does Beth Owen in the second article, also argue that the courts discriminate against women who work and that men who are abusers or batterers often end up with custody.

FATHERS MATTER
Jayne Keedle

The Elian Gonzalez custody case made international news in 1999–2000. For further information see the box on page 90.

YES

✓ If Elian Gonzalez had been taken from Cuba, not by his mother, but by his father, he would have been returned to Cuba within days of getting a clean bill of health from the hospital, no questions asked.

It's a point of irony in fatherhood support groups across Connecticut as they draw parallels between their own situations and that of Elian's father. They, too, have found themselves facing unfounded allegations of abuse and questions about whether they are capable of raising a young child. And they have had to battle agencies, relatives and longstanding medical and legal viewpoints that assume, at least in questions of child welfare, that mother knows best. The U.S. government may have sided with the father in Elian's case, but in many of theirs, government agencies have sided with the mother.

The gender bias?

This gender bias is not just the men's perception.

"I think they're right," says Patricia Wilson-Coker, acting commissioner of the Connecticut Department of Social Services. "Systematic constraints have inadvertently been built up to separate fathers from children. There's a lack of advocates in the court, a lack of connection between child support and visitation. Frankly, that a father should be thought of as no more than a paycheck is what we're working against." …

The author uses a quotation to back up the point that society is biased toward mothers. Do you agree that such a bias exists in society?

"There's cultural bias within society that moms are essential and dads are incidental," says Bill Pinto, director of youth development for the Department of Children and Families. "Within our system it's really clear we're focussed on the mothers because the mother is the custodial parent."

One of the things the advisory board set out to discover was what institutional barriers keep these men away. Pinto notes that some DCF forms don't even include a space for the name of the father. Nor is this the only agency to have such obvious biases. The Department of Correction has programs for mothers to help them become better parents, but few for fathers. Even the prison's [sic] designs are different. The women's prison has colorful murals of animals and a play area where moms visit with their children. The men's visiting rooms are stark and definitely not kid-friendly.

Schools send information about children addressed only to the mother. Some divorced fathers complain that when they go to their children's school to discuss their child's performance, they're told by school principals that they need the mother's permission to get any information. Although this is not the law, many fathers aren't aware of their rights, and so they leave feeling frustrated.

"Early childhood centers haven't really been welcoming to fathers," says Connecticut Women's Education and Legal Fund's Amy Miller, who coordinates a father-oriented child support pilot program in Litchfield, Hartford and New Haven. "Dad comes to pick up Johnny and is told, 'Tell your wife Johnny needs diapers.' It's [implied] that mom is primarily the caretaker."…

The Connecticut Women's Education and Legal Fund (CWEALF) is a non-profit organization concerned with equal opportunities for women. To find out more, visit www.cwealf.org.

How the state views fathers

The state's view of fathers as sources of income and little else begins at birth.

Because so many babies are born out of wedlock, fathers are now asked to sign an acknowledgement of paternity at the hospital. While the new mother is offered child care advice, or directed to child development programs and baby exercise classes, fathers are given a legally-binding piece of paper to sign that deals with finances exclusively. It warns they will be financially liable for their children and could have their wages garnished and their tax returns taken by the state to pay towards child support.

Should a father decline to sign the piece of paper, he could be forced by court order to take a paternity test. In such cases, he's entitled to legal representation because this is a quasi-criminal proceeding in which the man is technically "found guilty" of paternity.

The author argues that fathers and mothers are treated differently after their child's birth. Would it be possible to make both parents accept financial responsibility for their child?

Then there's the term "deadbeat," referring to fathers who don't pay child support. The move to attach wages and tax returns, threaten to take away drivers' licenses and throw men in jail for non-payment of child-support was necessary because some men have abandoned their families. But these sanctions are imposed even if there are legitimate explanations, ranging from unemployment to imprisonment, for why a man may fall behind in payments. Many men, for instance, don't know they can go to court to modify their child support orders. Others have called support enforcement to ask about this procedure and been confronted with rude and unhelpful "enforcers."

COMMENTARY: The Elian Gonzalez case

On November 22, 1999, five-year-old Elian Gonzalez, his mother, his stepfather, and 11 others left Cuba on a 16-foot (4.9m) motorboat in a bid to escape to the United States. On the next day the boat capsized in the Atlantic Ocean, and 11 of the passengers, including Elian's mother and stepfather, perished. Two days later fishermen came across Elian floating on an inner tube near Fort Lauderdale, Florida.

The U.S. Immigration and Naturalization Service (INS) sent Elian to live in the Little Havana district of Miami with his great-uncle Lazaro Gonzalez, who applied for the boy to be granted asylum in the United States. Elian's relatives in Miami felt that Elian should stay because he would have a better life in the United States than in Cuba. Meanwhile, Elian's father, Juan Miguel Gonzalez, who had been divorced from the boy's mother and had remarried, requested that Elian be returned to Cuba to live with him.

In early January 2000 the INS decided that Elian belonged with his father, who did not support the boy's application for asylum. Elian's great-uncle immediately and successfully applied in the Florida state courts for temporary custody and challenged the INS ruling in the federal courts, requesting that Elian be granted an asylum hearing. The courts dismissed this lawsuit in late March, but the boy's U.S. relatives were determined not to give up and lodged an appeal. The courts ordered that the boy should stay in the United States until the appeals process was completed.

Meanwhile, Elian's father had arrived in Washington, D.C. The government ordered the Miami relatives to hand over Elian so that he could be reunited with his father during the appeals process. Faced with the relatives' refusal to comply, the government had the temporary custody order revoked, and on April 22 federal agents launched an armed raid on Lazaro Gonzalez' Little Havana house. Elian was flown to Washington. Eventually, the 11th U.S. Circuit Court of Appeals in Atlanta, Georgia, sided with the INS decision to deny Elian asylum; and despite further appeals by the boy's Miami relatives, including a last-ditch plea to the Supreme Court, Elian and his father returned to Cuba on June 28.

"I'm not saying I'm in any way soft on men who don't pay child support," says Wilson-Coker, "but there's beginning to be a greater recognition that they're not so much deadbeats as dead broke...."

At the Dads Do Make A Difference Program, and other support groups across the state, paying child support is a main topic of conversation during meetings. They don't object to supporting their children financially. What galls them is they're paying for children they don't see....

"It's a nightmare," says Shayn Turner, who describes himself as a "Mr. Mom" prior to his divorce. "My children are just as important to me as if I were a woman. There's instantaneous discrimination simply for the fact you're a male. In the court's eyes, the best interests of the child are that the child is raised by the mother."

Infants better off with mom?

Bob Tompkins, deputy director for regional services of the court support services division, would dispute that. He says that surveys conducted regarding custody show that, in Connecticut, fathers have some form of custody in about 45 percent of the cases. But while he believes that the court tries hard to make sure both parents are actively involved in raising their children, he concedes there is a bias in favor of the mother when the child is an infant. These are the so-called "tender years" and the prevailing wisdom was that up until the age of five, a child was better off with the mother.

Although this is no longer written into law, as it once was, many working in the family services division of the courts still believe that babies shouldn't stay overnight with their fathers.

"One of the standard debatable issues that come up in court is at what age should the child be allowed overnight visitation," says Tompkins. "My personal answer would be at birth. If you expect a father to connect and get involved with parenting, you can't say, yeah, but your first three years have to be a couple of hours at a time." ...

The mother's reluctance to relinquish custody, even temporarily, to the father, isn't always motivated by an overly-developed maternal instinct.

"What happens in divorces is that parents use the power they have," says Tompkins. "Moms have the power of kids. Dad has the power of money. That's the vehicle both sides have, if they chose [sic] to use them." ...

"Unfortunately, when these cases get into family court, children are looked at as property. They're chattel. Until we view children differently, we're going to have a lot of problems in our family courts deciding these issues," says Pinto.

The term "Mr. Mom" derives from the 1983 MGM movie of the same name, starring Michael Keaton as a homemaking dad.

Is this rule unconstitutional? See http://www.thelib.org/2703/27_03_org_01.htm for an article on fathers suing the state of Michigan for violating their constitutional rights.

A "chattel" is a legal term for an item of personal property.

THE WOMEN'S VOTE, A NEWSLETTER: COVERING ISSUES RELEVANT TO WOMEN
Beth Owen

The author immediately catches the readers' attention by making several emotional, dramatic statements.

For more information on the American Judges Foundation, Inc., and to view its online booklet on domestic violence, visit http://aja.ncsc.dni.us/domviol/booklet.html.

NO

X … Contested custody encapsulates every single feminist issue. Women are jailed for attempting to protect their children from abusive fathers. They're made financially destitute by fathers successfully using the courts to harass them. Fit and loving mothers no longer have any right to children they chose to bear and for whom they have been the primary caregivers. Further obliterating the mother's role, in some states even third parties can gain custody.

The largest segment of men who go for custody are batterers. According to the American Judges Foundation, Inc.: "Studies show that batterers have been able to convince authorities that the victim is unfit or undeserving of custody in approximately 70% of these challenged cases." Statistics of fathers gaining custody go as high as 84%. Many women are not able to get due process because they can't afford the thousands of dollars for lawyers' up front fees. A lawyer can be appointed in a criminal case, not in civil (custody) cases.   In covert court operations abusive fathers are frequently granted custody to children they are physically and/or sexually abusing in spite of hard evidence of this abuse.…

Myths vs. reality
First, let's dispose of three widely held assumptions:
1) That mothers usually get custody,
2) That a mother must be unfit to lose, and
3) That babies and young children are given to the mother if she is fit.

By "this century" Beth Owen means the 20th century. She wrote this article in 1996. Go to www.google.com, and see if you can find more current statistics.

Historically fathers almost always got custody, up until this century. However, for a few decades, in the 1920's, 30's, 40's and 50's, mothers were generally granted custody, only because the fathers were discouraged from attempting it, and usually a mother had to be declared unfit to lose. All this changed in the 1960's, in a backlash to the women's movement. Women's legitimate right to equality was turned

Dustin Hoffman and Justin Henry starred as Ted and Billy Kramer in the 1979 Kramer vs. Kramer, *a film about a father fighting for the custody of his son.*

back against them. This is how it came to be that a mother can be declared fit and loving and still lose.

The general public has the notion that mothers usually get custody. This can be true when a case is not contested. Fortunately, a number of men are too decent to pursue custody, when in fairness, they know their wives have been the primary caregivers. And many men don't want custody, as raising the children has not been a significant part of their lifestyle. However, when the cases are contested, the father has a far better chance than the mother of winning. Statistics vary from 70% to 84%.

The author states that when cases are contested, fathers have a better chance of winning. Do you think this is because those fathers who do pursue custody are more aware of the requirements— whether they meet them or not?

Even in uncontested cases, women are often bullied or terrorized into accepting decisions that are the worst for their children, for example, joint custody when it is not mutually agreeable. A couple of joint physical custody scenarios that come to mind are, one in which a 1½-year-old girl spends two weeks with her mother and two weeks with her father. In another case, a four year old child, who's been living with her mother and stepfather, is now required by the court to spend one year with her mother and one year with her natural father, to whom her mother was never married....

Does the fact that a father and mother were not married matter? Why do you think Owen mentions it?

Why women suffer

In an attack on working women, the media has incorrectly presented the argument that women will just have to decide which they most want, a career or motherhood. In actuality most statutes don't recognize the parent who has been the primary caretaker of the child as a major reason for granting custody. Further, it's not only career women who are losing; stay at home mothers are losing as often.

Betty Friedan (1921–) is an American feminist. Her best-known work, The Feminine Mystique (1963), put forward the view that society expected women to live their lives through their husbands and children.

Betty Friedan has described some of the mistakes women have made in their zeal for rights. "In the early days of the American movement, we fell into a trap when we said, 'No Alimony!' because housewives who divorced were in terrible straits. We fell into another trap by accepting the no fault divorce without provision for a mandatory economic settlement."

What we have now is the trap of equal rights to custody, which is really no fault custody. However, this equal right is arbitrary, not based on who has been the child's primary caregiver....

Gender bias

An illustration of judicial gender bias is revealed by a tactic sometimes used by fathers. It is to keep a child after visitation, go to court [and] make false allegations against the mother and in this manner often successfully gain custody. On the other hand, if a mother prevents a child's return to the father to protect him or her from abuse, she risks being charged with kidnapping and facing a jail sentence.

Another strategy that sounds so fair and egalitarian, often to the feminist ear, is joint custody. Joint custody, is a backlash to the attempts to enforce child support. Frequently men are told by their attorneys that if they have sole custody, joint custody or significant visitation (the percentage of visitation being equal to the amount of child support required) they will pay no child support or very little. Instead their ex wives will often, with their 72 cents to the man's dollar, if they work, pick up this slack.

Most important, however, joint physical custody doesn't work. One wouldn't send a puppy back and forth between houses, so why a child?

The real issue

Recently there has been a specious attempt to blame father absence as the cause of crime, mental illness, delinquency and suicide. It is more likely these ills are caused by bad fathers, those who beat their wives and physically or sexually abuse their children. It is mother absence, which is becoming so common, that is a much more serious problem.

A triumvirate that sustains the power of men and represses women includes: the legislatures, the courts, and the media. The legislature [sic] pass laws supporting the ideologies and interests of men. The courts, with their male values and power, often buttressed by case law promoted by fathers' groups, translate these laws and case laws into decisions favorable to men. The media (another institution dominated by the interests of men), continually promotes and indoctrinates the public into the ideologies of men.

The hidden agenda in this misogynist age is to destroy women. What better and more effective way than to win in the battlefield of contested child custody?

For information on child support issues visit the Federal Office of Child Support Enforcement home page at www.acf.dhhs.gov/ programs/cse.

A "misogynist" is a man who has or shows a hatred of women. Bearing in mind that this article was written in 1996, do you believe you are living in a misogynist age? Are men discriminated against, too?

Summary

Jayne Keedle is convinced that gender bias still exists, and that it is men who are discriminated against when it comes to parental rights. She argues that even when couples are still together, schools, the welfare system, and government agencies treat fathers as incidental to their children's lives. The mother is seen to be the only essential parent from an emotional, psychological, and physical viewpoint. By contrast, most agencies and institutions see fathers merely as a means of financial support for their children. She points out that fathers are even more marginalized if the parents are an unmarried couple or when the child is very young. As a result, after a divorce or relationship breakdown many fathers simply give up trying to be a part of their children's lives, a situation that, for Keedle, cannot be in the "best interests" of the child.

In her piece Beth Owen argues that fathers have more than enough parental rights. For her, fathers often have too many rights because the courts, the media, and other institutions are biased in favor of male values and power. She contends that this results in the award of custody of children to men who may be unsuitable parents, such as batterers and abusers. At the same time, courts frequently rule against women in contested custody cases, particularly in situations in which a mother has chosen to return to work or to a career after having her children. This is the case regardless of whether the mother has been the primary caregiver in the child's life until the custody case. Further, Owen argues that the award of joint custody to parents does not work because what children really need is a single stable base and home.

FURTHER INFORMATION:

Books:

MacCoby, Eleanor E., and Robert H. Mnookin, *Dividing the Child: Social and Legal Dilemmas of Custody*. Cambridge, MA: Harvard University Press, 1994.
Knox, David, Ph.D., with Kermit Leggett, *Divorced Dad's Survival Book: How to Stay Connected with Your Kids*. Cambridge, MA: Perseus Publishing, 2000.
Ricci, Isolina, Ph.D., *Mom's House, Dad's House: Making Two Homes for Your Child*. New York, NY: Fireside, 1997.

Useful websites:

www. deltabravo.net/custody/
Home page of SPARC (Separated Parenting Access and Resource Center).
www.mothercustody.org/
Resource site for mothers fighting for custody of their children.

The following debates in the Pro/Con series may also be of interest:

In this volume:

Topic 1 Does society support family values?

Topic 3 Is marriage essential to the family unit?

Topic 4 Is the two-parent family best?

Topic 5 Do gay couples make good parents?

SHOULD FATHERS HAVE MORE PARENTAL RIGHTS?

YES: Courts will usually rule that it is in the "best interests" of a child to remain with his or her mother, particularly if the child is very young

YES: Even when couples are still together, schools, government, and welfare agencies often treat fathers as being unimportant in their children's emotional lives

BIAS IN COURTS
Does the legal system discriminate against fathers?

MEAL TICKET
Does society see a father's role as being merely a financial one?

NO: Where custody of a child is actually contested by the father, he usually wins the case. Statistically, mothers are more likely to get custody of their children because most fathers choose not to contest custody in the courts.

NO: Throughout history women have been marginalized by society in their role as mothers. Even today institutions such as the media are actually biased in favor of men and fathers' rights as parents.

SHOULD FATHERS HAVE MORE PARENTAL RIGHTS?
KEY POINTS

YES: A father who is prevented from seeing his children or is made to feel incidental in their lives is more likely to drop out of their lives altogether and refuse to pay child support

YES: Statistics show that children brought up by their mother alone are more likely to have behavioral disorders, suffer depression, drop out of school, and get into trouble with the law

ESSENTIAL ROLE
Is it essential that fathers are a part of their children's lives?

NO: It is more important that children have a good male role model in their lives. However, he does not have to be the biological father.

NO: Fathers themselves often choose not to be involved with their children because they do not want the financial or emotional responsibility and commitment

Topic 8

SHOULD PARENTS BE HELD RESPONSIBLE FOR THE BEHAVIOR OF THEIR CHILDREN?

YES

"DELINQUENT PARENTS SPAWN TEENAGE CRIMINALS"
WWW.TRINICENTER.COM/RAFFIQUE/2001/JUN/17062001.HTM
RAFFIQUE SHAH

NO

FROM "YES, I AM PLEADING FOR MY SON'S LIFE"
ONLINE FOCUS: OKLAHOMA BOMBING TRIAL, JUNE 11, 1997
TIM SULLIVAN AND JIM LEHRER

INTRODUCTION

Toward the end of the 20th century a trend emerged in the United States to hold parents responsible for the actions of their children, and various types of legislation were enacted or strengthened to enable the courts to do this. Children who commit crimes cannot always be punished. Sometimes they are too young to be responsible legally. Yet even when the children could be subject to legal punishment, many people believe that the parents should pay for their offspring's actions, whether it be by making good the damage caused by children's vandalism or by paying fines or going to prison for failing to adequately supervise their children's lives.

Advocates of enforcing parental responsibility want to put the onus on parents to nurture their children. In their opinion too many parents shirk their duties and blame their children's bad behaviors on external factors such as poverty or television violence. In the first of the following articles, for example, Raffique Shah contends that parents should ask themselves: "What did you do to guide your son or daughter during his or her formative years?"

The idea that the sins of the children should be visited on the parents is based on the view that parents get back exactly what they give. Good parents have decent children, whereas negligent parents give rise to criminal children. This opinion is contentious, and those who disagree with it are convinced that the parent–child relationship is much more complex. They argue that although some young lawbreakers come from delinquent or neglectful backgrounds, not all do. Young criminals may come from law-abiding families, just as Republican parents may have children who vote Democrat, and nonsmokers may have children who smoke. For example, Oklahoma City bomber Timothy McVeigh, whose case is discussed in the second article here, had decent parents. What seems to have turned him into a murderer was his anger at the perceived injustice of the American government's actions at the siege near Waco, Texas, in 1993.

> *"Parents shall not be put to death for their children, nor shall children be put to death for their parents; only for their own crimes may persons be put to death."*
> —DEUTERONOMY 24:16

Morality is learned behavior—no one has it naturally from birth—but can it be taught, as table manners are taught? Those who would hold parents responsible for their children's actions might argue that values can and should be instilled. They can point to cases in which parents have set an inappropriate example or failed to see warning signs that their children were going off the rails.

Those against parental responsibility legislation contend that the desire to be a good citizen must come from within the individual, asserting that while it is undeniable that mothers and fathers influence their children, no parenting—good or bad, attentive or negligent—can absolutely determine the behavior of the young. Opponents of such legislation question just how much control parents should be expected to exert over their children. How much

should they be expected to know about their kids' activities or their associates, especially since children can be past masters at hiding information? These people argue that there is a world of difference between negligent parenting and just not knowing what children are getting up to. Furthermore, according to some experts, many adults today simply do not know how to be parents, and even those who do can achieve little if a child refuses to abide by the rules. Also, some parents complain of being confused about how they are supposed to bring up their children. On the one hand, they are told to behave in an enlightened way toward their offspring and not use corporal punishment, say, while on the other hand being threatened with court action if their kids step out of line.

The question of whether parents should be held responsible for their children's actions is ultimately about the attribution of blame. Those in favor of greater parental responsibility would have the parents take the blame when their children offend because it is the parents who have been neglectful in their duties. A counterargument is that legislation against parents does not attack the root of the problem of juvenile crime and runs the risk of lashing out at the innocent, making the response worse than inaction.

The following two articles explore both sides of the argument. In the first Raffique Shah calls for legislation to make delinquent parents "culpable for the misdeeds of their children." The second article, on the other hand, is from a transcript of a television news show and describes the testimony of Timothy McVeigh's parents at their son's trial for the Oklahoma City bombing of April 19, 1995.

DELINQUENT PARENTS SPAWN TEENAGE CRIMINALS
Raffique Shah

YES

✓ The scene was as graphic as it was poignant: A relatively young mother of a 16 year-old youth who was shot dead by the police following a robbery, screaming, "I want justice for my son!" The boy was allegedly one of three armed bandits who robbed a Lotto outlet in downtown Port of Spain. Unluckily for him and his accomplices, the police, under pressure from city merchants who faced burglaries and robberies almost every night, had the area under tight security. So when the bandits pounced on the Lotto agent, they were quickly drawn into a running battle with the police. When the drama was over, Charleston Byron was found dead in a nearby drain.

Port of Spain is the capital of the Caribbean republic of Trinidad and Tobago. The city is situated in the northwest of the island of Trinidad.

Any mother or father faced with similar circumstances might have reacted the same way Byron's mom did. She was sure her "little boy" could not have been part of a gang of robbers, and even if he was, "De police couldn't shoot him in his leg?" She hinted that her son might not have been part of the robbery at all, just an innocent victim of recklessness on the part of the police. This latter claim has its merits since there are many instances in which the police arrest or shoot the wrong person and make up for their errors by pinning a crime on the victim.

A dispute with his father

But in this case, because the robbery was staged early in the night, there were many witnesses to the incident. And those who spoke with reporters commended the policemen for their reaction time and the way they pursued the bandits. Maybe we shall never know if Byron was part of the gang since dead men, or as is more applicable today, dead boys, tell no tales. Still, there are indications that the boy had drifted into the netherworld of crime. Not only did he drop out of secondary school (which says nothing, really, since there are thousands of dropouts), but he later abandoned working with his father "after a dispute between them". Did his parents monitor his activities after that, or did they abdicate their responsibilities, leaving him to fall prey to elements that took him down the "fast lane" to quick bucks and equally quick death?

COMMENTARY: Parental responsibility laws

Numerous laws exist in the United States that make parents responsible for their children's actions. For example, under some state civil parental liability statutes parents may be sued by those who have suffered as a result of their children's delinquency. Since this is civil legislation, the parents do not face a fine or imprisonment if they lose, but they may be required to pay financial damages to the plaintiff.

Criminal responsibility

U.S. criminal parental-liability legislation dates back as far as 1903, when Colorado enacted the country's first such law. Other states followed suit. Criminal prosecution of parents for their children's actions, however, remained unusual until the rise in juvenile crime in the late 1980s led to a tougher stance being adopted, including firmer sanctions against the parents of wayward adolescents. The result was the enactment of a range of criminal legislation and the expansion of existing laws.

The first state to introduce measures was California, which passed the Street Terrorism Enforcement and Prevention Act (STEP) in 1988. This law was aimed at controlling gang crime. STEP allows for a maximum fine of $2,500 and a one-year prison sentence for parents found guilty of failing "to exercise reasonable care, supervision, protection and control over their children." Since 1988 many more states and communities have introduced legislation enabling the prosecution of parents for their children's crimes (although some states have struck down parental responsibility laws because their wording was too vague). In 1994 the Detroit suburb of St. Clair Shores introduced its parental responsibility ordinance. Two years later the community became the focus of the nation when it prosecuted Anthony and Susan Provenzino for failing to supervise their teenage son, Alex, and the parents opted for a jury trial. Alex had been arrested for burglarizing churches and assaulting his father with a golf club. Despite the parents' assertions that they had done their best to control their son, and testimony from Alex that he had done his best to hide his activities, the six-person jury took less than half an hour to find the Provenzino parents guilty. Each of them was fined $100 and ordered to pay $1,000 in costs, although the convictions were later reversed.

Other liability legislation

Certain states may hold parents criminally liable if their children gain access to firearms—for example, if a loaded weapon is not stored safely, or if the parent knows a child has a gun but does nothing about it. Other liability laws may require parents to attend juvenile court proceedings, to pay their cost, or even to meet the cost of their children's time in the justice system. In some states the parents may be imprisoned for their children's truancy.

The signposts to Hell loomed large in the short life of this boy. Yet the mother, upon learning of his death at the hands of the police, sobbed as if he were an innocent teenager. Over the past two decades or so, more or less coinciding with the crime spiral that has frustrated the police and successive governments, we have repeatedly seen bereaved parents weep over their dead children. Their tears, which I won't classify as "crocodile", (hell, I, too, am a parent) beg the question: what did you do to guide your son or daughter during his or her formative years? What sort of values did you instill in your children? Did you leave them to their wiles as you partied away, almost abandoning them?

Shah puts forward the central theme of his argument in the form of questions. The device enables an author to make a point without making a direct accusation.

Education, discipline, and example

I've always argued that while poverty is not a crime, it is also no excuse for committing crime. I myself come from a background of relative poverty, like so many others, especially those from my generation. Our parents, illiterate as they were in many instances, were certainly not dumb when it came to aspiring to lift their children out of persistent poverty through education, discipline and example. While it is true that times have changed, that consumerism and television and video arcades have forever altered the values that were once the cornerstones of our society, it is also true that parenting is something alien to most of today's parents.

Are there any circumstances in which poverty might be an excuse for crime? If so, what sort of crime?

Shifting focus from the slain Byron to the two Ste Madeleine girls who were involved in an incident that led to one being stabbed to death, one needs to ask the same questions. Because this matter has reached the courts and a mother's-milk-in-the-face girl has been charged with murder, I cannot comment as freely as I would want to. Still, is it the norm for teenage girls involved in an altercation to resort to violence, or, as happened in this instance, reach for weapons? I don't know if Waynisha Williams was without sin, or if her assailant is a sinner. Whatever their backgrounds, the stark reality is that one girl lies buried in a cemetery and another is incarcerated with no chance of getting bail. Incidents of serious violence in the nation's schools have become so frightening (to both teachers and students), the no-licks Minister of Education, Kamla Persad Bissessar, has all but approved the introduction of "stun guns" in certain schools.

Do you think that Shah believes this, or is it irrelevant whether the girls were or were not without sin?

Really, when such a measure is even considered, when teachers flee schools because of fear of students, when hundreds of teenagers are arrested or killed because of criminal activities, we need to seriously take stock of the root causes of such rampant delinquency. It is a real "cop out" to cast blame on the ubiquitous television (too much sex and violence), on peer pressure, on poverty, on anything else but the truth. And that truth, sadly, lies squarely in the laps of parents, both mothers and fathers, but more so the latter. So today, as gifts and praises are showered on fathers—which some deserve—I want to rain on the Fathers' Day parade.

Abandoned responsibilities

In most instances fathers have abandoned their responsibilities at home. Mothers, too, have followed suit. Today's parents know about "manufacturing" children, which is the easy part of the job. But once they bring the poor souls into the world, if they don't dump the infants into latrines or the sea, they abandon them to the environments in which they must survive without parental guidance. And this unhealthy situation does not exist only in depressed, poor communities. It is rampant in the upper echelons of society. I've seen some prominent persons honoured for parenting, but whose children are as delinquent as those coming out of the "slums".

Would Shah's assertions be more credible if he used evidence to support them?

One can argue that this is a global problem and that there is no easy way out. To that I say, "Bull!" The authorities need to focus more on parents and parenting, since delinquent children invariably come from delinquent parents. It is time we put in place legislation that will make such parents culpable for the misdeeds of their children, especially if the latter are minors. Because when the police shoot these kids dead, or when they are imprisoned, their parents remain free to continue making more children, increasing the pool of potential delinquents. It is the latter, not the former, we need to focus on. Which is why I believe Fathers' Day, like Mothers' Day, is so much "bull."

Is it possible for the law to make good parents out of bad?

YES, I AM PLEADING FOR MY SON'S LIFE
Tim Sullivan and Jim Lehrer

NO

On April 19, 1995, 168 people died and 500 were injured when a truck bomb exploded at the Alfred P. Murrah Federal Building in Oklahoma City. Timothy McVeigh was executed on June 11, 2001, for his part in the incident. For more information go to www.time.com/time/2001/mcveigh.

Tim Sullivan: Well, Jim, it began with Mildred Frazer, Tim McVeigh's mother, who is now divorced from Tim McVeigh's father. She made a plea to this jury to spare her son's life. It was very brief testimony really in which she read a short statement. And in that statement she said—she began by saying, "I cannot even imagine the pain and suffering the people of Oklahoma City have endured since April 19, 1995." She went on to say, "I still can't believe that my son could have caused such devastation." She said, "There are still too many unanswered questions." And then she said, "Yes, I am pleading for my son's life. He's a human being, just like we all are. He's not a monster." And she concluded by telling the jury, "You have a very difficult decision to make about my son's life or death, and I pray that God will help you make the right decision."

Jim Lehrer: Yeah, go ahead.

Tim Sullivan: I was just going to say she was followed by her ex-husband.

Jim Lehrer: Let me—was she cross-examined in any way by the prosecution?

Tim Sullivan: No, Jim, she was not cross-examined. She was only up there for a few minutes, and actually two of the five women on the jury were crying as Mrs. Frazer read that statement.

Jim Lehrer: All right. Now, go on. The father was then next....

Tim Sullivan: Yes. Bill McVeigh, Tim McVeigh's father, testified. He also was not on the stand very long. His testimony included the playing of a videotape that the defense put together. It's a compilation of old home movies that Tim McVeigh's grandfather made when Tim McVeigh was a small boy and a recent video that the defense made of McVeigh's hometown, of Pendleton, New York, and Lockport, New York, where he grew up, showing the school he went to, the church he went to, et cetera.

Jim Lehrer: All right. Now, Tim, we have a one minute, twenty-five second excerpt from that. The tape, itself, was fifteen minutes long, but we have a one minute, twenty-five second excerpt—edited excerpt—from it that we want to look at now.

William McVeigh [on excerpt of video used by defense]:

I think he enjoyed school. He was a good student, although he never got the marks that he was capable of getting, I don't think. In high school he got an award when he graduated for never missing a day. In four years, he never missed a day of school. The first time Tim worked I think was the beginning of his senior year. He went to work at Burger King. After he was out, he got a New York State—$500 New York State Regents Scholarship. He went to Brian and Stratton. It's a business school. And he didn't feel he was learning more than he already knew, so he decided to go back to work. And then after that, he got a job at the Burger King in Lockport. He worked for Burger King—I don't know—maybe a year—and after that he got a job for Park Security, driving an armored car. He got the job there because he had a pistol permit. Tim graduated, and he said at the graduation that quite a few of the kids were going into the military. He come home one day and said he was going in the service, and I says, "When," and he says, "Tomorrow." That's about all I can tell you about when he went in the service, or over to the Persian Gulf. He didn't seem to mind going, and he was ready to go when the time come, and they went to Kuwait. And I believe it was right around the end of '91, Christmastime in '91 or so. And he come back, he seemed to be happy when he come home.

> *William McVeigh's testimony builds up an image of his son as a normal, everyday American boy. How does his evidence affect the idea that his son's childhood may have led to his subsequent actions and views?*

> *Timothy McVeigh joined the U.S. Army on May 24, 1988, and served with the 1st Infantry Division during the Gulf War of 1991. See Health, pages 188–189, for more information on the Gulf War.*

Jim Lehrer: Now, Tim, what was the impact of that tape, or is it hard to measure?

Tim Sullivan: Well, it was a bit hard to measure, Jim. You know, the gallery watched carefully, the jury paid close attention to it, of course. We didn't see any overt reaction from the jurors. Tim McVeigh sat pretty solemnly and perhaps a bit sad while that was being shown. When it was done, the defense just asked Bill McVeigh a few questions. They then showed a photograph of Bill McVeigh with his son in the kitchen of his home in Upstate, New York. It was taken in about 1992—the two of them with their arms around each other, big smiles on their faces. And Richard Burr, the defense attorney, asked Mr. McVeigh, "Is that Tim McVeigh in that picture the Tim you know and love," and he said, "Yes, it is." And then he was asked, "Do you still love your son," and he said, "Yes, I do love my son." And then he said, "Do you love the Tim McVeigh who is in this courtroom," and Mr. McVeigh said, "I do." And then he was finally asked, "Do you want him to live," and he said, "Yes, I do." And that was the end of that testimony, Jim, and he wasn't cross-examined either.

Jim Lehrer: Now, what was the reaction of Tim McVeigh when his mother testified? Was it any different than when his father did?

On April 19, 1993, FBI agents used tear gas against the headquarters of the Branch Davidian Christian sect near Waco, Texas, which had been under siege by federal agents since February 28. During the operation fire engulfed the buildings, and 80 members of the sect died. For more information go to www.pbs.org/wgbh/pages/frontline/waco.

Tim Sullivan: It was a bit different. He sat very still, with his hands folded, sitting back in his chair. A couple of times while his mother was reading that statement, he reached to his eye with one finger and wiped his eye. And there's some disagreement among the many of us who were in the courtroom as to whether he was actually crying. I will say this, Jim. He was much more emotional yesterday when a video—a tape was played of a song about the children who were killed at Waco, Texas, in the Branch Davidian compound there. And he was very close to tears, it seemed, while that song was being played about the dead children at Waco.

Jim Lehrer: Yeah. To summarize, Tim, the case that the defense has made for not executing Timothy McVeigh rests on that, more than anything, does it not, his anger over what happened at the Branch Davidian compound?

Soldier of Fortune: Journal of Professional Adventurers is a magazine. It "focuses on news and adventure based on firsthand reports from all over the world."

Tim Sullivan: Yes, it does, Jim. You know, they began with all these army buddies of Tim McVeigh's coming and testifying about what a good soldier he was, about his service in the Persian Gulf, the fact that he won a bronze star and performed well in the two brief battles he was in—skirmishes really—over there. But then it went on to Waco, and the heart of the defense case here was that he was so inflamed and so passionate about what happened at Waco, and he so strongly believed that the federal government through the FBI and the ATF had committed murder there, had declared war on the American citizens, as he put it, that he was driven to react to that. And I think what they want the jury to see is that—they put in a lot of evidence that he was not alone in those beliefs—*Soldier of Fortune* articles and videotapes about Waco—just to try to portray him as a person among many people who felt that way.…

Should parents be held responsible for the behavior of their children?

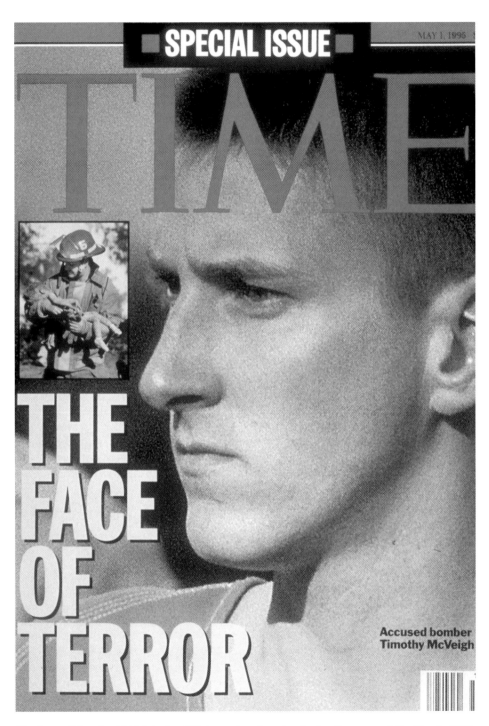

The face of Timothy McVeigh, the Oklahoma bomber, dominates the cover of the May 1, 1995, issue of Time *magazine.*

Summary

The first article begins by describing the reaction of a mother whose 16-year-old son has been shot dead by police after a robbery in Port of Spain, Trinidad. The author, Raffique Shah, has little sympathy with her cry for justice because he suspects that this tragedy and others like it, one of which he also describes, would not have happened if parents took greater responsibility for their children's upbringing and welfare. Shah dismisses the notion that violence and robbery are problems of global society and asserts that poverty is no excuse for committing crime. He says that although he himself had a relatively impoverished upbringing, that did not make him a criminal because he had good parents. By contrast, he says, "delinquent children invariably come from delinquent parents." The article is strongly worded, and some readers might find parts of it callous or offensive; as a polemic, it contains more assertion than evidence.

The second piece is a transcript of PBS television news anchor Jim Lehrer's interview with reporter Tim Sullivan, who was in court to hear Timothy McVeigh's parents plead for clemency for their son, who faced the death sentence for the 1995 Oklahoma City bombing. Unlike Shah's piece, this is a dispassionate report but no less effective for that. It shows not only that the parents loved their son but also that they had no idea why he carried out his act of terrorism. The article implies that McVeigh became a criminal by his own choosing, independently of any parental influence.

FURTHER INFORMATION:

Books:

John, Ramona Freeman, *Children and the Law in Texas: What Parents Should Know*. Austin, TX: University of Texas Press, 1999.

Kelleher, Michael D., *When Good Kids Kill*. Westport, CT: Praeger Publishing, 1999.

McCord, Joan, Cathy Spatz Widom, and Nancy A. Crowell (eds.), *Juvenile Crime, Juvenile Justice*. Washington, D.C.: National Academy Press, 2001.

Useful websites:

www.calbar.org/2pub/3kids/4kids-19.htm
State Bar of California's page on parents' rights and responsibilities.

http://crime.about.com/library/blfiles/bljuvc.htm
about.com juvenile crime page.

www.silverton.or.us/pro1.htm
City of Silverton, Oregon, Parental Responsibility page, referring to the city's parental responsibility ordinance.

www.ojjdp.ncjrs.org/pubs/reform/contents.html
"Juvenile Justice Reform Initiatives in the States 1994–1996," online publication by the Office of Juvenile Justice and Delinquency Prevention. Site also includes other relevant articles.

The following debates in the Pro/Con series may also be of interest:

In this volume:

 Topic 1 Does society support family values?

 Topic 2 Is the family the source of prejudice?

SHOULD PARENTS BE HELD RESPONSIBLE FOR THE BEHAVIOR OF THEIR CHILDREN?

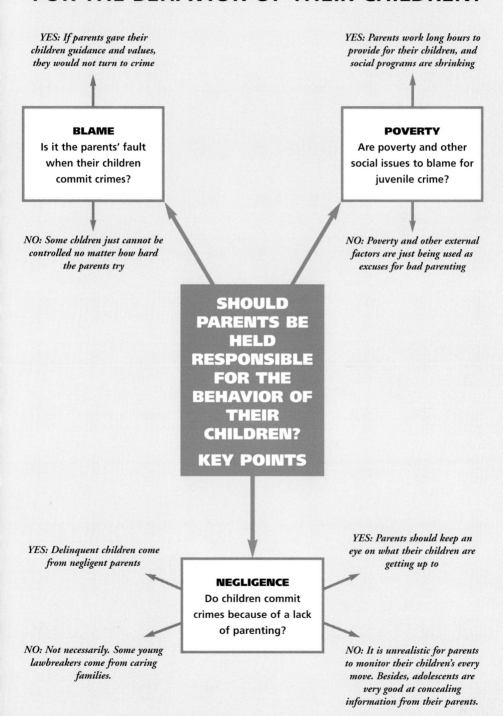

YES: If parents gave their children guidance and values, they would not turn to crime

YES: Parents work long hours to provide for their children, and social programs are shrinking

BLAME
Is it the parents' fault when their children commit crimes?

POVERTY
Are poverty and other social issues to blame for juvenile crime?

NO: Some chldren just cannot be controlled no matter how hard the parents try

NO: Poverty and other external factors are just being used as excuses for bad parenting

SHOULD PARENTS BE HELD RESPONSIBLE FOR THE BEHAVIOR OF THEIR CHILDREN?

KEY POINTS

YES: Delinquent children come from negligent parents

YES: Parents should keep an eye on what their children are getting up to

NEGLIGENCE
Do children commit crimes because of a lack of parenting?

NO: Not necessarily. Some young lawbreakers come from caring families.

NO: It is unrealistic for parents to monitor their children's every move. Besides, adolescents are very good at concealing information from their parents.

109

PART 3

THE YOUNG AND THE OLD

INTRODUCTION

Age is an important topic in the United States. This section deals with four of the main issues in the debate about the young and the old.

Demographics
A combination of factors, including the post-World War II Baby Boom, later marriages, a decline in the birthrate, and people living longer, have resulted in a disproportionately large elderly population in the United States. By 2040 it is estimated that more than a quarter of the population will be over 65 years of age. This has led many people to question who will pay for the elderly's support. Should the state foot the bill, or should they pay for themselves?

At the other end of the spectrum are the young. According to the Food Research and Action Center, in 1999 children under 18 accounted for around a quarter of the population. Around 25 percent of them resided in single-parent homes, and almost 17 percent lived in poverty. While the majority enjoyed good health and had health care, almost 13 percent had no health coverage at all.

Responsibility
Historically, in the traditional family those of working age were expected to support children, the infirm, and the elderly; today, critics claim, much of that burden falls on the state. They argue that the state's resources are already overstretched and that there is not enough money to support families in crisis. That fact, they assert, is reflected in the neglect of the elderly, rising crime rates, and teenage delinquency. Others argue that the state has a responsibility to nurture, educate, and look after society's dependents if families cannot do so themselves, and that outside institutions, such as government agencies, welfare departments, and schools, should step in to help. They claim that punishing people when they go wrong and educating them about what is right will benefit society as a whole.

What schools can teach
Some sociologists believe that children learn their behavior from the family and from their peer group. They claim that problems arise when antisocial behavior in young people remains uncorrected. But if the family is not able to correct behavioral problems, be it from neglect or from lack of time, who should? In practice it is often left to schools to fill the gap.

The United States is one of the few industrialized countries to still allow corporal punishment in schools. This is an area of great controversy, since many people believe that children should not be physically punished at all, while others assert that corporal punishment is a parental responsibility. Topic 9 examines this issue in greater depth.

In the "yes" article author Tom Larimer remembers back to his school days when he was paddled by a teacher. He argues that it in no way diminished his respect for that teacher and refers to paddling as "an awesome education aid." Authors Adah Maurer and James S. Wallerstein, on the other hand, argue that corporal punishment has a detrimental effect on children and leads to all kinds of problems in later life.

Corporal punishment is not the only contentious issue when it comes to the role of what schools should or should not do. The issue of sex education is also controversial.

with head on. In the "yes" article in Topic 10 BUPA's medical team considers whether sex education really works. Drawing on recent research, they argue that teenagers who receive good sex education often delay the experience of having sex. But the "no" article, by Pamela DeCarlo of the Center for AIDS Prevention Studies, argues that providing young people with information on sex does not deter them from engaging in early sexual activity.

Topic 11 deals with the related issue of whether teenagers should have a right to contraception without parental consent. The "yes" article from the

---

"The old believe everything; the middle-aged suspect everything; the young know everything."

—OSCAR WILDE (1854–1900), IRISH DRAMATIST AND NOVELIST

The promotion of abstinence-only education by President George W. Bush's administration and the allocation of $135 million to the program in the 2003 budget have fueled discussion further. While advocates point to the fact that something has to be done to reduce current teenage pregnancy rates and that abstinence education gives the young an option, critics argue that teenagers need to make informed decisions when it comes to sex and that sex education is therefore important. They claim that sexually transmitted diseases are on the increase, and that of the 13 million people who have some form of STD in America, around eight to nine million of them are below 25. This indicates that a lot of young people are sexually active and that the issue needs to be dealt

Center for Reproductive Law and Policy argues that parental consent for contraception threatens both teenage constitutional rights and teen health. Peter Brandt in the "no" article argues that abstinence education would be more effective.

The elderly

The final topic in this section looks at whether the elderly should be made to pay for their own health care, as many advocates argue. Peter G. Peterson argues in the first article that there is simply not enough money to sustain the increasingly old population and that some self-financing is inevitable. Jonathan Cohn, however, argues that the elderly simply cannot afford to pay and that most young working people believe it is right to support them.

Topic 9
SHOULD SCHOOLS BE ALLOWED TO USE CORPORAL PUNISHMENT?

YES
FROM "CORPORAL PUNISHMENT MAKES IMPRESSION"
DAILY NEWS JOURNAL, MARCH 4, 2001
TOM LARIMER

NO
FROM "THE INFLUENCE OF CORPORAL PUNISHMENT ON CRIME"
PROJECT NOSPANK, 1987
ADAH MAURER AND JAMES S. WALLERSTEIN

INTRODUCTION

School corporal punishment is the use of physical means to assert authority and instill discipline in children and young adults. Punishment can take the form of hitting, slapping, punching, pinching, shaking, or using different objects, such as wooden paddles, belts, and rulers, to inflict pain on a student or child. Corporal punishment has been a form of disciplinary action since colonial times in the United States, although New Jersey banned its use in 1867. However, it is really only in the last 20 years or so that there has been mounting pressure on a national scale to prohibit the practice in schools. It comes against a background of increasing reports of institutional child abuse and concerns about the rights of the child.

The United States is one of the few industrialized countries, along with Canada and one state in Australia, to still allow school corporal punishment. The American Academy of Pediatrics (AAP)

is just one of a number of important bodies that have publicly denounced the practice.

In August 2000 the AAP estimated that there had been between 1 and 2 million cases of corporal punishment in U.S. schools. In an article in its journal *Pediatrics* the association stated that corporal punishment "may adversely affect a student's self-image and school achievement and that ... may contribute to disruptive and violent student behavior."

The American Orthopsychiatry Association and the American Civil Liberties Union (ACLU) sponsored a big conference on corporal punishment in 1972, a year after Massachusetts joined New Jersey in formally banning it in schools. Two years later the American Psychological Association passed a resolution prohibiting school corporal punishment, and the Task Force on Children's Rights was established to look into the matter further. Yet the main obstacle to a complete ban on school corporal discipline in the United States is the underlying belief that it is legally acceptable.

In 1977, for example, in *Ingraham v. Wright,* a case that looked at the constitutional rights of students in a disciplinary setting, the court ruled that while the Eighth Amendment pronouncement on cruel and unusual punishment could be applied to those individuals who have committed a crime, it did not apply to students being disciplined. The court stated that there was enough public surveillance in schools to minimize the incidence of abuse. Since then any attempts to use the court system to prove that corporal punishment is unconstitutional or abusive have largely failed.

"Excessive bail shall not be required, nor excessive fines imposed, nor cruel and unusual punishments inflicted."

—EIGHTH AMENDMENT,
THE CONSTITUTION

In a 1985 poll on the elimination of corporal punishment in schools 47 percent of the U.S. population and 60 percent of teachers, administrators, and board members supported its continued use. Other advocates include the National Association of Secondary School Principals, the National Federation of Teachers, and some fundamentalist churches. Supporters of corporal punishment in schools, such as Tom Larimer, author of the first following article, argue that this form of discipline results in better behaved, more controlled children who learn to appreciate authority. Many also believe that its existence gives teachers the support they need in dealing with increasingly unruly students and that to take it away would lead to higher crime and more social problems among young adults. Such arguments underline the belief that schools have a moral and legal right to provide discipline.

Conversely, critics argue that there is no evidence to show that school corporal punishment serves to instill better values in students.

In fact, Adah Maurer and James S. Wallerstein, authors of the second article, claim that corporal punishment has a detrimental effect on children, leading to underachievement in education, "poor impulse control, and spontaneous violent outbursts." They provide evidence that it can even lead to crime in later life.

Critics also argue that research has found that about half of those punished suffer from educationally induced post-traumatic stress disorder (EIPSD), a stress-related mental disorder whose symptoms include feelings of sadness and worthlessness, and bouts of anger, resentment, and aggression. Many students have, they claim, had to receive medical attention after punishment. Supporters of corporal punishment, on the other hand, argue that disorders such as EIPSD are symptomatic of how politically correct the United States has become. They argue that juvenile crime rates are soaring, and corporal punishment enables teachers to discipline unruly pupils and to instill moral values. The following articles examine the debate.

CORPORAL PUNISHMENT MAKES IMPRESSION
Tom Larimer

YES

Do you agree with the author that corporal punishment gives children a very clear message that their behavior will not be tolerated?

The author uses casual language and a personal memory to enforce his argument. This is a good way to engage the audience while making a point.

Getting the point across

There are probably more "positive" ways to help a public school student modify his or her behavior than paddling, but none that drives the point home so succinctly.

I can recall definintely "getting the point" while having my backside lit up by educators using anything from a tennis shoe to a wooden paddle with holes drilled in it to punctuate the point of the administration of corporal punishment.

Yes, message received. Ouch!

The lesson

Exel Smith was an educator with over 30 years of experience. He was superintendent of a tiny high school in Northwest Arkansas, retired, moved to our little community, and went back to work as a science teacher in our little high school.

Obviously of the old school, Mr. Smith had no qualms about taking paddle in hand to mete out some attitude adjustment to students. He also was of the opinion that public paddling, using the rest of the class as "witnesses" to the paddling, was the best way to get the most mileage out of a paddling.

Once that was established, it would be hard to imagine a more disciplined and orderly classroom, or a better learning environment. And learn we did.

Bullying or discipline?

Do you think it strengthens or weakens the author's argument when he tells the reader that he was a model student?

Now, keeping in mind that I was a model student, it is also necessary to know that as a student leader, it fell to me to test the boundaries with the "new" teacher … Mr. Smith.

It didn't take long for him to have me in front of the class, paddle in hand. When the first swat fell, I let out a howl that echoed down the halls of the little high school, despite the fact that I'd had harder swats from a 9-year-old girl. Mr. Smith was cool. He strategically placed himself between me and the class, so that only I could see his face or hear what he was saying.

COMMENTARY: U.S. school punishment

The tradition of corporal punishment in U.S. schools was originally brought from England (the last European country to make the practice illegal in 1998). It has been used since colonial times to discipline children.

New Jersey became the first state, in 1867, to pass a law banning school corporal punishment. It took 104 years for the next state, Massachusetts, to follow suit, in 1971. However, soon after there were large-scale protests as organizations banded together nationwide to make school corporal punishment illegal.

Organizations against school corporal punishment

In 1972 the American Civil Liberties Union (ACLU), along with the American Orthopsychiatry Association, set up a conference on corporal punishment. By 1974 the American Psychological Association made a formal statement in support of banning school corporal punishment and started the Task Force on Children's Rights. The National Education Association soon followed with a report condemning school corporal punishment and recommending its abolishment.

Almost a decade later, in 1987, an organization called the National Coalition to Abolish Corporal Punishment in Schools was formed, which included the American Bar Association, the American Academy of Pediatrics (AAP), the American Medical Association, the Parent-Teacher's Association, the National Center on Child Abuse Prevention, the National Education Association, and 20 other groups. Its activities continue to involve meetings on a national and local level, as well as articles and newsletters aimed at raising public awareness about corporal punishment.

Current status of school corporal punishment by state

The work of such organizations has had an effect. Since 1974, 27 states have passed laws banning corporal punishment in schools. Yet it is still legal in Alabama, Arizona, Arkansas, Colorado, Delaware, Florida, Georgia, Idaho, Indiana, Kansas, Kentucky, Louisiana, Mississippi, Missouri, New Mexico, North Carolina, Ohio, Oklahoma, Pennsylvania, South Carolina, Tennessee, Texas, and Wyoming.

In 2000 the number of students recorded as having received corporal punishment at school was 365,058. Statistics for the same year report that the states with the greatest incidence of the use of school corporal punishment are Mississippi (10.1 percent of children were hit by educators), Arkansas (9.2 percent), Alabama (6.3 percent), Tennessee (4 percent), Oklahoma (3 percent), Louisiana (2.7 percent), Georgia (2.13 percent), Texas (2.07 percent), Missouri (1 percent), and New Mexico (0.9 percent). The statistics also note that black students are hit twice as often as white students.

"Do that again and I'll give you licks that will really make you howl," he said softly.

I didn't do it again. After all, like I say, I was a model student.

History repeating itself

Years later, I ended up Mr. Smith's next-door neighbor. Life does take some crazy turns.

He's gone now, and so is Curly White. Curly, a junior high teacher with a paddle that hung prominently in his classroom, had a reputation for particularly painful paddlings.

That wasn't hard to believe if you'd seen his paddle. It was carved from a hickory tree that had been struck by lightning, and was about a half-inch thick. The wide, "business" end of the paddle had holes drilled through it to add some sting to the swats.

Do you think that using a paddle with holes in it to "add some sting to the swats" could be considered unnecessary cruelty?

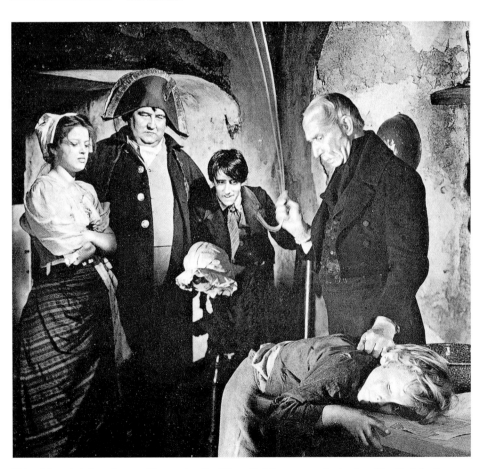

This picture is taken from a film poster for Oliver Twist, *an award-winning film that features corporal punishment in Victorian England.*

Curly insisted students call him by his nickname ... Curly. He was the only teacher I ever had who insisted we call him what everyone else did. Just to spite him, I'd call him Mr. White. I guess I showed him.

Curly's paddlings were legendary. He didn't think he'd done his job if he didn't leave marks, and it wasn't hard to do with that hickory paddle.

I only had to have the Curly paddling experience once. That was all most students who ran afoul of Curly's rules needed to see the error of their ways. Once.

Years later, long after Curly retired, I did a story for our community newspaper on Curly, who was raising coon dogs in his retirement. We sat in his living room for the interview, he in his favorite recliner. Hanging prominently over the recliner was "old hickory," the board of education that put so many young students back on track.

I could still remember the sting that came with a swat from that awesome education aid.

A lasting impression

I have from time to time wished I'd assured both Mr. Smith and Curly that what they did helped me a lot more than it hurt me. They were both no-nonsense educators who weren't going to let even a model student like me prevent them from trying to stamp out ignorance.

I had some great teachers. Not all of them used corporal punishment. These two did, but it in no way diminished my respect for them or their abilities to teach.

They definitely made a big impression on me. And it didn't hurt me a bit.

Well, maybe a little at the time.

> Many people use the argument that "It did me no harm." Is there anything wrong with that point of view?

THE INFLUENCE OF CORPORAL PUNISHMENT ON CRIME
Adah Maurer and
James S. Wallerstein

NO

X The last legal flogging of a convicted felon in the United States occurred in Delaware in 1952. The barbaric practice was made illegal in that year, but Delaware waited until 1972 to formally remove the whipping post from the state penitentiary.

Flogging in the Navy for drunken or disorderly conduct was abolished in 1853. The Marines finally forbade all forms of physical punishment in 1957, after a drill sergeant led a disciplinary march into a bog where six young men were drowned. Military instructors now may not touch the person or the clothing of a recruit and "Any fracture, concussion, contusion or welt shall be considered prima facia evidence of excessive force...."

Slavery and involuntary servitude had always been maintained with the help of whips, but that disappeared in the United States with the Emancipation Proclamation issued by President Lincoln, January 1, 1863.

Spousal abuse used to be termed "reasonable chastisement of wives" and was presumed necessary to maintain the sanctity and stability of the family. All states now have laws against such assaults, and law enforcement and the courts have begun to take seriously, complaints of spousal battery.

Only children

Now, in 1987, physical punishment is considered too severe for felons, murderers, criminals of all kinds and ages, including juvenile delinquents, too demeaning for soldiers, sailors, servants and spouses. But it remains legal and acceptable for children who are innocent of any crime.

The reasoning behind this curious discrepancy has been the belief that physical punishment will prevent the child from becoming a criminal. The frequent headlines, "Rising Tide of Juvenile Delinquency" usually attribute the situation to a decline of the use of corporal punishment in schools and homes. "Permissiveness," or letting the child do as he pleases,

The authors begin the article by giving the historical background of physical punishment for other members of society, so that when they make their point about children, it will have a more powerful effect.

118

assumed by some to be the only alternative to hitting, is pervasively believed to be the primary cause of anti-social behavior. In the good old days, it is said, "old fashioned discipline" kept children in line. There was very little crime. Harmony reigned. Or did it?

The truth about the "good old days"

There are no reliable statistics on the extent of crime a hundred or a hundred and fifty years ago. From all reports, however, crime in the U.S. was extensive, especially violent crime and crimes among the young. The good citizens of 19th-century America were also alarmed. They looked back to the good old days of simple rural life, before the growth of the cities. The crowded and crime-ridden Eastern cities were contrasted unfavorably with the "wide open spaces" of the West—the West, that is, of Jesse James and Billy the Kid!

Discipline in the one room schoolhouses was violent. Often the teacher engaged in a bare knuckle fight with the biggest student as a warning to the others of what would happen to them if they provoked his wrath. Horace Mann, the Father of American education, fulminated against the number of floggings per day, sometimes more than the number of scholars. Most of our great grandparents were satisfied with a fourth grade education and eighth grade was the end for all but five percent. The lawless mountain men of the Old West were recruited from the 14-year-olds who high-tailed it after one thrashing too many. Bands of outlaws stole horses, and plagued the defenseless. Public hangings and lynchings were commonplace while pickpockets worked the crowds. Only the militia and the sheriff's posse maintained any semblance of order.

Yet the myth remains that only woodshed discipline in early youth keeps boys from a life of crime, and that respect for authority is promoted only by painful procedures that induce fear and resentment of authority.

What is the truth? Let's take a good hard look at the facts about the effects of corporal punishment on crime.

After effects of physical punishment

Adrenalin output increases sharply during fear, anger and physical punishment. When this is prolonged or often repeated, the endocrine balance fails to return to baseline. The victim becomes easily angered and prone to poor impulse control and spontaneous violent outbursts.

Educational achievement is affected both directly and indirectly. Studies of prisoners, delinquents, school drop-outs,

> The authors focus only on the argument that corporal punishment prevents crime. But is that the only purpose of corporal punishment in the classroom? What other purposes might it have?

> The authors take a common myth—that there was less crime in the "good old days"—and stand it on its head. How many people do you know who still hark back to this myth?

> Hormones such as adrenalin are produced by cells and glands in the body that are collectively known as the endocrine system. These hormones are then transported to their target tissues in the body via the bloodstream.

college freshmen and successful professionals are compared in the following composite report [see chart below].

Taking part in this survey were: 200 psychologists who filled out anonymous questionnaires, 372 college students at the University of California, Davis and California State University …, 52 slow track underachievers at Richmond High School. Delinquents were interviewed by Dr. Ralph Welsh in Bridgeport, Connecticut and by Dr. Alan Button in Fresno, California. Prisoner information was by courtesy of Hobart Banks, M.S.W., counselor of difficult prisoners at San Quentin Penitentiary, San Quentin, California….

The Belt Theory

Dr. Ralph Welsh, who has given psychological examinations to over 2,000 delinquents, has developed what he calls. "The Belt Theory of Juvenile Delinquency." Dr. Welsh tells us: "The recidivist male delinquent who has never been exposed to the belt, extension cord or fist at some time in his life is virtually non-existent. As the severity of corporal punishment in the delinquent's developmental history increases, so does the probability that he will engage in a violent act."

Welsh's data also shows that the principal factor accounting for the over-representation of blacks in our prisons is the greater amount and severity of the physical punishment they endure as children. Black parents who do not use belts, boards, extension cords or fists, however, have

A "recidivist" is someone who relapses into a previous condition or mode of behavior. The word is often used to describe habitual criminals.

Relationship between corporal punishment and educational achievement

DEGREE OF PHYSICAL PUNISHMENT

	Never	Rare	Moderate	Severe	Extreme
Violent inmates at San Quentin	0%	0%	0%	0%	100%
Juvenile delinquents	0%	2%	3%	31%	64%
High school dropouts	0%	7%	23%	69%	0%
College freshmen	2%	23%	40%	33%	0%
Professionals	5%	40%	36%	17%	0%

children no more prone to criminal violence than the children of whites who do not use belts, etc.

> Might other causes, such as racial prejudice, also explain this fact?

Driving under the influence

Car crashes caused by drunk driving are increased by a hidden factor. Bottled up anger, when combined with alcohol is the largest cause of the highway death toll which comes to 25,000 deaths every year, or one every 20 minutes. An investigation by Donald C. Pelz of the Institute for Social Research at the University of Michigan in 1973 led to his finding that: "For the young male, anger toward the adult world is likely to find vent in dangerous driving.... Hostility tends to multiply with their attitude toward the educational system.... Those who had rejected the school system ... are likely to reject the highway system." In fact he concluded that abiding anger was even more dangerous than drinking per se, but that the combination was the most deadly. The insult to high school boys of an embarrassing paddling raises the adrenaline level, which if repeated often enough stays high all the time. They are the timebombs whose battlefield casualties litter the roads and intersections of our country....

Institutional abuse

Institutional punishments lack even intermittent moments of pride and belonging, that might in some cases mitigate slightly the worst effects. Charles Manson, the child of a 15-year-old single mother had his first contact with police when he was 7 and spent the rest of his life in a series of foster homes, reform schools and prisons. He could have survived the rejection of his mother, he says, if reform school of officials hadn't been institutionally cruel, whipping, beating and raping him, and letting other inmates do the same.

> The authors use the example of a famous criminal they know will be familiar to most of their readers. This can be an effective way to drive home a point.

A survey of 3,900 people in Houston as to what effect school corporal punishment had on their lives found that 76 percent of them said the effects had been negative and that they continued to resent what happened to them. That leaves about a fourth of them who were able to shrug it off and a mere handful who felt grateful for the timely punishment that "saved me from a life of crime." Thus, the one who testifies that "I was paddled when I was a kid and I turned out okay," must be labelled a survivor and congratulated on the strength of character that enabled him to make a life in spite of early mistreatment. Physchologist Robert Fathman, has offered this apt analogy: "Many people grew up in homes that had outhouses and they turned out okay. But do outhouses get the credit?"

> The authors employ an exaggerated analogy for their finale to make those who advocate corporal punishment look ridiculous. Do you think this technique is effective?

121

Summary

Many countries have banned school corporal punishment on the grounds of human rights, but many states continue to allow it. The issue has caused much heated debate.

In the first article Tom Larimer looks back at his own experience of receiving corporal punishment. A model student, he decided to test the waters with a new teacher, Exel Smith; he received a paddling for his behavior. As Larimer says, he had received harder blows from nine-year-old girls, but he never misbehaved again. But Larimer also mentions Mr. "Curly" White, who had a specially carved paddle and only believed he had punished a child correctly if he left marks. In spite of this Larimer insists that he wished he had told them that they did him more good than harm and that "it in no way diminished my respect for them or their abilities to teach."

Adah Maurer and James S. Wallerstein, on the other hand, argue that it is unreasonable that although it is illegal to inflict corporal punishment on criminals, soldiers, servants, and spouses, it still remains legal to inflict it on children—the most defenseless members of society. The authors go on to argue that instead of school corporal punishment instilling in children discipline and respect for authority, as is claimed by its supporters, research indicates that it is more likely to lead to poor educational progress and criminal behavior. The authors conclude with statistics from a survey of 3,900 people who had gotten corporal punishment at school—76 percent claimed the effects had been negative and still resented it.

FURTHER INFORMATION:

Books:

Hyman, Irwin A., *Reading, Writing and the Hickory Stick: The Appalling Story of Physical and Psychological Abuse in American Schools.* Lanham, MD: Lexington Books, 1990.

Hyman, Ronald T., *Corporal Punishment in Schools, No. 48: Reading the Law and the Principals' Decision.* Dayton, OH: Education Law Association, 1993.

Useful websites:

www.adolescenthealth.org/html/corporal_punishment_in_schools.html
Position paper of the Society of Adolescent Medicine.
www.nasponline.org/information/pospaper corppunish.html
National Association of School Psychologists (NASP)
Position Statement on Corporal Punishment in Schools.
www.corpun.com/
World Corporal Punishment Research.

www.stophitting.com/disatschool/
National Coalition to Abolish Corporal Punishment in Schools (NCACPS) website.
www.sparethechild.com/
Spare the Child organization website.

The following debates in the Pro/Con series may also be of interest:

In this volume:

 Topic 1 Does society support family values?

In *Media*

 Topic 5 Does movie and television violence cause social violence?

SHOULD SCHOOLS BE ALLOWED TO USE CORPORAL PUNISHMENT?

YES: The Eighth Amendment protects people against "cruel and unusual behavior." Corporal punishment qualifies as this.

YES: Schools do not have the right to physically punish students. That is the jurisdiction of the parent.

CHILDREN'S RIGHTS
Is school corporal punishment unconstitutional?

PARENTS
Should corporal punishment be applied by parents and not by schools?

NO: Various legal cases have established that the Eighth Amendment does not cover disciplinary action in schools

NO: All corporal punishment is wrong. There are other methods of disciplining children and young adults.

SHOULD SCHOOLS BE ALLOWED TO USE CORPORAL PUNISHMENT? KEY POINTS

YES: Corporal punishment can lead to educational underachievement and even criminal behavior later in life

YES: Many students who are physically punished end up having to receive medical treatment. In 1987-1988 around 10,000 students who were punished were treated for their injuries.

LONG-TERM EFFECTS ON BEHAVIOR
Does school corporal punishment have negative effects on children's behavior in the long run?

ABUSE
Is school corporal punishment a human rights abuse?

NO: It gives them a sense of discipline and a respect for authority that will prove beneficial later in life

NO: Instilling discipline and a code of conduct in young people is not abusive—children need to learn right from wrong, especially in a climate of rising crime

123

Topic 10
DOES SEX EDUCATION WORK?

YES
"SEX EDUCATION PAYS"
BUPA.CO.UK, MAY 31, 2001
BUPA'S MEDICAL TEAM

NO
"FACT SHEET: DOES SEX EDUCATION WORK?"
CENTER FOR AIDS PREVENTION STUDIES, UNIVERSITY OF CALIFORNIA,
PAMELA DECARLO

INTRODUCTION

Sex education—also known as sexuality education and sex and relationships education—involves learning about and forming attitudes and beliefs about sex, sexual identity, relationships, and intimacy. It has two main functions: to help young adults make informed choices about sex and also to reduce the potentially negative effects of having sex, such as unwanted pregnancies and sexually transmitted diseases (STDs). But sociologist and writer Barbara Dafoe Whitehead, author of several books on family and social issues, argues that sex education should also serve "not simply to reduce health risks to teenagers but also to build self esteem, prevent sexual abuse, promote respect for all kinds of families, and make little boys more nurturant and little girls more assertive."

Although many people believe that sex education is essential, the subject has resulted in much heated debate as critics argue, on the one hand, that it is ineffectual, since anyone intending to have sex will do so regardless of any education they receive to the contrary, and on the other, that sex education just encourages sexual activity. Supporters, however, claim that even if the first argument is true, it is better that young people engage in sexual activity knowing about contraception and the subsequent effects of having unprotected sex.

Although sex education remains a controversial issue in the United States, SIECUS (Sexuality Information Education Council in the United States) claims that almost 90 percent of Americans support sex education in high schools, while 80 percent support its teaching in middle or junior schools.

Similarly, the Alan Guttmacher Institute (AGI) published a study based on two national surveys of 7th- to 12th-grade public school teachers of sex education. It found that 86 percent of those interviewed believed that sexually active students taught to use contraceptives were more likely to use them than students who had not received similar instruction.

While many teachers now consider that contraceptive use should be taught to students at an older age than it was in the late 1980s, 93 percent still favor covering the subject, and 50 percent believe it should be taught in the 7th grade or earlier. And 89 percent of teachers also believe that students should be told where to go for birth control, while 82 percent believe students should be taught the correct way to use a condom.

"Given a choice between hearing my daughter say 'I'm pregnant' or 'I used a condom,' most mothers would get up in the middle of the night and buy them herself."

—JOCELYN ELDERS, FORMER SURGEON GENERAL (1993–1994)

However, the AGI also found that four out of ten teachers in 1999 cited abstinence as their most important message to their pupils, a rise from a figure of one in four in 1988. Seven in ten teachers also believed that students who were taught the need for abstinence were less likely to have intercourse than those who were not.

But is abstinence-only education really the answer? Certainly many Americans think so because support for it has increased in recent years, especially from government bodies. On January 31, 2002, Secretary Tommy G. Thompson announced in a Department of Health and Human Services (HHS) press release that "President Bush's budget for 2003 will increase funding for abstinence education programs to $135 million to ensure that more children receive the message that abstinence is the best option for avoiding unintended pregnancies and sexually transmitted diseases." Congress set aside $50 million a year over five years for abstinence-only school programs, and every U.S. state has applied for federal funding.

But will abstinence help reduce teenage pregnancy, STDs, and sexual activity among young people? AGI President Sara Seims claims that one-quarter of the decline in recent teen pregnancies may be thanks to abstinence, but the rest are due to improved contraceptive use. She also argues that "the teenage pregnancy rate and rates of STDs remain high."

The Centers for Disease Control (CDC) found that the United States currently has the highest teenage pregnancy rate of all developed countries: about one million teenagers become pregnant each year. Over 95 percent of those pregnancies are unwanted, and almost 30 percent of them end in abortions. Similarly, the National Institute of Allergy and Infectious Diseases (NIAID) estimates that around 13 million people in the United States suffer from STDs, such as gonorrhea, and that almost two-thirds of those people are aged under 25. Those statistics indicate that many young people are engaging in unprotected sexual activity. And many people are asking whether the problem actually lies in the lack of relevant sex education available.

The following two articles examine the pros and cons of the subject in greater detail.

SEX EDUCATION PAYS
BUPA's Medical Team

YES

Teenagers who receive good sex education will delay experimenting with sex, according to a new report from the USA.

National Campaign to Prevent Teenage Pregnancy

The study for the National Campaign to Prevent Teenage Pregnancy reviewed 73 studies of over 250 pregnancy prevention programmes in the USA and Canada. It found that sex education that discusses contraception does not encourage teenagers to try sex, or increase the frequency of sex or sexual partners. This counters the belief held by some that talking about sex to children will encourage them to try it sooner.

Jan Barlow, Chief Executive of Brook says: "These findings confirm what we already know in the UK. Effective sex and relationship education and greater openness, combined with access to confidential services, are more likely to lead to a delay in first sex and greater contraceptive use."

According to Brook, all the research indicates that openness when discussing sex with young people leads to informed decisions, rather than a desire to experiment earlier.

Does education work?

The Sex Education Forum says that good quality sex and relationship education can help reduce the number of teenage pregnancies. Information officer Caroline Ray says: "There are a number of new initiatives in this country which is good news, but the reality is that sex and relationship education is patchy. The main issue in schools is time and whether it begins early enough."

The Sex Education Forum advocates talking to children about sex and relationships from a very early age—from as young as nursery age onwards—as long as it done in an age-appropriate way.

"Sex education should be conducted both by parents and by schools. Many parents are willing and keen to provide sex education for their children, but there is not much advice on how to go about it", explains Ray. "It is not just a case of sitting down once and telling them everything, you should

Brook is a UK registered charity organization set up by in 1964 by the late Helen Brook to provide free, confidential sex advice and contraception to young people. Brook has 18 centers throughout the UK and a website called Brook Online at www.brook.org.uk.

The Sex Education Forum is the UK national authority on sex and relationships education (SRE), devoted to providing information and support for effective sex education. For more information see their website at www.ncb.org.uk/ sexed.htm.

COMMENTARY: Differing approaches to sex education in the United States

Debate is raging in schools about the best way to teach teenagers about sex. The adversaries generally form two groups: those who believe in the abstinence-only approach, in which teenagers are encouraged to abstain from sex until they are married or in a mature and responsible relationship; and the comprehensive approach, in which abstinence is advised along with information on sexually transmitted diseases (STDs) and contraception.

Abstinence-only programs

Abstinence-only (also known as abstinence-only-until-marriage) programs originated in 1981 with the Adolescent Family Life Act (AFLA), also known as the "Chastity Law." The aim of the act was to prevent teenage pregnancy by promoting chastity and self-discipline. In its first year it was allocated $11 million in government funds, increasing to $19 million by 2000. The first programs taught teenagers that abstinence was the only solution in preventing unwanted pregnancies and STDs, and promoted specific religious values. In 1983 the American Civil Liberties Union (ACLU) accused the AFLA of violating the separation of church and state defined by the Constitution and filed a suit against it. The courts ruled in the ACLU's favor in 1985, but it was only in 1993 that the Supreme Court ruled that all AFLA-funded sex education programs must be medically accurate, respect the principle of self-determination regarding contraceptive referral for teenagers, not include religious references, and not allow programs to use church premises or parochial schools during school hours for their programs or presentations. In 1996 a provision attached to the welfare-reform law gave federal funding of $50 million per year for five years for state-run abstinence-only programs. Currently, approximately $100 million, including matching state funds, is spent annually on state programs that have "teaching the social, psychological, and health gains to be realized by abstaining from sexual activity" as their exclusive purpose. The main methods used in these programs involve teaching teenagers to say "no" to sex, to resist peer pressure, and that around 50 percent of teenagers have never had sex and only 36.3 percent are currently sexually active.

Comprehensive programs

Comprehensive programs combine the promotion of abstinence with fact-based advice on contraception. They are based on the belief that some teenagers will choose to be sexually active despite advice to the contrary and that these teenagers should therefore be equipped with the means to protect themselves. They accuse abstinence-only programs of abandoning teenagers who choose to be sexually active or lack self-discipline, thereby causing higher rates of unwanted teenage pregnancies and STDs.

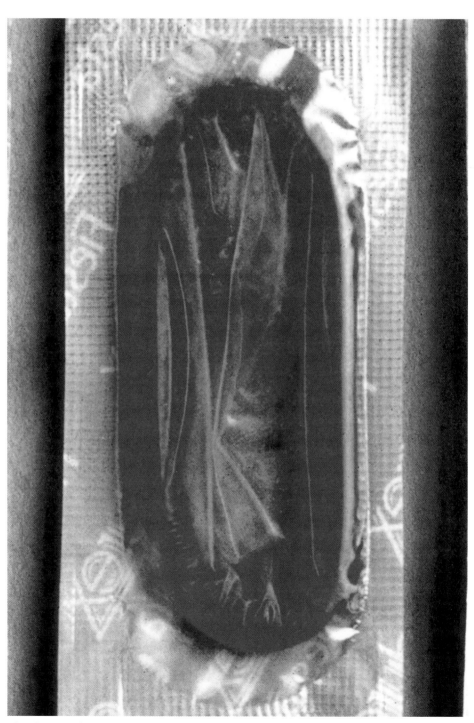

The photograph is a closeup of an advertisement for condoms.

give children small pieces of information and talk to them rather than at them. Discuss the issues with them and find out how much they already know," she concludes.

Last year the government issued a framework for sex and relationship education. Jan Barlow of Brook says: "We are very supportive of this framework—it is a significant step forward in making sex education in schools relevant, although there is still a huge disparity on how it is taught from school to school. In this country there seems to be a culture of fear surrounding the issue of sex and young people and these guidelines are trying to overcome this in an appropriate way."

How old were you when you were given sex education in school? Do you think it would have been more useful if you had been younger or older than that?

FACT SHEET: DOES SEX EDUCATION WORK?
Pamela DeCarlo

NO

✓ **Should sex education be taught in schools?**
The question is no longer should sex education be taught, but rather how should it be taught. Over 93% of all public high schools currently offer courses on sexuality or HIV. More than 510 junior or senior high schools have school-linked health clinics, and more than 300 schools make condoms available on campus. The question now is are these programs effective, and if not, how can we make them better?

Why do youth need sex education?
Kids need the right information to help protect themselves. The US has more than double the teenage pregnancy rate of any western industrialized country, with more than a million teenagers becoming pregnant each year. Teenagers have the highest rates of sexually transmitted diseases (STDs) of any age group, with one in four young people contracting an STD by the age of 21. STDs, including HIV, can damage teenagers' health and reproductive ability. And there is still no cure for AIDS.

Why do you think HIV infection is increasing most rapidly among young people?

HIV infection is increasing most rapidly among young people. One in four new infections in the US occurs in people younger than 22. In 1994, 417 new AIDS cases were diagnosed among 13-19 year olds, and 2,684 new cases among 20-24 year olds. Since infection may occur up to 10 years before an AIDS diagnosis, most of those people were infected with HIV either as adolescents or pre-adolescents.

The author is implying that it is not enough to try to change the way teenagers think about sex, it is their behavior that must be changed. In psychology this approach is called behavioral therapy.

Why has sex education failed to help our children?
Knowledge alone is not enough to change behaviors. Programs that rely mainly on conveying information about sex or moral precepts—how the body's sexual system functions, what teens should and shouldn't do—have failed. However, programs that focus on helping teenagers to change their behavior—using role playing, games, and exercises that strengthen social skills—have shown signs of success.

In the US, controversy over what message should be given to children has hampered sex education programs in schools. Too often statements of values ("my children should not have sex outside of marriage") come wrapped up in misstatements of fact ("sex education doesn't work anyway"). Should we do everything possible to suppress teenage sexual behavior, or should we acknowledge that many teens are sexually active, and prepare them against the negative consequences? Emotional arguments can get in the way of an unbiased assessment of the effects of sex education.

Other countries have been much more successful than the US in addressing the problem of teen pregnancies. Age at first intercourse is similar in the US and five other countries: Canada, England, France, the Netherlands, and Sweden, yet all those countries have teen pregnancy rates that are at least less than half the US rate. Sex education in these other countries is based on the following components: a policy explicitly favoring sex education; openness about sex; consistent messages throughout society; and access to contraception.

Why do you think that the United States has a higher teen pregnancy rate than these other countries? Can you think of any reasons why Americans might have more problems in their approach to sex education?

Often sex education curricula begin in high school, after many students have already begun experimenting sexually. Studies have shown that sex education begun before youth are sexually active helps young people stay abstinent and use protection when they do become sexually active. The sooner sex education begins, the better, even as early as elementary school.

What kinds of programs work best?

Reducing the Risk, a program for high school students in urban and rural areas in California, used behavior theory-based activities to reduce unprotected intercourse, either by helping teens avoid sex or use protection. Ninth and 10th graders attended 15 sessions as part of their regular health education classes and participated in role playing and experimental activities to build skills and self-efficacy. As a result, a greater proportion of students who were abstinent before the program successfully remained abstinent, and unprotected intercourse was significantly reduced for those students who became sexually active.

Postponing Sexual Involvement, a program for African-American 8th graders in Atlanta, GA, used peers (11th and 12th graders) to help youth understand social and peer pressures to have sex, and to develop and apply resistance skills. A unit of the program also taught about human sexuality, decision-making, and contraceptives. This program successfully reduced the number of abstinent students who

The Postponing Sexual Involvement program uses older peers to teach young adolescents about sex. Can you think of another environment in which this process tends to occur in a more natural way?

initiated intercourse after the program, and increased contraceptive use among sexually experienced females.

Healthy Oakland Teens (HOT) targets all 7th graders attending a junior high school in Oakland, CA. Health educators teach basic sex and drug education, and 9th grade peer educators lead interactive exercises on values, decision-making, communication, and condom-use skills. After one year, students in the program were much less likely to initiate sexual activities such as deep kissing, genital touching, and sexual intercourse.

AIDS Prevention for Adolescents in School, a program for 9th and 11th graders in schools in New York City, NY, focused on correcting facts about AIDS, teaching cognitive skills to appraise risks of transmission, increasing knowledge of AIDS-prevention resources, clarifying personal values, understanding external influences, and teaching skills to delay intercourse and/or consistently use condoms. All sexually experienced students reported increased condom use after the program.

A review of 23 studies found that effective sex education programs share the following characteristics:

1. Narrow focus on reducing sexual risk-taking behaviors that may lead to HIV/STD infection or unintended pregnancy.
2. Social learning theories as a foundation for program development, focusing on recognizing social influences, changing individual values, changing group norms, and building social skills.
3. Experimental activities designed to personalize basic, accurate information about the risks of unprotected intercourse and methods of avoiding unprotected intercourse.
4. Activities that address social or media influences on sexual behaviors.
5. Reinforcing clear and appropriate values to strengthen individual values and group norms against unprotected sex.
6. Modeling and practice in communication, negotiation, and refusal skills.

What still needs to be done?

Although sex education programs in schools have been around for many years, most programs have not been nearly as effective as hoped. Schools across the country need to take a rigorous look at their programs, and begin to implement more innovative programs that have been proven effective. Educators, parents, and policy-makers should avoid emotional

> For more information on the AIDS Prevention for Adolescents in School program see www.socio.com/srch/summary/pasha/passt09.htm.

> In what ways do you think the media influence the sexual behavior of teenagers?

misconceptions about sex education; based on the rates of unwanted pregnancies and STDs including HIV among teenagers, we can no longer ignore the need for both education on how to postpone sexual involvement, and how to protect oneself when sexually active.

A comprehensive risk prevention strategy uses multiple elements to protect as many of those at risk of pregnancy and STD/HIV infection as possible. Our children deserve the best education they can get.

Do you think that these two types of education can be easily combined, or can you see ways in which they might actually conflict with each other?

Summary

The preceding articles examine whether sex education, as it is currently taught, actually works. This is a topical issue, especially in light of the high incidence of teenage pregnancy and STDs among teenagers. In "Does Sex Education Work?" Pamela DeCarlo argues that although 93 percent of schools give some kind of course on sex education, the statistics show that this is not having a significant enough effect. She proposes that giving teenagers information on sex and its consequences is not enough to change teenagers' risky behavior and that only programs that help teenagers change their behavior, through role-playing, games, and exercises that enhance social skills and confidence, will have the desired effect. DeCarlo examines policies that have worked, such as Reducing the Risk, Postponing Sexual Involvement, and AIDS Prevention for Adolescents in School, and analyzes what characteristics they share that may be responsible for their success. The BUPA health team, on the other hand, argues that teenagers who get good sexual education will delay sexual experimentation. They assert that openness in talking about sexual issues is essential and that discussing contraception does not encourage teenagers to try sex or increase sexual activity. They also point to the crucial role that parents play in teaching their children sex education and that what both parents and schools need most is a specific framework and guidelines in order to teach sex education effectively.

FURTHER INFORMATION:

Books:

Levine, Judith, and Jocelyn M. Elders, *Harmful to Minors: The Perils of Protecting Children from Sex*. Minneapolis, MN: University of Minnesota Press, 2002.

Useful websites:

www.siecus.org/pubs/fact/fact0001.html
Sexuality Information and Education Council of the United States' (SIECUS) fact sheet on adolescence and abstinence.
www.ncac.org/cen news/cn80sexeducation.html
National Coalition Against Censorship's article on its launch of an anticensorship campaign on sex education.
www.mathematica-mpr,com/3rdLevel/abstinence.htm
"The Evaluation of Abstinence Education Programs Funded under Title V, Section 510" report.
www.share-program.com/teen.htm
The SHARE organization teen abstinence website.
www.theatlantic.com/politics/family/failure.htm
Atlantic online article "The Failure of Sex Education" by Barbara Dafoe Whitehead, Institute of American Values.

www.avert.org/schsexed.htm
Center for AIDS Prevention Studies Fact Sheet: "Should We Teach Only Abstinence in Sexuality Education?"
www.sexrespect.com
The Sex Respect abstinence-only organization website.
www.cfoc.org/3 teen/3 abstinence
Campaign For Our Children, Inc. abstinence teen website.

The following debates in the Pro/Con series may also be of interest:

In this volume:

Topic 1 Does society support family values?

Topic 11 Should teenagers have the right to contraception without parental consent?

DOES SEX EDUCATION WORK?

YES: *Statistics show that sexually active teenagers who are given information about contraception do use it*

YES: *The high incidence of STDs and teenage pregnancy shows that teenagers are experimenting with sex at an earlier age and that information about sex encourages them to engage in sexual activity*

TEENAGE PREGNANCY
Does sex education help reduce teenage pregnancy?

MORALITY
Does sex education encourage teenagers to experiment with sex?

NO: *The United States has the highest rate of teenage pregnancy among industrial countries despite the fact that 93 percent of public high schools offer courses in sex education, proving that sex education is failing to educate teenagers effectively*

NO: *Teenagers engage in sexual activity for a number of reasons, including love, curiosity, peer pressure, and the media*

DOES SEX EDUCATION WORK? KEY POINTS

YES: *The government has invested millions of dollars in abstinence education in the belief that it will help the current teenage pregnancy and STD problems*

YES: *Abstinence education teaches teenagers moral and social values and may enable them to resist peer pressure to have sex until they are in a married or mature, responsible relationship*

ABSTINENCE
Is abstinence education the way forward?

NO: *Other factors affect the sexual choices of teenagers. Teaching them to abstain from sexual practice does not mean that they will necessarily do so.*

NO: *Current sex education may not completely work, but it does provide sexually active teenagers with contraceptive knowledge, which can prevent pregnancy and protect their health*

A HISTORY OF CONTRACEPTION

"It is surprising ... how little every day conversation there is about safer sex."

—JILL LEWIS, ASSOCIATE PROFESSOR OF LITERATURE AND FEMINIST STUDIES, HAMPSHIRE COLLEGE, AMHERST, MASSACHUSETTS

Since time began people have used some method of contraception to prevent pregnancy. One of the earliest references is in the Bible, in Genesis, Chapter 38, where Onan "spilled his semen on the ground to keep from producing offspring." Although withdrawal is still used as birth control today, there are also many other contraceptive devices available on the market, ranging from condoms to the pill. The following timeline lists the main events in the history of contraception.

1839 Rubber condoms become available for use, although the ancient Egyptians made prophylactics from animal intestine.

1873 The Comstock Law bans the dissemination of contraceptive information.

1915 The Dutch invent the diaphragm.

1916 Feminist Margaret Sanger founds the American Birth Control League (known today as the Planned Parenthood Federation of America).

1917 The first birth-control clinic is opened. Sanger is arrested under the Comstock Law. It is illegal to import diaphragms.

1918 British family-planning pioneer Marie Stopes sells rubber caps by mail order.

1923 Sanger opens the first legal family-planning center.

1925 J. Noah Slee, Sanger's husband, finances the manufacture of diaphragms.

1930s In Germany the intrauterine device (IUD) becomes available. It is made of silver rings and silkworm thread.

1936 The ban on importing contraceptive devices is lifted by the Supreme Court.

1937 Doctors are able to legally provide information on birth control to married couples. North Carolina becomes the first state to recognize birth control and to provide contraception to mothers through its public health program.

1950s Scientists develop synthetic hormones that can block ovulation.

1960 The Food and Drug Administration (FDA) approves the first contraceptive pill.

1966 Around one million illegal abortions per year, resulting in about 5,000–10,000 deaths, are reported in the United States.

1967 Colorado becomes the first state to liberalize abortion in cases of rape, incest, when the mother's health is at risk, or when the child is damaged; North Carolina and California quickly follow.

1968 Pope Paul VI publishes *Humanae Vitae,* in which he predicts a general decline in moral standards among those people practicing contraception.

1972 The U.S. Supreme Court rules in *Eisenstadt v. Baird* that states cannot prohibit the distribution of contraceptive devices to single people.

1973 In *Roe v. Wade* state laws against abortion in the first trimester are invalidated on right-to-privacy grounds.

1978 People in the United States, Sweden, Tanzania, and Haiti begin showing signs of what becomes known as HIV/AIDS.

1981 President Reagan endorses the Human Life Amendment (HLA), a constitutional amendment aimed at banning abortion, the IUD, and some forms of birth control.

1982 Around 71 percent of all sexually active teenage girls in the United States report using contraception.

1983 Courts prevent the Department of Health and Human Services from implementing the "squeal rule," under which government-funded clinics have to notify parents when teenagers seek prescription contraceptives.

1985 Many manufacturers withdraw IUDs from sale following reports of infections and deaths. An international teenage pregnancy study concludes that those countries that have extensive contraceptive services and sex education have lower pregnancy rates.

1986 Following a report on HIV/AIDS, Surgeon General Everett Koop calls for

sex education to help prevent the spread of the disease.

1988 France becomes the first Western nation to approve the use of RU-486, the so-called abortion pill.

1989 President George Bush vetoes a bill approved by the House and Senate that would permit the use of Medicaid funds to pay for abortions for poor victims of "promptly reported" rape or incest. An FDA advisory committee approves Norplant, a long-acting contraceptive that protects a woman from pregnancy for up to five years when implanted under the skin.

1990 A study by the Institute of Medicine reports that the United States has fallen significantly behind other countries in developing new methods of birth control. Around 750,000 of the abortions performed annually are reported to have resulted from contraceptive failure.

1997 The Centers for Disease Control (CDC) claims that condoms have helped prevent the spread of HIV/AIDS and other STDs.

2000 The UN Population Fund estimates that 50 percent of couples use modern methods of contraception. The Sexuality Information and Education Council of the United States (SIECUS) estimates that around 65 million people have incurable sexually transmitted diseases.

2002 The government is already spending $571 million annually on pregnancy prevention. In May President George W. Bush promises to provide $138 million in new spending to fund health programs promoting abstinence-until-marriage. The Department of Health and Human Services reports that teenage birthrates have fallen 22 percent since 1991.

Topic 11
SHOULD TEENAGERS HAVE A RIGHT TO CONTRACEPTION WITHOUT PARENTAL CONSENT?

YES
"PARENTAL CONSENT AND NOTICE FOR CONTRACEPTIVES THREATENS TEEN HEALTH AND CONSTITUTIONAL RIGHTS"
APRIL 2001
CENTER FOR REPRODUCTIVE LAW AND POLICY

NO
FROM "DATA CONFIRMS THAT THE ABSTINENCE MESSAGE, NOT CONDOMS, IS RESPONSIBLE FOR THE REDUCTION IN BIRTHS TO TEENS"
NATIONAL COALITION FOR ABSTINENCE EDUCATION, MAY 17, 1998
PETER BRANDT

INTRODUCTION

Recent research shows that in America nearly one million women per year between the ages of 15 and 19 become pregnant, 70 percent of teenage mothers drop out of high school, and 20 percent of sexually active teens contract a sexually transmitted disease (STD) each year. With statistics like these, adolescent sexual behavior has been the subject of much debate, provoking passionate and diverse opinions from various experts, including those working in health care, youth advocacy, and policy-making.

Debate has focused increasingly on the sexual behavior of teenagers in an attempt to learn what might reduce the number of unplanned pregnancies and STDs among teenagers. Opinion is divided. Currently the main argument is whether it is better to teach teenagers

the values of abstinence or to offer free, confidential contraception and advice to those who wish to have sex.

Current legislation allows teenagers free, private access to contraception. Precedent for this was established in 1977 in *Carey v. Population Services International*, which centered on a New York law prohibiting the sale of condoms to anyone under 16. The court ruled that the "right to privacy in connection with decisions affecting procreation extends to minors as well as adults," and that the state interest in discouraging teenage sex would not be helped by withholding the means to protect themselves. As a result, the U.S. Constitution now protects the teenager's right to privacy in obtaining contraceptives and any advice on them. Yet those committed to promoting abstinence argue that what teenagers need is a sustained, focused message to abstain from sex until they are in a responsible adult relationship, and that confidential contraceptive health care and advice counteract this message by encouraging sexual activity. This view is supported by the Consortium of State Physicians Resource Councils, which commissioned a report on the rates of teenage pregnancy, birth, and abortion in the 1990s. The report concluded that it was abstinence and decreased sexual activity in teenagers, and not increased contraception, that were responsible for the decline in adolescent pregnancy, birth, and abortion rates in the 1990s.

> "Mandatory parental consent means more teens won't use birth control, more will get pregnant, and more will have abortions."
> —PLANNED PARENTHOOD AFFILIATES OF CALIFORNIA

However, opponents of abstinence-only campaigns argue that there is no conclusive evidence that they work. A research review by the National Campaign to Prevent Teen Pregnancy found that none of the abstinence-only programs reviewed had any consistent or significant effects on delaying the onset of intercourse. Without evidence that these programs are successful, opponents argue that there are no clear benefits to be gained from witholding contraception advice from teenagers.

A central premise of the abstinence argument is that parents and society play a key role in teaching family values and responsible behavior. The Helms amendment, filed in 2001, took this notion a step further. It proposed a change in legislation in which the funds in Medicaid and Title X, the two key sources of federal funds for family planning and health care for low-income women, should not be used for emergency contraception for a teenager without written parental consent.

Medical experts argued that the amendment was potentially harmful to teenagers. Pointing out that emergency contraception is a very time-sensitive service and needs to be used within 72 hours of intercourse, they feared young people might lag in getting family planning if required to obtain parental consent. They also feared the amendment would affect low-income teens most, those who could not afford private health care.

Other medical and advocacy bodies, such as the American Medical Association, expressed alarm at the wider ethical implications of requiring parental consent, arguing that such legislation would breach patient–physician confidentiality, that some teenagers might face harm from their families if they disclosed their sexual activities, and that healthy family communication can not be created by mandate. For such reasons care for teenagers would be most effective if their confidentiality were protected.

The following articles discuss the subject in greater detail. The first piece argues that parental consent for contraceptives threatens teen health and constitutional rights. The second piece argues that advocating abstinence and not contraception will tackle sexually risky behavior more effectively.

PARENTAL CONSENT AND NOTICE FOR CONTRACEPTIVES THREATENS TEEN HEALTH AND CONSTITUTIONAL RIGHTS
Center for Reproductive Law and Policy

YES

 No law currently requires parental consent for contraception

Increasingly, proposals are being introduced to restrict teens' access to reproductive health care by calling for parental consent or notification. Currently, no state or federal laws require minors to get parental consent in order to get contraception.

Examples of minors who would face harm

Teens in a variety of circumstances would be affected if required to obtain parental consent for contraception:

Birth control pills are a contraceptive that is taken orally, and DepoProvera is a contraceptive that is taken by a shot in the arm or buttocks; both drugs contain a hormone that prevents the ovaries from releasing an egg, so that fertilization cannot occur. A diaphragm is made of rubber. It is inserted into the vagina over the cervix (the opening to the uterus) to prevent the male's sperm from reaching the egg.

- A young woman seeking contraception from a clinic— birth control pills, DepoProvera, diaphragm—would be forced to obtain parental permission
- A minor who buys condoms at a pharmacy could be turned away without parental consent
- A teen who seeks emergency contraception because of forced or unanticipated intercourse would need approval, even though emergency contraception must be used within 72 hours of unprotected intercourse.

Two types of mandatory parental contact for contraception are sometimes proposed:

- Mandatory parental consent would force teenagers to get permission from one or two parents before getting contraception.
- Mandatory parental notification would require young people to tell one or two parents about their plans to get contraception. Mandatory notification poses the same danger of discouraging contraceptive use by teens as does the requirement of consent. If a minor is fearful about discussing contraception with a parent, there is no difference between 'telling' the parent and getting parental permission.

Federal programs require confidentiality for teens

Two federal programs—Title X and Medicaid—protect teens' privacy and prohibit parental consent requirements for teens seeking contraception. Title X provides funds to states for family planning services; Medicaid covers health care services for low-income women. Both programs mandate that, in exchange for receiving monies from the federal government, health care services treat all patients confidentially, including teens.

Attempts by states to implement parental consent requirements for contraceptive services that are funded by these programs have been invalidated when challenged in court. Courts find that the requirements impermissibly conflict with federal program requirements. Federal program rules mandating confidentiality preempt state efforts to make new requirements.

Both consent and notification damage teens

Parental contact requirements discourage teens from seeking contraception, even though they may already be sexually active. Confidentiality can be a determining factor for teens deciding whether or not to seek contraceptive protection.

Do you think that the teenagers you know would be discouraged from seeking contraception if they had to have their parents' consent?

Teenagers need access to contraceptive services

More than half the women in the United States have intercourse before their 17th birthday. While the teen pregnancy rate today has dropped slightly in the past twenty years, almost one million teens become pregnant each year. A sexually active teen using no contraception has a 90% chance of becoming pregnant within a one year period, according to the Alan Guttmacher Institute.

Lack of contraception increases the chances of unintended pregnancy. Nearly 80% of teen pregnancies are unplanned in the U.S. Teen pregnancy rates are much higher in the U.S. than in other industrial countries—double the rates in England; nine times as high as the Netherlands. Lack of contraception also increases the possibility of exposure to sexually transmitted diseases. About three million U.S. teens acquire a sexually transmitted infection every year.

These statistics were compiled from research data in the Alan Guttmacher Institute's 1995 National Survey of Family Growth.

Parental contact laws threaten teens' health

Supporters of measures forcing teens to notify or get consent from their parents argue that they promote the best interests of young women and improve family communications.

These arguments are out of touch with reality. These proposed laws threaten adolescent health and well-being.

COMMENTARY: Legal proposals for mandatory parental consent for teenage contraception

Since 1997 there have been attempts to pass legislation in Congress to make it illegal for teenagers to seek contraception without their parents' consent. At present, teenagers are protected under Title X of the Public Health Service Act of 1970 and Medicaid's Title XIX of the Social Security Act of 1965. They get full confidentiality when seeking reproductive health care, contraception, and contraceptive advice. However, in both 1997 and 1998 Illinois Republican Representative Donald Manzullo introduced a bill proposing an amendment to Title X that would require teenagers to obtain parental consent for contraception. Around the same time, Texas Republican Representative Kevin Brady introduced a similar bill that would allow states participating in programs funded by Medicaid and Title X to bar minors from purchasing contraceptives without parental consent. Although neither representative succeeded in having his bill passed in Congress, this was only the beginning of continuous attempts to change minors' rights to confidentiality in obtaining contraception.

In May 2001 Pennsylvania Republican Representative Melissa Hart proposed an amendment to the Labor/HHS appropriations bill that would prevent teenagers from receiving emergency contraception at school-based health centers without their parents' written consent. The same month, Republican Senator Jesse Helms filed a similar amendment to the Elementary and Secondary Education Act. Emergency contraception in this context refers to what is commonly called "the morning-after pill," which must be taken within 72 hours after unprotected sex to be effective.

Many medical and public health organizations point out that because of the time-sensitive nature of this method of contraception, the time taken to obtain parental consent could make it practically useless. In 2002 seven states—Alaska, Florida, Georgia, Idaho, Kentucky, Maryland, and South Carolina—attempted to introduce state legislation requiring parental involvement in teenage contraception.

Even teens who could comply with parental consent requirements will face delays in getting contraceptive services. Additional clinic visits, missed school or work time, and increased expense will result.

Many young women live in nontraditional situations— with one parent, a stepparent, other relatives, or on their own. Contact with biological parents, if required by law, may be impossible.

Some teens face violence or other severe consequences from parents as a result of informing their parents that they are seeking contraceptive services. Minors fearful of retribution may forgo using contraception altogether, even though they are already sexually active.

Teens who seek contraceptive services are generally sexually active already. They benefit from meeting with health care providers, who can provide screening, counseling about sexually transmitted diseases, and education about other reproductive health concerns.

States may not impose additional restrictions on Title X programs

Several courts have found that state parental consent requirements may not be imposed on federally funded family planning programs. Where states accept Title X and Medicaid funds, they cannot require minors to obtain parental consent prior to using those services.

Parental consent for contraception is unconstitutional

Minors have a right to privacy that includes their ability to use contraception. The U.S. Supreme Court said in 1977 that denial of contraception is not a permissible way to deter sexual activity. Although states may require parental consent for a minor's abortion when sufficient alternatives, such as judicial bypass, are in place, the same reasoning does not apply to contraception. According to the U.S. Supreme Court, "The states' interest in protection of the mental and physical health of the pregnant minor, and in protection of potential life are clearly more implicated by the abortion decision than by the decision to use a nonhazardous contraceptive."

Access to contraceptive services is considered a fundamental privacy right and has remained so for over three decades.

This 1977 court case, Carey v. Population Services International, overturned a New York state law prohibiting the sale of condoms to minors under 16. The judge, Justice Stevens, said that the attempt to deny teenagers access to contraception in an effort to impress on them the evils of underage sex was as irrational as if "a state decided to dramatize its disapproval of motorcycles by forbidding the use of safety helmets."

Summary: teens' lives would be endangered by bad policy and bad law

Placing barriers on teen access to contraception is dangerous to the health and welfare of young women because it increases their risk of unplanned pregnancies. The costs to society from teen pregnancy are enormous.

While programs with federal family planning money are forbidden from requiring parental consent or notice for teen services, teens also have a constitutional right to privacy that encompasses their decision to obtain contraception, a right that lawmakers should acknowledge and respect.

What do you think are the costs to society that are caused by teen pregnancy?

DATA CONFIRMS THAT THE ABSTINENCE MESSAGE, NOT CONDOMS, IS RESPONSIBLE FOR THE REDUCTION IN BIRTHS TO TEENS
Peter Brandt

NO

X On April 30, 1998, the National Campaign to Prevent Teen Pregnancy released a substantial amount of new data and analysis dealing with the issue of adolescent sexual risk behavior. The data was from a variety of sources, including Campaign-sponsored research and the National Center for Health Statistics (NCHS). The release of this data received wide and extensive media coverage. I have now had time to review the Campaign and its data and press releases. I would like to share some observations.

Decline in teen birthrate

The author begins his argument by setting out the statistics and data that he will use to substantiate his argument.

The data reflect a very favorable trend. The data released by the Campaign reflects the first change in the trend of adolescent sexual activity in several decades. The teen-age birthrate has declined 11.9 percent from 1991 to 1996 (from 62.1 to 54.7 births per 1,000 young women aged 15 to 19). The birthrate for African-American teens fell 21 percent.

All 50 states witnessed a decline in the teen birthrate. Twelve states saw teen birthrates decline more than 12 percent, five of them had birth rates drop more than 16 percent. Source: "Teenage Births in the United States: National and State Trends, 1990-1996," National Center for Health Statistics.

Decline in abortions

This trend is especially encouraging since the decline in births to teen-age women has not come at the expense of more abortions. In fact, the number of abortions in the U.S. declined by 15.3 percent from 1990 to 1995.

To view the full report, go to www.welfare-reform-academy. org/conf/papers/ sonenste.pdf.

Too much credit by the media and some experts is given to contraceptives.... But to credit contraceptive use for the decline in teen birth and abortion rates simply doesn't square with the evidence. There are three reasons to link the decline in birth rates, at least in part, to increased abstinence.

Three reasons to link birthrate declines to abstinence

First, condom use is up, but total contraceptive use is flat. In a report issued on May 1, 1998 by Joyce Abma from the National Center for Health Statistics and Freya L. Sonenstein from the Urban Institute, the authors stated: "Between 1988 and 1995 there has been little change in the proportion of currently sexually active teens reporting that they used no method of contraception at the last intercourse."

The actual percentage of teens reporting the use of some form of contraception at last intercourse has actually decreased, particularly among female teenagers. This decrease is most likely even larger than reported when the dual use of oral and barrier contraception is considered. It is likely that dual use increased from 1988 to 1995 due to the awareness of pregnancy and HIV/AIDS.

> What the author means when he refers to "the dual use of oral and barrier contraception" is the use of both birth-control pills to avoid pregnancy and condoms to avoid sexually transmitted diseases.

Thus, to attribute the decline in teenage birth rates to increased contraception use is not intellectually honest.

Second, teenage sexual behavior has decreased. The percentage of teenagers who have ever had sexual intercourse has decreased, according to Abma and Sonenstein. Males in 1988 who have had sexual intercourse was 60 percent; in 1995 this percentage dropped to 55 percent. Females in 1988 who have had sexual intercourse was 51 percent; in 1995 this percentage dropped to 49 percent. Source: "Teenage Sexual Behavior and Contraceptive Use: An Update," Abma and Sonenstein, 1998

Third, there is broad societal support for abstinence. Several studies released in the past year point to two conclusions:

There is broad parental and societal support for abstinence. Parents have a significant influence on their children's behavior.

On April 30, 1998 the Campaign released the results of an in-depth survey of parents and adolescents regarding sexuality issues. Here are some of the findings from the Campaign's study:

> Do you think that parents are the best people to advise young people on sexual behavior? Who else might provide advice?

87 percent of parents said that teens should be at least 16 before they begin steady, one-on-one dating.

Only 6.8 percent of parents answered the question that sex in high school is generally OK as long as contraception is used.

95 percent of both adults and teens thought that it is either very important or somewhat important for teens to be given a strong message from society that they should abstain from sex until they are at least out of high school.

This data is consistent with an opinion survey done by the Wirthlin Worldwide research firm. The results of the telephone poll, released in February, 1998, showed that 71 percent of adults believe that couples should wait to have sex until marriage.

The [health study] published September 10, 1997 in the *Journal of the American Medical Association* reported parental connectedness as a strong protective factor against adolescent risk behavior. In the study, parental disapproval of adolescent sex and parental disapproval of adolescent contraceptive use were powerfully associated with a delay in the age of sexual debut.

Abstinence gaining society's acceptance

The abstinence message is gaining acceptance from society. Longtime abstinence advocates tell stories about getting laughed at in public meetings ten years ago when they suggested abstinence, well, times are changing. Abstinence is becoming recognized, and in some cases even embraced, as the only 100 percent effective way for teenagers to avoid pregnancy and STDs.

What do you think are some of the factors that may have changed society's attitudes toward abstinence within the past 10 years?

This renewed acceptance of abstinence is coming from across the board—parents, the genera public, the media, even the public health community. Consider the following excerpt from the May 5, 1998 *USA Today* article:

"The public health director for Riverside Country credits welfare reform for convincing some teenagers to abstain from sexual intercourse. Teenage girls are having less sex … [this] is a victory for those who have long argued that convincing teenagers to forgo intercourse can help cut the number of young girls who have babies."

The cultural consensus in America is definitely moving towards the abstinence message. Sure there are still those in the media and safe-sex cartel who stubbornly refuse to accept it. But their position on teenage sexuality is based on the ideological belief in unhindered sexual liberation not on medical facts. For these individuals to move toward the abstinence message would require them to admit that they have devoted their lives to a lie. But, there are many in the public health field who are re-thinking their stand on condoms and moving towards abstinence as their primary prevention message….

Summary

The decline in teen pregnancy is likely due to a combination of factors including:

Greater societal awareness of the problems of teen pregnancy and STDs.

More conservative cultural views toward illegitimacy.
Changes in state and national welfare policy.

The efforts of abstinence-education programs by such organizations as crisis pregnancy centers and *True Love Waits* whose reach has expanded dramatically in the 1990s.

There are many studies that prove that "safe-sex" programs increase the total number of condoms used. This fact is undisputed. But the cartel has not proven a link between an increase in condom usage and a reduction in pregnancies or STDs. There is absolutely no evidence that contraception programs have appreciably reduced teen pregnancy or STDs. Absolutely none. I have recently asked public health officials and cartel members to provide me with any and all research studies that prove the ability of condom programs to reduce pregnancy or STDs. I have not received a thing. Why? Because no such study exists.

Is it possible to prove such a link exists? Does common sense suggest that there is or is not a link?

There is evidence that the abstinence message is making an impact. For example, in the past year about 700,000 teens signed *True Love Waits* pledge cards. Another 1.5 million teens were exposed to abstinence education provided by crisis pregnancy centers.

For more information on the international True Love Waits campaign go to www.lifeway. com/tlw.

The acceptability of abstinence until marriage as the most beneficial lifestyle choice for America's young people is growing rapidly. Abstinence is becoming mainstream. The reason is that ABSTINENCE WORKS.

Summary

The Center for Reproductive Law and Policy asserts that teenagers' constitutional right to privacy when seeking contraceptive advice should be acknowledged, respected, and upheld. It argues that supporters of legislation promoting parental consent are out of touch with reality, which is that it will deter teenagers from seeking contraception and greatly increase the chance of unwanted pregnancy and sexually transmitted diseases. It proposes that such legislation will also block access to important public health provisions, such as Title X and Medicaid. It stresses that there are myriad reasons why a young person may be afraid to tell their family about their sexual activities and that these reasons are varied and complex. Legislation that forces parental contact does not take this into account and may put young people at greater risk of abuse, disease, and unwanted pregnancy.

In the opposing article Peter Brandt does not accept that the recent decline in teenage pregnancy rates is due to increased contraceptive use. He argues that although "safe-sex" programs do increase condom use, there is no proven link between condom usage and a reduction in pregnancies or STDs. By contrast, he argues, the abstinence message is having an effect not only on teenagers, but also on the cultural ethic of American society, citing recent statistics showing that 95 percent of adults and teens believe there should be a strong message to abstain from sex until they are at least out of high school. He suggests that parental disapproval of adolescent sex and contraceptive use encourages teenagers to delay intercourse and is therefore a key factor in promoting abstinence. For Brandt the data suggests a society in which there is a much greater level of awareness about teenage pregnancy and sexual health, and in which abstinence is increasingly the lifestyle choice for teenagers and a viable intervention strategy in state and welfare policy.

FURTHER INFORMATION:

Books:

Endersbe, Julie K., *Teen Sex, Risks and Consequences (Perspectives on Healthy Sexuality)*. New York: Lifematters Press, 2000.

Mucciola, Gary, *Everything You Need to Know about Birth Control*. New York: Rosen Publishing Group, 1998.

Useful websites:

www.aclu.org
Site of the American Civil Liberties Union.
www.crlp.org/
Site of the Center for Reproductive Law and Policy.
www.teenwire.com/index/asp
Planned Parenthood's site for teens.

The following debates in the Pro/Con series may also be of interest:

In this volume:

Part 1: The family

Topic 1 Does society support family values?

Topic 8 Should parents be held responsible for the behavior of their children?

SHOULD TEENAGERS HAVE A RIGHT TO CONTRACEPTION WITHOUT PARENTAL CONSENT?

SHOULD TEENAGERS HAVE A RIGHT TO CONTRACEPTION WITHOUT PARENTAL CONSENT? KEY POINTS

YES: Many teens will therefore not seek contraception, and statistics show that teenagers who do not use contraception have a 90 percent chance of becoming pregnant within a year

YES: Minors have as much right to privacy and confidentiality as adults in matters regarding their own health and welfare, and the law upholds these rights

TEEN PREGNANCIES
Will parental consent requirements cause more teenage pregnancies?

MINORS' RIGHTS
Do minors deserve the same rights to privacy in obtaining contraception as adults?

NO: There is no evidence that confidential contraception programs reduce teen pregnancies. Teenage birthrates are decreasing because more teenagers are abstaining from sex, not because of increased contraceptive use.

YES: Confidential contraceptive health care conflicts with the abstinence message by encouraging teenage sexual activity

NO: Teenagers are too young to manage their own sex lives. Parents and society need to encourage responsible behavior.

YES: Teenagers who cannot ask their parents will suffer from unwanted pregnancies and STDs; others may risk physical harm from their parents if they do ask them

ABSTINENCE
Does teenage access to contraception interfere with the promotion of abstinence?

HEALTH RISKS
Does requiring parental consent for teenage contraception put teenagers' health at risk?

NO: Teens who seek contraception are usually already sexually active, and there is no proof that abstinence-only programs really work

NO: Parents will have a beneficial influence on teenagers' behavior, and this will improve family communication

149

Topic 12

SHOULD THE ELDERLY PAY FOR THEIR OWN HEALTH CARE?

YES

FROM "WILL AMERICA GROW UP BEFORE IT GROWS OLD"?
THE ATLANTIC MONTHLY, MAY 1996
PETER G. PETERSON

NO

"SECOND OPINION"
THE NEW REPUBLIC ONLINE, JUNE 25, 2001
JONATHAN COHN

INTRODUCTION

From 1946 to the end of the 1960s there was an unprecedented growth in the number of births, a period known as the Baby Boom in America. During the 1950s there were four million live births a year, resulting in 1976 in nearly 34 million teenagers. At the time, this seemed little more than a demographic oddity. Today, however, as all 76 million of that generation grow older, economic planners are becoming increasingly concerned about who should pay for their health care: the state, the family, or the elderly themselves?

At the heart of the problem is the fact that in the last 50 years or so there have been so many advances in health care and medical science that life expectancy is higher than ever before. In 1920, for example, the average American lived for around 45 years; today a woman's average age at death is 80 and a man's 73. By 2040 it is estimated that between 20 and 25 percent of the population will be over 65, and most of them will be supported to some extent by government entitlements. Politicians are being forced—rather belatedly, in the opinion of some—to address the problem of how to pay for an aging population.

Historically, since the decline of the traditional extended family unit and the realization that the family could no longer take care of its own, care of the elderly has been funded by Social Security financed by taxes. Social Security programs are financially self-sustaining, supported on a pay-as-you-go basis through payroll taxes collected in equal amounts from employees and employers during a worker's years of active employment, in accordance with the Federal Insurance Contribution Act (FICA). Participation in Social Security is compulsory, and benefits are paid as an earned right.

Because Social Security is earnings-linked, most of the money raised comes from people at the top of their career earning curve—typically those aged between 30 and 50. But while that system worked well in the 1960s, when there were five times more taxpayers than Social Security beneficiaries, since the end of the Baby Boom the birthrate has fallen sharply, and it is predicted that by 2040 there will be no more than two taxpayers for each Social Security claimant. In the worst-case scenario the welfare state will simply be unaffordable.

"I encourage you to go on living solely to enrage those who are paying your annuities."
—VOLTAIRE, 18TH-CENTURY FRENCH PHILOSOPHER AND AUTHOR

While supporters of state provision of elderly health care claim that many old people live below the poverty threshold, critics argue that many of the Baby Boom generation had financially successful careers and can now afford to support themselves without funding from the state. Under the present system, however, those people will be supported in retirement by money taken from people born after 1970, many of whom were badly hit by the recession of the early 1990s.

One of the many suggestions for alternative funding of elderly heath care is raising the retirement age from 65.

But in order to maintain Social Security at its present levels, people would have to stay at work until they were around 74. Although this would be an effective method of ensuring that old people contribute more to their own health care, there is little evidence that such an initiative would be welcomed by either workers or employers.

Similarly, a new tax could be levied on savings, but it might not produce the funding required since Americans retain only about 5 percent of their disposable income. Moreover, the sudden imposition of such a tax could undermine confidence in investment, and make it difficult for people to plan their own financial futures.

Critics argue that Medicare, the system of health insurance for the over-65s provided by the U.S. government, could be restructured. At the moment, apart from an initial sum paid by the patient, Medicare covers all expenses for the first 60 days of hospitalization and a proportion of hospital costs for a further 30 days. It does not pay for prescription drugs, extended nursing-home care, or the costs of chronic illness. But while some older people are able to bridge the financial gaps left by Medicare through alternative means, such as private health insurance, others are forced to exhaust their assets before they can qualify for Medicaid, the medical program for the indigent.

Under a proposed new system Medicare could fund prescription drugs, which are now much more expensive proportionally than when Medicare was introduced in 1965. That would make it easier for the state to restrict benefit payments to those who need them most.

The following two articles look at the pros and cons of making the elderly pay for their own health care.

WILL AMERICA GROW UP BEFORE IT GROWS OLD?
Peter G. Peterson

YES

In the 1930s the United States suffered severe economic and social decline in a period that came to be known as the Great Depression. In 1934 President Franklin D. Roosevelt announced his intention to provide a program of Social Security. The subsequent 1935 Social Security Act created several general welfare provisions and set up a social insurance program designed to pay retired workers aged 65 or older an income after retirement.

Using bullet points is an effective way to clarify the points you want to make.

Demographics is destiny

Within the next fifteen years the huge generation of Baby Boomers, whose parents brought them into the world with such optimism, will begin to retire. As they do, they will expect the munificent array of Entitlements that were guaranteed (again with such optimism) to every retiring American with no anticipation of the ever-growing length of retirement as life expectancy increases or the ever-rising expectations of independence, affluence, health, and comfort of life in retirement. But consider who is expected to pay for this late-in-life consumption: the relatively small "bust" generation in whose productive capacity we have failed to invest. Neither the founders of Social Security 60 years ago nor the founders of Medicare 30 years ago imagined the demographic shape of America that will unfold over the next several decades.

Ponder the following:

- With 76 million members, the Baby Boom generation is more than half again as large as the previous generation.... [T]he number of Social Security beneficiaries will at least double by the year 2040.
- In 1900 only one in twenty-five Americans was over sixty-five. The vast majority of these people were completely self-supporting or supported by their families. By 2040 one out of every four or five Americans will be over sixty-five, and the vast majority will be supported to some degree by government entitlements.
- In 1960 there were 5.1 taxpaying workers to support each Social Security beneficiary. Today there are 3.3. By 2040 there will be no more than 2.0—and perhaps as few as 1.6.
- The number of "young old" (sixty-five to sixty-nine) will roughly double over the next half century, but the number of "old old" (eighty-five and over) is expected to triple or quadruple—adding the equivalent of an entire New York City of over-eighty-five-year-olds to the population. Nearly three quarters of those over eighty-five will be single,

divorced, or widowed—the groups most likely to need extensive government assistance.

- In 1970 children under five outnumbered Americans aged eighty-five and over by twelve to one. By 2040 the number of old old will equal the number of preschool children, according to some forecasts.
- The extraordinary growth of the old old population will add especially to federal health costs. This is because the average annual medical-care bill rises along a steep curve for older age groups. The ratio of Medicare and Medicaid spending on the old old to spending on the young old is about 2.5 to 1.
- In 2030 only about 15 percent of the over-sixty-five population will be nonwhite. But about 25 percent of younger Americans will be nonwhite. This will create a potentially explosive situation in which largely white senior Boomers will be increasingly reliant on overtaxed minority workers.
- In order to provide the same average number of years of retirement benefits in 2030 that were contemplated when Social Security was set up, in the 1930s, the retirement age would have to be raised from sixty-five to seventy-four by 2030. But this projection—daunting as it is—assumes that future gains in longevity will slow as average life expectancy approaches the supposed "natural limit" to the human life-span. Many experts now question whether such a limit really exists. Summing up research at the National Institute on Aging, the demographer James Vaupel goes so far as to suggest that we are now on the threshold of a "new paradigm of aging," in which the average life expectancy could reach 100 or more.

Why should the race of Social Security contributors and claimants be an issue?

James Vaupel is the director of the Program on Population, Policy, and Aging at the Terry Sanford Institute of Public Policy, Duke University, NC.

Age wave

Of course, the United States is not the only country facing an "age wave." Indeed, the age waves in most industrial countries are approaching faster than ours, and—to judge by official projections—could have an even worse impact on their countries' economies and public budgets. But these other countries enjoy long-term defenses that we lack.

Unlike the United States, most can actually budget their public spending on health care, and so have much greater control over this potentially explosive dimension of senior dependency. Unlike the United States, most generally tax public benefits as they do any other income. And unlike the United States, most have fairly healthy household savings rates (generally well over 10 percent

Can you think of any explanation for the relatively low savings rates in the United States?

Should affluent Americans refuse benefits they do not need, even if they are entitled to them?

Should a balanced budget take priority over the welfare and health care of the elderly population?

The author states that over 70 percent of the elderly population expect to have a similar or better lifestyle in retirement than what they had when they were working. Is such an expectation unrealistic?

of disposable income, as compared with about five percent here), and so can absorb public-sector deficits much better than we can....

Obligations vs. reality

Social Security was established to protect the elderly from indigence late in life—to prevent a "poverty-ridden old age," in the words of Franklin D. Roosevelt. If we allow it to go bankrupt by paying benefits to middle-class and affluent Americans, many of whom can live well enough without these benefits, what will happen to those who really need them?

Among Social Security recipients whose incomes are under $20,000, Social Security accounts for more than half of the total. In spite of this sobering dependence, many political leaders imply by their inaction that it's fine to wait until trillion-dollar deficits have devastated our economy, and then slash benefits at the last minute.

By doing so we would then deprive Americans at all income levels of the chance to plan for their futures. Millions of lower-income beneficiaries would be stranded in what might be called a demographic Depression, as the safety net that Social Security was enacted to provide suddenly vanished. Future historians may record that Social Security's "defenders" were the ones who most wanted to exempt the program from a balanced-budget amendment and thus from gradual and timely reform....

America's savings gap

When it comes to our retirement plans, we are a nation in denial. About nine out of ten Boomers say they want to retire at or before age sixty-five (about six out of ten before age sixty). More than two thirds say they will be able to live "where they want" and live "comfortably" throughout their retirement years. A stunning 71 percent expect to maintain in retirement a standard of living the same as or better than what they enjoyed during their working years....

B. Douglas Bernheim, of Stanford University, concludes that Boomers on average must triple their current saving if they want to enjoy an undiminished living standard in retirement. And if one assumes a 35 percent reduction in Social Security benefits (which seems more than likely if not inevitable), then Boomers will have to quintuple their saving. A recent study by the [nonpartisan organization] Committee for Economic Development, *Who Will Pay for Your Retirement? The Looming Crisis*, comes to a similarly stark conclusion....

Prospect of inheritance

Finally there is the prospect of inheritance, that magic cure-all for any generation's retirement worries.

In recent years Boomers have been cheered by a spate of upbeat stories about the "$10 trillion inheritance boom" that today's affluent seniors are expected to pass on.... But ... for most of this generation the typical inheritance will just about cover the costs of settling Dad's estate and pay off a few lingering medical bills....

SECOND OPINION
Jonathan Cohn

NO

Congress won't take up Medicare prescription drug coverage for at least a few weeks, or maybe longer if the Bush White House has anything to say about it. But on such an important issue, it's never too early to take on a critic —particularly when the critic happens to be a colleague or, ahem, your boss.

Peter Beinart's articles

To see these articles, go to www.the newrepublic.com.

I refer here to an aside—actually, two asides—in recent articles by *New Republic* editor Peter Beinart. One appeared in his otherwise fine "Punditry" column about the death penalty that appeared here at TNR Online two weeks ago; the other appeared in an unsigned staff editorial about Democratic Party priorities, which ran in *The New Republic's* print edition earlier this month. (What, you didn't know the magazine's editor had something to do with those editorials?)

The first aside that got my attention was Peter's statement that a prescription drug benefit constituted part of "the meekest, safest Democratic agenda in years," one driven by "the preferences of a focus group." The second was a dismissal of the prescription drug benefit as "not worth fighting for," because it "continues the Democratic Party's unfortunate trend toward redistributing wealth not from rich to poor but from young to old."

I mention these two small, seemingly insignificant comments not because I'm obsessed with health care reform—or, at least, not only because I'm obsessed with health care reform. I mention these comments because I'm pretty confident that other pundits on the center-left will soon be making the same essential argument: That prescription drugs are just a sop to a powerful Democratic interest group, the elderly, who really don't need the help.

Do you agree that the media tend to take two opposing sides of an argument? How does this affect the information the public receives?

How do I know this? For one thing, the media loves symmetry. If Republicans oppose an drug plan for some craven political reason—namely, to score points with the pharmaceutical lobby—then the pundits will insist Democrats have an equally craven reason for supporting it —namely, to score points with the elderly lobby. Plus, there's a strong element of neoliberal groupthink in Washington punditry, and it's an article of neoliberal faith that the big entitlement programs like Medicare lavish too many resources on the relatively affluent elderly. Finally, Peter is a really swell guy who is right about most things. People are bound to heed his arguments, as, in most cases, they should.

This time, though, I'm not so sure. It's true, as Peter notes, that prescription drug coverage is very popular with seniors. But can you blame them? The rising prices of prescription drugs represent a real public crisis that will only get worse unless government addresses it. The typical senior citizen now spends around $1,200 a year on prescription drugs: That's more than twice as much as in 1992, and the number will likely double by 2010, according to a recent and persuasive report by Families USA, the liberal health care advocacy group. At the same time, only about half of all senior citizens have year-round prescription drug coverage. More than one-third lack any drug coverage whatsoever.

Why foot the bill?

Critics like Peter typically ask why it's up to the rest of us (that is, non-elderly taxpayers) to cover this bill, particularly since seniors are so relatively well-off. Well, for starters, they're not as well-off as you might think. Despite the popular images of wealthy retirees living off fat stock portfolios in South Florida condominums, 70 percent of people enrolled in Medicare have annual incomes of less than $25,000. That's why there have been so many articles about retirees coping with high drug bills by running up huge credit card debt, forgoing basic necessities like groceries, or even their medication itself—with sometimes disastrous results.

In some ways, the situation today is analogous to 1965, when half of all senior citizens had no health insurance at all. It was to remedy this crisis that the federal government first created Medicare. The program's goal was to make sure every senior citizen got basic health care, on they very logical theory that the elderly are among those people least able to finance such coverage on their own. Nobody thought to include prescription drug coverage in 1965 because, back then, prescriptions were a relatively minor part of treating disease and because they were far cheaper. Today, by contrast, treatment for some cancers can consist almost entirely of prescription drugs— and rather expensive ones at that. So, when you think about it, including prescription drugs in Medicare isn't really adding some lavish new benefit to the program. It's adapting the program so that it can fulfill its original mission, now that the practice (and cost) of medicine has changed. Or, to put it

The author sets up Beinart as an expert whose arguments should be heeded and then proceeds to show why they actually should be disregarded.

To view Family USA's conclusions, go to http://www. familiesusa.org/ media/press/2000/ prdrugod.htm.

Is it true that removing prescription coverage would undermine Medicare itself? What other benefits would be left?

The photograph shows an elderly man in the hospital being treated by a nurse.

another way, if you want to argue we shouldn't have prescription coverage in Medicare, then you are really arguing against the whole premise of Medicare.

But the moral case for prescription drug coverage goes well beyond respecting the terms of an old contract. The whole notion that this is a big transfer of money from the young to the old obscures one obvious reality: We all get old eventually. Today, we pay for our grandparents; tomorrow, our grandkids will pay for us. This is one reason the idea of creating a prescription benefit in Medicare has such overwhelming support—74 percent in the latest *New York Times* poll— that transcends age. Younger people like myself aren't being snookered; we simply grasp our own future stake in this fight.

Of course, people my age don't have to wait until we retire to benefit from drug coverage—or to be harmed by the lack of it. When senior citizens struggle to pay for their prescriptions, younger family members end up bearing some of the financial and emotional burdens. Inevitably, it is those seniors and those families with the least money that suffer disproportionately. A prescription drug benefit would spread this cost across society, in the form of the taxes that finance Medicare. As such, it would do exactly what Peter and other neoliberals say it wouldn't: transfer wealth from rich to poor. Indeed, the mix of subsidies, insurance premiums, and co-payments in the leading Democratic proposals subsidize coverage almost completely for the least affluent while forcing those of greater financial means to bear a significant fraction of the cost.

None of which is to say that we should never reduce government payments to retirees, particularly as medical advances prolong Americans' economically productive years. (That's why, for example, it may make sense to raise the retirement age for Social Security.) Nor is it to say that prescription drugs (or, the other big health care issue today, HMO reform) are the most compelling use of political or economic resources. As Peter and others have written, by far the most important item on the health-care agenda today is one that isn't even on it: universal coverage. But that probably has a lot more to do with public ambivalence about the role of government than to a lack of sufficiently enthusiastic advocacy by Democrats. And that's why, far from precluding the enactment of universal health insurance, creating a prescription drug benefit might just increase its political prospects: It would demonstrate how a smart, well-run government program can deliver a tangible benefit to the public. With all due respect to Peter and the many pundits I expect will follow his lead, there's nothing "meek" about that.

Do you agree that the main reason why the majority of people support the creation of a prescription benefit under Medicare is that they see it as a reciprocal agreement?

Should government policies aim to redistribute wealth? How else is wealth redistributed in society?

HMO (health maintenance organization) reform legislation known as the Patients' Bill of Rights was passed on October 8, 1999. It grants all Americans enrolled in managed health-care plans certain consumer protections, such as allowing a consumer to sue HMOs that deny them access to care.

By introducing other issues in the debate, such as "universal coverage," the author presents a balanced argument.

Summary

In 2011 the first of the Baby Boomers will turn 65. Most of them will then retire. At that point they will expect to be able to reap the benefit of the funds they have put into Social Security throughout their working lives.

Yet so many people were born between 1946 and 1970, and so many of them have survived, that, according to Peter G. Peterson, unless something is done, there will soon be an intolerable strain on social services. The ratio of retired people receiving Social Security to taxpaying working people is becoming more and more unbalanced—in 1960 there were 5.1 taxpaying workers for every Social Security recipient, while currently there are 3.3 to 1. By 2040 this ratio will be an estimated 2 to 1. Peterson states that there is just not enough money available to maintain health care at its historic level since the demand for it is about to become greater than ever before. He suggests that those elderly people who are relatively well off should pay for health care themselves so that those more needy can be helped.

Although Jonathan Cohn recognizes the problems incurred by the Baby Boomers' cost to Social Security, he contests the view that a significant number of elderly people are well off enough to pay for their own health care. He points out that the cost of prescription drugs has skyrocketed and that elderly people are often more dependent on such drugs. He advocates that it is therefore only fair that prescription drugs should be paid for by Medicare and claims that, according to a *New York Times* poll, 74 percent of younger working people support this view because they realize that they too will be old eventually and will then need the same financial support.

FURTHER INFORMATION:

Books:

Barry, R.L., and G.V. Bradley, *Set No Limits: A Rebuttal to Daniel Callahan's Proposal to Limit Health Care for the Elderly*. Urbana, IL: University of Illinois Press, 1991. Winslow, G.R., and J.W. Walters, *Facing Limits: Ethics and Heath Care for the Elderly*. Boulder, CO: Westview Press, 1993.

Useful websites:

www.census.org
Contains up-to-date statistics on the elderly population.
ww.thenewrepublic.com
Contains articles on the elderly population, including Jonathan Cohn's.
http://ssw.unc.edu/fcrp/Cspn/vol5_no1/what_is_family
_support_mvmt.htm
Article on family and welfare.

The following debates in the Pro/Con series may also be of interest:

In *Government:*

 Topic 2 Are all human beings created equal?

In *Science:*

 Topic 6 Should governments limit the price of drugs?

In *Economics:*

 Topic 5 Should welfare be abolished?

SHOULD THE ELDERLY PAY FOR THEIR OWN HEALTH CARE?

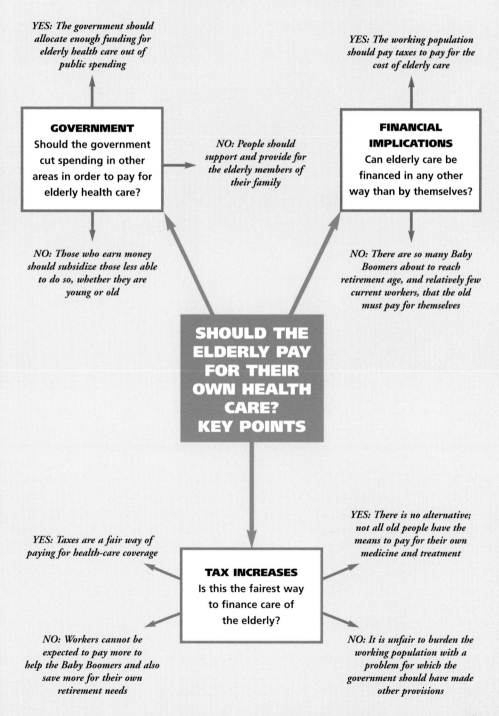

YES: The government should allocate enough funding for elderly health care out of public spending

YES: The working population should pay taxes to pay for the cost of elderly care

GOVERNMENT
Should the government cut spending in other areas in order to pay for elderly health care?

NO: People should support and provide for the elderly members of their family

FINANCIAL IMPLICATIONS
Can elderly care be financed in any other way than by themselves?

NO: Those who earn money should subsidize those less able to do so, whether they are young or old

NO: There are so many Baby Boomers about to reach retirement age, and relatively few current workers, that the old must pay for themselves

SHOULD THE ELDERLY PAY FOR THEIR OWN HEALTH CARE? KEY POINTS

YES: There is no alternative; not all old people have the means to pay for their own medicine and treatment

YES: Taxes are a fair way of paying for health-care coverage

TAX INCREASES
Is this the fairest way to finance care of the elderly?

NO: Workers cannot be expected to pay more to help the Baby Boomers and also save more for their own retirement needs

NO: It is unfair to burden the working population with a problem for which the government should have made other provisions

PART 4
THE FAMILY AND SOCIETY

The last section in this book deals with the family and its place in society. The provision of welfare to poorer families or government initiatives to limit the size of families raise important issues about the family's place in a changing society. For many observers, even more important questions relate to the extent to which government and the state should be involved in regulating or influencing family life. Some people argue that it is the government's responsibility to support the family as an institution—for example, by giving tax breaks to married couples or by providing welfare support to poor families. Others argue that what happens inside the home is not the preserve of government but reflects individual lifestyle choices.

The family's role in society is of particular concern because it inevitably reflects changes in the structure of the family itself. The traditional model of the nuclear family—a mother and father with their biological children—has increasingly been challenged by other models. In 1997, 50 percent of all marriages ended in divorce; around 9.8 percent of all adults—19.4 million Americans—had been divorced at least once. Such high levels of divorce and remarriage have created larger numbers of step families in which children live with one nonbiological parent and often with step siblings. An increase in adoption has also led to more children living with nonbiological parents.

The number of single-parent households in the United States rose from 5 percent in 1970 to 9 percent in 1990. Around a quarter of all American children are now born to unmarried mothers. Meanwhile, with the nuclear family apparently eroding, increasing numbers of people are falling back on the support of extended families—grandparents, uncles, aunts, and other relatives—which is a family model more familiar in cultures from, say, Asia and Latin America.

Given such fundamental shifts in the makeup of the family, what should the government do? If these changes are perceived as marking a decline in society, as some people argue, should the government discourage couples from separating? Or should Americans simply accept that the shape of the family is changing and that this change is both natural and in itself is not negative and may even be positive?

Welfare

One of the fundamental ways in which government is involved in family life is by giving welfare assistance to the needy. Welfare encompasses programs such as health insurance and income allowances. Particularly relevant to the family is the childcare benefit, which allows parents to work while their children are cared for. Around 15 million Americans are eligible for childcare benefits, but fewer than 2 million actually claim them.

Many critics argue that welfare in general encourages people not to work, and that childcare in particular makes it easier for couples to break up who might otherwise stay together for financial reasons. Others disagree, arguing that most of the 5.8 million people who rely on welfare would

women, into the workforce. For many single parents this creates a need for childcare, an issue considered in Topic 14. The "yes" article claims that, even though only a small percentage of eligible children get federal childcare subsidies, the government is nevertheless underfunding childcare. Susan Benitez in the "no" article claims that childcare should be a mother's priority, not keeping up a career.

"There is no doubt that it is around the family and the home that all the greatest virtues, the most dominating virtues of human society, are created, strengthened and maintained."

—WINSTON CHURCHILL, BRITISH POLITICIAN

---

prefer not to. Recent legislation has also had the effect of decreasing welfare dependency. In return, the government has undertaken to provide health insurance, childcare, and income allowances. Welfare recipients rose to over 5 percent of the population in the early 1990s but are now only a little over 2 percent.

Welfare, childcare, and wages

Topic 13 considers whether the welfare system does enough to support the family. The "yes" article looks at a state-run family resource program in North Carolina. Marcia K. Meyers, in the "no" article, argues that much family support remains unclaimed since people are unaware of their entitlements and because the procedures for claiming are often overcomplicated.

Changes in welfare legislation have directed more people, particularly

The number of single-parent households headed by women—7 million in 1990—is rising, and the income earned by them is crucial. However, some people argue that in spite of equal-pay legislation, women are still paid less than men doing the same job. Topic 15 examines this issue and asks if fewer families would live in poverty if men and women received equal pay.

Population

The final topic in this section looks at the wider issue of world population and government moves to limit family size. Janet Larsen examines the success of the Iranian government's program, which has led to a declining birthrate and improved social conditions. P. Dean Russell's article, however, looks at alleged human rights abuses committed under China's similar One-Child policy.

Topic 13

DOES THE WELFARE SYSTEM PROVIDE ENOUGH SUPPORT FOR THE FAMILY?

YES

"WHAT IS THE FAMILY SUPPORT MOVEMENT"?
CHILDREN'S SERVICES *PRACTICE NOTES*, VOLUME 5, ISSUE 1, APRIL 2000
NC FAMILY AND CHILDREN'S RESOURCE PROGRAM

NO

FROM "HOW WELFARE OFFICES UNDERMINE WELFARE REFORM"
THE AMERICAN PROSPECT, VOLUME 11, ISSUE 15, JUNE 19–JULY 3, 2000
MARCIA K. MEYERS

INTRODUCTION

Successive administrations since the 1980s have attempted to get people off welfare and into work. However, the government was never under the illusion that everyone would be able to earn enough to live at a socially acceptable standard, so a new form of state welfare was introduced. Although its rules are complicated, the basic rationale is that the government will help keep people above the poverty line for as long as they can be seen to be making an effort to help themselves. In the last 20 years Congress and state legislatures have restricted access to welfare and liberalized spending on support services designed to serve as a transition from reliance on welfare to independence of welfare.

Since the 1990s parents have been expected to support themselves and their children by leaving welfare and going to work. The government has undertaken, in return, to provide health insurance, childcare assistance, and income allowances to ensure that the jobs parents take are worth their while. That is meant to put an end to the old "Catch-22" in which people might lose more benefits by going to work than they would earn in wages.

The contemporary approach to welfare is not necessarily an attempt to create a nation in which the watchword is "every man for himself." It is more often seen as a largely humanitarian attempt to tackle social privation and exclusion at its roots.

Yet some commentators fear that the plan is not working. The problem is not philosophical but practical. Although the government claims to be making money available to families in need, it is not clear that there is an infrastructure enabling the benefits on offer to be delivered to the working poor. The bureaucracy involved prevents people from getting their entitlements. The red tape is not cut away because it serves the needs of elected officials—anything that stops claimants from claiming helps politicians restrict spending.

Evidence suggests that if old-style welfare is to be ended, the family must be able to control its own destiny as much as possible, not only financially but also practically. When families have problems, they must know what to do and where to go before their difficulties turn into crises. Grants may be available, trained professionals may be sitting in offices waiting for the call to help, but if no one knows they exist, what good are they?

> *"On welfare you get food, clothing and shelter—you get survival, but you can't really do anything. You can't control your life."*
>
> —JOCELYN ELDERS, FIRST WOMAN SURGEON GENERAL

Parents need to be active directors of their children's well-being. One obstacle that currently makes this objective difficult is the compartmentalization of social services—people are often bounced from one municipal office to another in search of the services they need and that are available if only they could find them.

It has been proposed by some, such as the authors of the first of the following articles, that services of this type should be a continuum—in other words, job ads, the address of the local library, and bus route maps of the downtown area should be obtainable in the same location and from the same

people as counseling on mental health and substance abuse.

But while some people say that child welfare and family support are inextricably linked, others maintain that although the former is essential, the latter is an unaffordable luxury.

However, it is not difficult to make the case that the money for family support is there. Congress raised the minimum wage in 1996. Federal and state governments spend more than ever before on childcare assistance. There is a safety net to protect low-earning working families.

In the view of many the most vulnerable group in society is the one-parent family. It is widely believed that one-parent families deserve state support, and single mothers currently do make most of the claims. Yet according to some statistics quoted in the second of the following articles, since the new regulations came into force, the number of single mothers receiving welfare has dropped, while the number of such women in employment has increased enormously. Work and welfare are supposed to be complementary, not mutually exclusive; there are grants these mothers should be getting no matter how well paid their jobs. There are several possible explanations for this trend, but it seems likely that childcare subsidies are so complicated that many give up on trying to claim them.

So, disadvantaged people may be keeping their half of the new social bargain, but the government may not be making welfare funds practically available. If the support cannot be reached by the intended recipients, why have any family welfare at all?

The following articles look at the question further.

WHAT IS THE FAMILY SUPPORT MOVEMENT?
NC Family and Children's Resource Program

The Smart Start initiative aims to help children under six years of age get a good start in education. For more information on North Carolina's Smart Start initiave see www.smart start-nc.org/ overview/ history.PDF. North Carolina's Families for Kids is designed to promote the adoption of children and reduce the amount of time they spend in foster care. For more information see http://ssw.unc. edu/fcrp/families_ for_kids.htm.

YES

When you hear the words "family support program" or "family support movement," you may think of the family preservation services offered by your county DSS or of a family resource center in your community. Or perhaps you think of the Smart Start initiative or North Carolina's Families for Kids. The family support movement in North Carolina is all these things, and more.

Origins and evolution of family support

In order to understand family support as it pertains to child welfare practice in North Carolina, it is important to look at both how this movement got its start and how it has evolved recently in North Carolina.

Family support emerged in the mid-1970s to fill gaps families were experiencing in their support. Combining knowledge about child development, family systems, and the impact of communities on families, this grassroots movement focused on preventing family crises and promoting healthy family functioning.

Most of these programs called themselves "family resource programs" to indicate their role as resources to be used as needed, on families' terms. They provided basic information about child development, activities for children and parents, and links to other family services in the community.

They fostered a welcoming environment so that parents could feel that in at least one place in the community, someone understood and valued the work they were doing with their kids (Best Practices Project, 1996). These programs emphasized family-to-family support rather than dependence on professional support systems, and their services were— and still are—entirely voluntary.

Family support programs are not just for at-risk families. They are founded on the belief that every family needs and deserves help, support, and access to resources. From a family support perspective, seeking help in parenting is a sign of strength. Such parents are seen as involved, concerned directors of their families' lives and children's growth.

A young mother plays with her son in a community-based family support center.

Yet the idea of what constitutes family support has changed recently in North Carolina. We still have "traditional" community-based family support centers (family resource centers), which are usually run by and for parents themselves. At the same time, family-support concepts and family-centered approaches have become more a part of DSS practice.

As a result, what constitutes family support to human services professionals in North Carolina has broadened to include family preservation (FPS) and intensive family preservation services (IFPS). Once seen as "after the fact" interventions, since to be eligible for these services a family must already be in crisis to some extent, FPS and IFPS are now viewed by many as part of a continuum of services designed to support and strengthen families.

Family support beliefs and training

The philosophy of family support is based on nine principles for practice (see "Principles Underlying Family Support"). These principles, which describe good family support practice, closely parallel the family-centered principles that form the basis of best practice in child welfare in North Carolina.

To Laura Weber, director of the N.C. Family Resource Coalition, an agency that conducts family support training

For "Principles Underlying Family Support" see http://lssw.unc.edu/fcrp/Cspn/vol5_no1/principles_underlying_family.htm.

across the state, the principles underlying family support practice are the family support movement. As she puts it, "Family support is not about a particular kind of program, job, or agency. It is not discipline-specific. No matter what job you do, you can implement the family support principles."

Accordingly, the N.C. Family Resource Coalition's family-support training is highly interdisciplinary. Its classes are attended by professionals involved in mental health, substance abuse counseling, transportation, public health, DSS, and especially family members. If we are serious about promoting partnerships with family members, Weber says, then family members must be involved at all levels of the system—especially in training.

The author argues that family members must be involved at all levels of the system, especially in training. Do you believe that families can really be taught how to act and interact?

Family support in North Carolina

Since they first took root in North Carolina in the mid to late 1980s, family-support programs have taken many forms. They were founded wherever people familiar with family support saw a need and were able to marshal the resources necessary to provide services.

In 1994 a big change came to North Carolina's family support community. At that time, the N.C. Department of Health and Human Services selected family support/family preservation programs in 55 counties and the Eastern Band of Cherokee Indians to receive state and federal funds to serve their communities. These programs use a variety of service models, including some of those outlined in "Family Support Service Models at Work in North Carolina." For a look at some of the services provided by North Carolina's family support agencies, refer "Services Provided by Family Support Agencies."

For "Services Provided by Family Support Agencies" see http://ssw.unc.edu/fcrp/Cspn/vol5_no1/services_provided_by_agencies.htm.

Another expansion of the family support community began in 1999, when, at the request of Governor Hunt, the state legislature provided funding to bring family preservation services to all of North Carolina's 100 counties.

James B. Hunt was governor of North Carolina from 1977 to 1985. He was responsible for making many educational reforms and introduced Agenda for Action, which focused on giving children a healthy start in life. He also introduced the Smart Start initiative.

Relationship with child welfare

To some, differences between the child welfare and family support communities are an obstacle. Viewed from the perspective of "traditional" child welfare, the sometimes time-intensive, family-centered approach and voluntary services offered by family support programs seem like unaffordable luxuries. And, because they want so badly to help families build themselves up, some involved in family support see child welfare workers as "the bad guys" or "baby snatchers" when they must exercise their authority to protect children.

Yet others see these differences as complementary rather than divisive. In the view of Becky Kessel, Families for Kids Coordinator for Buncombe County, North Carolina DSS, "We can't effectively do our jobs without family support programs." Kessel sees family support programs as an essential part of the array of services to families.

This perception of a "win-win" partnership with family support is in part a result of changes in North Carolina's approach to child welfare. In recent years training for child welfare workers has placed a greater emphasis on the importance of strengths-based thinking and a family-centered approach to working with families.

For more information about Challenge for Children see http:// ssw.unc.edu/fcrp/ Cspn/vol2_no2/NC_ issues_challenge. htm.

Initiatives such as North Carolina's Families for Kids and the Challenge for Children have also had an influence. In an effort to obtain positive outcomes for children and families, DSS's have begun to "open up" to their communities, embracing new approaches, such as family group conferencing, that are more inclusive of families and providers from other agencies.

In Laura Weber's opinion, this trend must continue. "Families hold the key to human services reform," she says. "We, the professionals, developed the system. We know the system is not perfect. But we will never be able to get the system to where it needs to be without the input of the people who use the system. Families are the missing piece."

HOW WELFARE OFFICES UNDERMINE WELFARE REFORM
Marcia K. Meyers

NO

Welfare and related policy reforms adopted by Congress in the 1990s seemed to strike an implicit bargain with low-wage working families. Parents were expected to meet their "personal responsibility" for supporting themselves and their children by leaving welfare and going to work. If they did, government would help out by providing a package of income, health insurance, and child care assistance to "make work pay," even for low earners. Four years out, there is disquieting evidence that government is not keeping its side of the bargain—largely because we have failed to develop the appropriate administrative systems and capacity to deliver assistance to the working poor. This ostensibly bureaucratic failure happens to serve the goal of many elected officials to avoid spending money on the poor. But if our commitment to "end welfare as we know it" without impoverishing families is genuine, these administrative problems must be addressed.

Do you agree with Marcia K. Meyers that the goal of many elected officials is to avoid spending money on the poor? Why might this be the case?

To understand why low-income working families are failing to get or keep the supportive assistance that was designed to help them achieve self-sufficiency, one needs to look beyond legislated policies to examine the details of program delivery. This is work that several colleagues and I are pursuing in our research on child care and welfare reform at the state and local levels—talking to program managers and staff, studying program operations, and observing the experience of program applicants and clients as they negotiate the system. What we have observed is disturbing: The state and local welfare systems that distribute support services to poor individuals remain ill-equipped to serve a new population of working poor families.

The author feels it is important for her to state that she is sympathetic to welfare programs. Is her sympathy apparent in her argument so far?

Let me say up front that I am a sympathetic observer of welfare programs.... [But w]hat I have not seen is a reformulation of the systems, administrative structures, and incentives to allow welfare offices to do a good job in keeping the government side of the welfare reform bargain.

Getting the word out

The first form of help that low-income individuals need is information. Learning about the benefits for which they may be eligible turns out to be a surprisingly difficult hurdle for many. Although low-income individuals are often portrayed as knowledgeable and savvy consumers of welfare services, more systematic research reveals that their information is often both limited and inaccurate.

Child care may be one of the most important, but least well-known, benefits available to low-income parents. In a 1995 survey of current and former welfare recipients in California, for example, my colleagues and I found that two-thirds to three-quarters of mothers did not know about employment-related child care subsidies. More recent studies in Florida, Massachusetts, and South Carolina reveal that, even in the wake of welfare reforms, 40 to 60 percent of former welfare recipients remain unaware of child care assistance for which they may be eligible. Given that recipients exiting the welfare system have been the primary target of new child care subsidy programs, knowledge is likely to be even lower among low-earning families who have had little contact with the welfare system. …

Helping individuals access the system

Unfortunately, those who know enough to seek benefits may face even more formidable hurdles when they encounter the welfare office. In some communities, there are now alternative entry points for the working poor to obtain nonwelfare assistance: Individuals may sign up for Medicaid at a local health clinic or for child care benefits through a Child Care Resource and Referral program. But for most individuals, and for any who hope to qualify for food stamps, the point of entry is still the local welfare office. (In fact, many areas still use a single application for all three programs, a by-product of earlier reforms designed to simplify the application process.) Once again, the welfare system turns out to be poorly equipped to help them. …

Helping applicants find the right services

Even if an applicant manages to make it into and through the arduous system of welfare application, her chances of getting the right information, referrals, and applications for supportive assistance remain uncertain. The rules governing entry to Medicaid have grown more complex over the years, as policies have changed, new rules have been adopted, and court decisions have codified rights for sometimes very narrowly defined groups. In many states, child care continues to be nearly as complicated, with separate rules for those in welfare, leaving welfare, or outside the welfare system. In

How might low-income individuals learn information about welfare services?

"Medicaid" is a health insurance program started in 1965 that is funded jointly by state and federal money, and that provides medical assistance to the needy and certain low-income people, including children, the elderly, and those who are blind or disabled.

What are the advantages for the government of making welfare applications "arduous"?

order to obtain these benefits, applicants need information, assistance, and often the time and goodwill of the workers who make eligibility determinations. Front-line workers, in turn, need both a detailed knowledge of the system and time to determine claimants' needs and match them to the right services. Unfortunately, many welfare workers have neither—even when they have plenty of goodwill. ...

Helping clients keep benefits

In many programs, it is nearly as hard to retain benefits as to obtain them. In studying the duration of child care assistance in a number of states, for example, we have found that children generally receive subsidies for only a few months. The reasons they leave the system are likely to be varied—parents may lose their jobs, change their schedules, lose their child care providers, or decide to go without assistance. But the complexity of keeping a child care subsidy appears to contribute to these exits as well. As in other areas of assistance to the working poor, welfare systems turn out to be better equipped to avoid processing errors that cost the state money than they are to help working families meet their needs....

The author states, not for the first time, that the welfare system concentrates more on saving the state money rather than helping families meet their needs. Do you think the state needs to shift its priorities?

When lawmakers in Congress and state legislatures set out to "reform" welfare, they started with the obvious targets. They restricted access to welfare and liberalized spending for supportive services designed to serve as a transition from welfare reliance to welfare independence. The reform was incomplete, however, because they left the delivery of these support services to a welfare system that has neither the incentives nor the organizational capacity to advertise and deliver them. As a result, many working families are not getting the help they need to achieve self-sufficiency on low wages. This is not inconsistent with the reluctance of many elected officials to spend money on the poor. But it is also not inevitable. Rather, it means that lawmakers committed to real reform of the system will need to consider changes not only in the rules and regulations, but in the delivery system as well. Fortunately, there are examples, in the United States and abroad, of alternative approaches. ...

In the United States, many disadvantaged parents are keeping their side of the welfare bargain, especially single mothers, who constitute the large majority of welfare recipients. Whether they have been pushed by more demanding welfare rules or pulled by a tight labor market, the number of single mothers receiving welfare has plummeted since 1996 while the number employed has increased at a remarkable rate.

On one level, government appears to have kept its side of the bargain as well. Congress expanded the EITC in the early 1990s and raised the minimum wage in 1996. Federal and state governments are also spending more on child care assistance. Congress has authorized new federal funds with a more generous matching rate to encourage states to expand health coverage for poor children. Considered together, these policies form a reasonably generous alternative safety net for working but low-earning families. The Council of Economic Advisers says that, with the EITC, a parent with two children who works full time for the minimum wage can now have income above the poverty line. If she and her children are covered by government health insurance, and if she has subsidies to cover her child care expenses, she has a reasonable chance to achieve self-sufficiency.

However, the operative word in this optimistic scenario is "if." Families can hope to achieve self-sufficiency on low wages if they receive the extra income from the EITC and food stamps, if they have health insurance, and if they receive child care subsidies. To date, the evidence suggests that far too many working but poor families are not receiving this package of assistance....

EITC is the abbreviation for the Earned Income Tax Credit—a refundable federal income tax credit for low-income working individuals and families. The legislation for EITC was approved in 1975 in order to alleviate some of the burden of Social Security taxes and provide an incentive to work.

Food stamps are benefits, either in the form of paper coupons or plastic debit cards, given to unemployed, part-time, or low-income families and individuals to help them afford to buy food. Food stamps can be used to buy eligible food from authorized food stores. Food stamps began in the 1930s and became a legislated nationwide program in 1971.

Summary

The first article outlines a best-case scenario in which the welfare system provides the family with adequate material and spiritual support, whereas the second article summarizes the practical problems that often get in the way.

The first piece focuses on modern family welfare practice in North Carolina. The state's "Families for Kids" initiative has pooled knowledge of all aspects of child development and family dynamics to create a social service that promotes healthy relationships and prevents crises in normal and dysfunctional families alike. The program is family-to-family, in other words, run by volunteers rather than reliant on professional support systems. Yet it is closely linked to services that deal with serious problems, which can be called in if necessary. This is part of an attempt to ensure that the services really are available to those who need them.

In the second article Marcia K. Meyers describes some of the pitfalls that North Carolina seems to have avoided. She points out that in many states child welfare and family support remain discrete functions when they should be complementary. She also notes other practical difficulties: a lack of communication between the social services and low-income earners, and the fact that not all the available childcare benefit is claimed, possibly because the intended beneficiaries do not know it is available. She makes the point that welfare offices are sometimes better at bureaucratic functions, such as weeding out fraudulent claims, than at paying what is due to deserving cases.

FURTHER INFORMATION:

Books:

Lasch, Christopher, *Haven in a Heartless World*. New York: W.W. Horton & Co., 1997.

Useful websites:

www.theatlantic.com/unbound/flashbks/welfare/welf.htm

The Atlantic Monthly online site about the welfare debate.

http://www.ahca.org/secure/top15.htm

Article on care of the elderly.

www.bcn.boulder.co.us/pss/welfare.html

"Project Self Sufficiency Welfare Reform: General Information" discusses the myths and realities of welfare, including discussion of women with large families, single-parent families, and so on.

www.irs.gov/businesses/display/0,il%3d2&genericID%3d13280,00.html

Overview of the Earned Income Tax Credit (EITC).

The following debates in the Pro/Con series may also be of interest:

In this volume:

Topic 14 Should there be more childcare facilities for people in need?

In *Health*:

Topic 1 Should the government implement universal health-care coverage?

In *Economics*:

Topic 6 Should welfare be abolished?

DOES THE WELFARE SYSTEM PROVIDE ENOUGH SUPPORT FOR THE FAMILY?

YES: It is up to individuals to make themselves aware of their entitlements

YES: The red tape surrounding family benefits is so tangled that there is no clear path through it

USAGE LEVEL
Is it enough that the government has put a welfare system in place?

BUREAUCRACY
Are too many government departments involved in welfare?

NO: Welfare does not get claimed by everyone who is entitled to it

NO: Childcare and family welfare are different functions that require different expertise; therefore they are organized and function separately

DOES THE WELFARE SYSTEM PROVIDE ENOUGH SUPPORT FOR THE FAMILY?

KEY POINTS

YES: As long as they can show that they are trying to work, they should be guaranteed a basic living

YES: For as long as some people remain unable to earn enough to live on, they must be maintained by the better-off in society

SOCIAL SAFETY NET
Should people who cannot help themselves be helped?

NO: People would not work if there was no incentive to do so

NO: The economy cannot afford to keep those who put nothing in to it

Topic 14

SHOULD THERE BE MORE CHILDCARE FACILITIES FOR PEOPLE IN NEED?

YES

FROM "NEW STATISTICS SHOW ONLY SMALL PERCENTAGE OF ELIGIBLE FAMILIES RECEIVE CHILDCARE HELP"
PRESS RELEASE, U.S. DEPARTMENT OF HEALTH AND HUMAN SERVICES
DECEMBER 6, 2000

NO

FROM "WANTED: MOTHER"
WOODBURY REPORTS, 1999–2001
SUSAN BENITEZ

INTRODUCTION

Childcare has become an increasingly pressing issue as more women enter the job market. The main argument for federally funded childcare, especially for poor families, is that it enables a greater number of parents—particularly mothers—to take jobs they would not otherwise be able to because of domestic commitments. Without subsidies, however, many parents have to spend most of their earnings on childcare and would be better off staying on welfare.

Those who support federally funded childcare claim that it benefits both individuals and society as a whole. They point out that it is currently desirable in the United States, where there are higher levels of employment than at any time for a generation, and many firms have more jobs than they can fill. Having parents at work also benefits the nation by taking people off welfare. Once people are free to go back to

work, even if they still receive some form of welfare payment, they are less of a drain on federal resources than they would be if unemployed. Since the United States needs more workers, providing childcare not only frees people to take new jobs or continue in their existing ones, but also creates jobs for nannies and nursery nurses.

Those who oppose childcare benefits object to them on various grounds. The most extreme view is that government has no business interfering in such matters—if parents want to work, they should organize their lives so that they can do their jobs and bring up their children as well. Those who want a family and a job should finance the childcare themselves.

Yet even those opposed to any increase in existing levels of federal childcare funding do not deny that the number of people receiving childcare benefits today is lower than the national commitment—the parents of 15 million children are eligible, but only about 1.8 million currently claim.

Yet the first of the following articles, from the U.S. Department of Health and Human Services, indicates that cost is still a problem. The authors admit that even though the United States is providing childcare to only 12 percent of those parents eligible to claim it, individual states are already using all the federal funds currently allocated to them for this purpose. Therefore, either the government is not channeling sufficient resources into childcare benefits, or it simply cannot afford to.

"To deny the need for comprehensive childcare policies is to deny a reality— that there's been a revolution in American life."

—EDITORIAL, *THE NEW YORK TIMES*, SEPTEMBER 6, 1983

The first article also claims, however, that unless parents have access to affordable and reliable childcare, they will be forced to give up their jobs and might not seek any further employment. They will then lose familiarity with the workplace, will cease to keep their skills up to date, and, if and when they ever return to employment, will be unaware of the latest developments and generally be less useful than they were when they left.

In the second article, however, Susan Benitez objects to federally funded childcare on the grounds that parents who are working are parents who are not where they should be—in the home bringing up their children. Although childcare may sometimes be necessary (for example, in one-parent families), Benitez argues that it should not be as widespread as it is currently because it is damaging to the children themselves. Benitez claims that while the harm absent parents causes to children may be hard to measure, it is no less real for all that. Many parents admit to feeling guilty about leaving their children with others so that they can go to work, and she cites this as an indication that they know that what they are doing is wrong.

There is some evidence to suggest that one-year-old infants who are minded for more than 20 hours a week are more likely to suffer psychological and emotional damage than children who are raised by their parents. Yet critics of this research maintain that the experimental method is flawed—most children in childcare centers come from poor families, and no conclusive evidence has been produced to prove that their problems were caused by childcare rather than by other factors in their background and environment.

Many modern parents say that they cannot afford not to work. They claim—or, at least, make themselves believe—that they perform a largely successful balancing act, satisfying the needs of their children while keeping up their careers. Yet, according to Benitez, they are merely unwilling to admit that whenever there is a conflict between the child's requirements and the employer's demands, it is the latter that prevail.

The following articles discuss both sides of the argument further.

NEW STATISTICS SHOW ONLY SMALL PERCENTAGE OF ELIGIBLE FAMILES RECEIVE CHILDCARE HELP
Press Release, U.S. Department of Health and Human Services

HHS is the abbreviation for Department of Health and Human Services—the government's principal agency for protecting the health of all Americans and providing essential human services, especially to those least able to help themselves.

YES

HHS Secretary Donna E. Shalala today released new statistics on childcare for low-income families showing that, because of a lack of federal funding, only 12 percent of eligible children received federal assistance in 1999, despite a slight increase in the number of children being served.

According to new state-reported statistics for fiscal year 1999, 1.8 million children in low-income families are receiving federal childcare subsidies on an average monthly basis. This is a slight increase from the 1.5 million children served in 1998. Yet, with 15 million children estimated to be eligible for federal support, only 12 percent of those children are receiving federal help due to limited federal funds.

For a copy of the full report go to http://cpmcnet. columbia.edu/dept/ nccp/subsidy_ substudy.html.

Many children are still missing out on childcare

A companion report, "National Study of childcare for Low-Income Families, State and Community Substudy," confirmed that even when additional state funds are included, many children still go unserved. The study also reported that, because of the strong economy and more parents working, states were spending significantly more for childcare, with a median increase of 78 percent from 1997 to 1999 in the states studied. Yet, a survey of 17 states showed that those states were only able to serve 15 to 20 percent of federally eligible children in 1999. The study, prepared by Abt Associates for HHS, also reported waiting lists in 12 of the 17 states.

For more information on the Child Care and Development Block Grant see http://aspe.hhs.gov/ cfda/p93573.htm.

"The information released today confirms that working families still do not have adequate access to safe and affordable childcare … something that is crucial if they are to keep their jobs," said Secretary Shalala. "Our appropriations bill now before Congress includes an $817 million increase in the Child Care and Development Block Grant. It is imperative that Congress pass this bill now and provide critical childcare support for America's working families."

This child is one of the three-quarters of children under six years of age whose mothers go to work and leave their children in some form of licenced childcare, such as this day-care center.

COMMENTARY: Recent developments in government-funded childcare

Government-funded childcare received a major overhaul during President Clinton's term of office (1992–2000) with the signing of the Personal Responsibility and Work Opportunity Reconciliation Act of 1996. This law encourages parents—particularly mothers—to join the workforce by offering state-funded childcare to working parents. The act replaced guaranteed state welfare entitlements to childcare benefits with a block grant called Temporary Assistance for Needy Families (TANF). TANF requires that: 25 percent of parents receiving state childcare assistance must be at work or have found work by the following year, and that this figure must rise to 50 percent by the year 2002; single parents must work at least 20 hours per week, increasing to at least 30 hours per week by 2000; and two-parent families must work at least 35 hours per week within a year of receiving assistance. For those receiving TANF benefits who are not yet at work, the state is required to make assessments of the recipients' skills and help them find the education, training, and job placement services they need to move into the workforce. After receiving childcare assistance for five continuous years, however, recipients are no longer eligible for benefits.

For a six-year period from 1996 the government allocated $14 billion for state-funded childcare—$3.5 billion more than the previous year's budget allocation. A further $1 billion per year is awarded to each state that proves successful in moving welfare recipients into jobs. In 1998 President Clinton also supported the expansion of the childcare tax credit, which allows childcare costs to be deducted from families' federal income taxes and even refunded to low-income families. President George W. Bush, however, in his 2002 budget proposal suggested cuts in state TANF funds.

Even though states are continuing to use all the federal funds available to them for childcare, today's findings demonstrate the extent that eligible children are going unserved. In fiscal year 1999, states spent $5.2 billion in federal funds, including transfers from their welfare block grant, and spent $1.6 billion from their own funds. During that time, only 1.8 million of the approximately 15 million children eligible for federal childcare support received federal funds.

Studies in Florida and North Carolina have found that increased childcare subsidies result in increased employment rates and earnings for low-income working families. Conversely, parents who have no childcare support are seven times more likely to rely on public assistance than employed parents who receive a subsidy. A study of Santa Clara, Calif.

showed that one-third of low-income parents were unable to work because they could not afford childcare, while another third reduced their work hours.

"Studies show that subsidized childcare helps parents stay employed while a lack of subsidies results in more parents giving up jobs or reducing their work hours," said Olivia A. Golden, HHS assistant secretary for children and families. "This is the reason that the administration has proposed a major increase in childcare funds, which is currently part of the bipartisan conference agreement on Labor-HHS appropriations before Congress. Prompt action by Congress is needed to ensure that these funds reach the working families who need them."

Need for childcare more critical than ever

Never before has the American economy been this strong and the need for affordable, quality childcare this critical, Golden noted. With the unemployment rate recently at a 30-year low, many employers are straining to find workers. Meanwhile, more parents are entering the work force. In 1996, 3 out of 4 mothers with children between 6 and 17 were working compared to 1 in 4 mothers in 1965. Two-thirds of mothers with children under 6 now work.

Do you think the low unemployment rate and the need to fill jobs will be a major factor in Congress's decision whether or not to allocate more funds for childcare?

The state-reported statistics released today highlight that 84 percent of all families who received childcare subsidies did so because the parents were employed. The majority of families, 68 percent, were responsible for co-payments at an average of 6 percent of their income. Nearly three-quarters of all children receiving subsidies were served in licensed care, while 15 percent of all children receiving subsidies were cared for by relatives. About two-thirds of the children were under 6 years old.

WANTED: MOTHER
Susan Benitez

NO

X   …In the traditional nuclear family, the father has the role of provider while the mother is nurturer of the children and keeper of the household. Throughout human history, sometimes it has been necessary for mothers with young children to work outside the home, most often due to the untimely deaths of their husbands. In recent decades, there is an ever- increasing, worldwide trend of married mothers entering the workforce or returning to work soon after the birth of a child. If these women are not working because they need to support their families due to the death of their spouse, then why are they choosing to work?

> *How many mothers do you know who go to work? Would you say that it is the majority or the minority?*

Some married women who work claim their family cannot survive financially with only one income. Others desire to "have and do it all," striving for success both in family and career. A third group works outside the home as a form of escape, recognizing just how challenging it is to both nurture children and maintain an orderly home full time, in other words, to be a homemaker. There is also a growing trend toward single parenting, mainly due to increasing rates of divorce and unmarried couples having children. In most cases this requires the custodial parent, usually the mother, to supplement alimony and child support payments with outside employment.

> *Among the young children that you know, have you noticed any difference in the behavior of those who attend day-care centers and those who are raised at home?*

The effect of working mothers on their children

How do these trends affect the children? Are children who spend significant portions of time in day care better adjusted and more independent and intelligent than their peers who are raised at home, as scores of studies would suggest? Are children better off being raised by one loving—but possibly overwhelmed—parent than by two parents who perpetuate a spirit of strife within the home? Where do we draw the line when balancing adults' needs with children's needs? These are the difficult issues at stake in the debate over modern family structure. Dr. Barbara Dafoe Whitehead, well known political and family-issues commentator, writes, "the social-science evidence is in: though it may benefit the adults involved, the dissolution of intact two-parent families is harmful to large numbers of children."

COMMENTARY: Strange Situation Test used to study effect of nonmaternal care on children

Jay Belsky's research group used a test called the Strange Situation Test to study the effect of nonmaternal care on young children. Child psychologist Mary Ainsworth at John Hopkins University designed the test in 1964 to study a one-year-old's relationship to its mother by observing the child during seven three-minute episodes. The episodes entail the child being left alone with its mother, then with its mother and a stranger, then with the stranger alone, then with the mother, then entirely alone, then with the stranger, and finally alone again with the mother. Observers watch the child throughout and judge how quickly it can be calmed by its mother when stressed and whether it exhibits any signs of avoidance or resistance toward her. Their judgments are based on the idea that children with insecure attachments to their mothers avoid their mothers or actually push them away, while those with secure attachments to their mothers seek their mothers out. Further research suggests that children who have an insecure attachment to their mother are at higher risk of developing future psychological problems than those who demonstrate secure attachments

Belsky found that children of 12 to 13 months old who routinely spent more than 20 hours a week in nonmaternal care were more likely to show insecure attachments to their mothers and linked that with "heightened aggressiveness, noncompliance, and withdrawal in preschool and early school years." However, Belsky's critics point out that the Strange Situation Test was invented to measure children's attachment to their mothers at a time when most children were raised at home, whereas children in day care are subjected to a "strange situation" every day when they are left with someone else, and naturally the child would form close attachments to others who care for it and show more independence from its mother.

This "harm" is not limited only to children whose families have been disrupted by death, divorce, or out-of-wedlock parenting. Preventing these circumstances, which affect significant numbers of children, is often beyond an individual's control. What can be controlled, is a securely married mother's choice to either work outside the home or remain home full time to nurture her young children.

Subjecting infants and young children to daily care by a surrogate so that its mother can work goes against the ingrained value system of most Americans, though most will not admit this publicly. Thus it is not surprising that there was an explosive public reaction to a review paper written by Jay Belsky, a developmental psychologist at Pennsylvania State University, titled "The 'Effects' of Infant Day Care Reconsidered."

The author makes a sweeping statement about the value system of most Americans. Do you think she is right in her assumption?

Belsky's research group, including Dr. Peter Barglow, psychiatrist with the University of Chicago Medical School and others, showed that twelve- to thirteen-month-old infants subjected to over twenty hours of nonmaternal care each week are at risk for future psychological and behavioral difficulties. Nonmaternal care includes day-care centers, family day care, and care in the infant's home by a babysitter or a relative. "These findings sent shudders of guilt through millions of parents." If these parents truly believe that the mother's decision to work outside the home was morally correct, then why do they shudder at such reports? Why is parental guilt a prevailing theme in dual-career households?...

It is clear that children's interests are best served by being raised at home in the presence of loving parents, as opposed to an institutionalized day care facility. Working parents pronounce themselves guilty of not spending enough time with their children, whether they consciously acknowledge it or not.

But if working creates such feelings of guilt, then why do significant numbers of modern mothers continue to work outside the home? Why don't mothers take advantage of family-friendly company policies, when available, that allow flexible or reduced hours, or job sharing? The most frequent and politically correct excuse is the family's inability to afford the reduced hours....

Mothers' personal fulfillment vs. their children's

Dr. Laura Schlessinger writes, "people don't want to be told that what they feel or believe they have to do (or simply want to do) is wrong and may injure their children and society.... [W]hitewashing the consequences to children is self-indulgent." Despite their guilt about not spending more time with their families, many mothers continue seeking the public recognition and personal fulfillment from the workplace that they feel is far greater than what they would ever achieve "only" being a parent.

Do you think that parents should always put the needs of their children before their own needs?

Fortunately, as the shifting social trends move between the various extremes of the swinging pendulum, very recently researchers note a change in working mother's attitudes. "In the late '70s, only about half of women ages 20–50 worked outside the home.... In the late '90s, three-fourths of women ages 20–50 worked.... Today, [working mothers] consider home and family as important as a career, want quantity more than 'quality' time with their kids ... feel less ambitious, career-driven and competitive," according to Edmonds. This prioritization of family over and in conjunction with career is a paradigm-shift described as "sequencing."

Can you think of any factors that may contribute to this shift in attitude toward parenthood at the beginning of the 21st century?

The sequencing mother's watchword is "balance." She gauges her success based on how her various activities make her feel, by listening to her inner voice—those pangs of conscience that were being ignored during previous decades. If her career demands are requiring too much time away from home, she chooses to prioritize home; but nevertheless seems to manage to have it both ways....

The sequencing mother may say that her family is firmly entrenched at the top of her priority list, but as long as she continues to work she maintains a meaningful commitment to her employer. As Janelle Phifer, former director of the Toledo (Ohio) Legal Aid Society states, if you are employed "...you don't say no to the bosses—you say no to your family."

Does the author provide any evidence to support this fact, or is it simply an opinion?

In the childcare debate, the question at the bottom line—and typically the least-addressed issue—is how does childcare, whether in or out of home, affect the child? Much debate on this issue centers on the mother's right to work or the quality of the day care program. But the individuals who are most affected—the children themselves—have no voice in the argument. Long-term consequences of day care on young children are yet to be definitively established by the scientific community, but the definitive guide currently available to all parents is conscience.

Do you agree with the author that conscience should be the definitive guide, rather than the findings of scientific research?

A perilous experiment

It will take years to further research childcare issues and draw informed conclusions. In the meantime our children are being subjected to an institution considered by some as little more than a perilous experiment. Suppose an individual is visiting his doctor for an annual checkup. At the end of the examination the doctor tells him that he needs an injection which will be either a) possibly very harmful, b) moderately harmful, or c) the effects are unknown. Do you suppose the patient will take the injection? Given those options, most people would not readily submit to their doctor's advice without first giving the matter extensive thought and most likely getting a second professional opinion. This analogy is applicable to the childcare debate: if we are not certain about the long-term effects of day care on young children, why put them at risk unnecessarily? Why treat them as guinea pigs merely to benefit the career aspirations of adults?...

Do you think the author's argument is enhanced by using the doctor-and-patient analogy? Do you think the analogy is appropriate?

Simply put, there is no substitute for the care that a child's own mother can provide; no other whose attention is more likely to be committed to that child's well being. If a mother gives her child's needs top priority, then mother and child will always be found together.

Summary

The first article is a government press release concerned mainly with the fact that only about one in eight families eligible for childcare funding actually claims the benefit to which it is entitled. It also draws attention to the fact that despite the low usage rate, some states are already using all the federal funds allocated to them for this purpose. It therefore points out the contradiction that although the government should want its citizens to claim all the benefits to which they are entitled, there would not be enough money available to pay them if they did. The article also makes the point that women are needed in the workplace because of the current high demand for employees in the United States, and that recent stastistics show that three out of four mothers with children between six and 17 are working, compared to one in four in 1965, making childcare support crucial.

The second article expresses the view that a woman's place is in the home. In support of this the author, Susan Benitez, cites the work of developmental psychologist Jay Belsky, whose research has found that children who are looked after by outsiders are at a greater risk of developing problems in later life than those who are cared for by their own parents. Benitez also quotes a doctor who has written that parents do not want to face up to the damage that the pursuit of their own careers may be causing to their children. The article concludes that mothers should not even try to strike a balance between family and job—a good mother is a mother who is always with her child. Thus the implication is that childcare facilities only encourage parents to neglect their child's real needs—their mother's undivided attention.

FURTHER INFORMATION:

Books:
Cohen, Sally S., and Christopher Dodd, *Championing Child Care (Power, Conflict, and American Policy into the 21st Century)*. New York: Columbia University Press, 2001.
Michel, Sonya, *Children's Interests/Mothers' Rights: The Shaping of America's Child Care Policy*. Hartford, CT: Yale University Press, 1999.

Useful websites:
www.theatlantic.com/issues/88aug/babe.htm
"Babes in Day Care" by Ellen Ruppel Shell from *The Atlantic Monthly*, August 1988.
www.edweek.org/ew/ewstory.cfm?slug=22care.h19
"Problems in Child Care Found to Persist" by Linda Jacobson, Education Week on the Web, February 9, 2000.
www.anxiousparents.com/images
Site giving definitions, categories of childcare, and other general information on this subject.

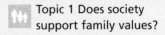

The following debates in the Pro/Con series may also be of interest:

In this volume:

Topic 1 Does society support family values?

Topic 4 Is the two-parent family best?

Topic 13 Does the welfare system provide enough support for the family?

SHOULD THERE BE MORE CHILDCARE FACILITIES FOR PEOPLE IN NEED?

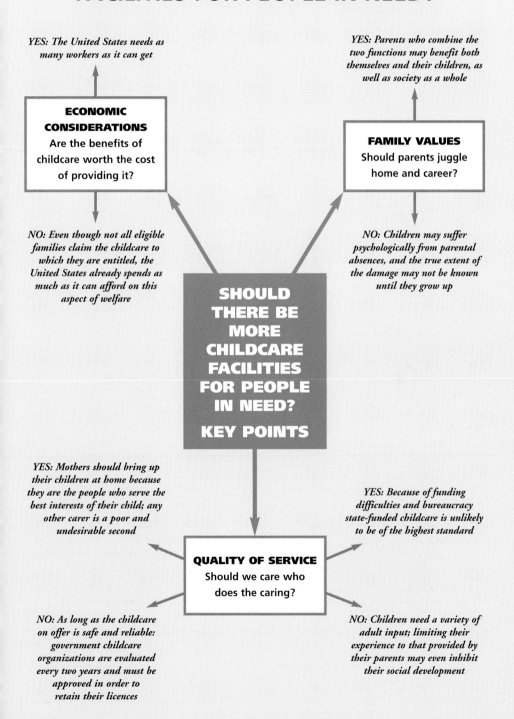

YES: The United States needs as many workers as it can get

YES: Parents who combine the two functions may benefit both themselves and their children, as well as society as a whole

ECONOMIC CONSIDERATIONS
Are the benefits of childcare worth the cost of providing it?

FAMILY VALUES
Should parents juggle home and career?

NO: Even though not all eligible families claim the childcare to which they are entitled, the United States already spends as much as it can afford on this aspect of welfare

NO: Children may suffer psychologically from parental absences, and the true extent of the damage may not be known until they grow up

SHOULD THERE BE MORE CHILDCARE FACILITIES FOR PEOPLE IN NEED?

KEY POINTS

YES: Mothers should bring up their children at home because they are the people who serve the best interests of their child; any other carer is a poor and undesirable second

YES: Because of funding difficulties and bureaucracy state-funded childcare is unlikely to be of the highest standard

QUALITY OF SERVICE
Should we care who does the caring?

NO: As long as the childcare on offer is safe and reliable: government childcare organizations are evaluated every two years and must be approved in order to retain their licences

NO: Children need a variety of adult input; limiting their experience to that provided by their parents may even inhibit their social development

Topic 15

WOULD FEWER FAMILIES LIVE IN POVERTY IF MEN AND WOMEN RECEIVED EQUAL PAY?

YES

"EQUAL PAY FOR WORKING FAMILIES: NATIONAL AND STATE DATA"
AFL-CIO

NO

EXECUTIVE SUMMARY, "POVERTY TRENDS FOR FAMILIES HEADED BY WORKING SINGLE
MOTHERS, 1993 TO 1999"
CENTER ON BUDGET AND POLICY PRIORITIES
KATHRYN H. PORTER AND ALLEN DUPREE

INTRODUCTION

To determine poverty, the Census Bureau uses the "poverty threshold," calculated as roughly three times the cost of a "basic food basket" (the minimum nutritional requirements for a healthy diet). Using this benchmark, the bureau estimated that in 2000, 11.3 percent of the population, around 31 million people, were "poor." Poverty tends to be concentrated in specific minority groups, especially nonwhite communities, but it is higher among women across all races.

According to the Census Bureau, the poverty rate in 2000 for married-couple families was 4.7 percent, for families headed by a single male it was 11.5 percent, whereas among families headed by a single woman the poverty rate was 24.7 percent. Similarly, the average income for a family maintained by a woman was $25,787 a year, far less than the $37,523 earned by a male-headed family or the average $59,187 earned by a married couple.

These statistics indicate a "feminization of poverty"—a phrase coined by Diana Pearce, a researcher at the University of Wisconsin who analyzed poverty trends in 1978 and discovered that between 1950 and 1970 more women than men had become poor. The Census statistics also show that families headed by women tend to live in poorer circumstances. Why should this be the case in a period in which both the female employment rate and women's educational qualifications have improved? Would equalizing women's wages help?

Some theorists argue that changes in the family structure have helped create this situation. Census Bureau figures show that between 1970 and 1998 the number of women living alone more than doubled from 7.3 million to 15.3

million. Traditional heterosexual-parented nuclear families have decreased, while there has been a rise in the numbers of single women and female-headed households.

One reason for this increase in the number of single women is that more women are opting out of unsatisfactory marriages, often with primary custody of their children. Similarly, many women are opting to marry later if they marry at all. In general, women today are self-supporting for far longer than were their 1950s counterparts, with many choosing to have children without the support of a partner.

> *"We are determined … to promote women's economic independence … to eradicate the persistent and increasing burden of poverty on women."*
> —FOURTH WORLD CONFERENCE ON WOMEN, SEPTEMBER 15, 1995

Another area of debate concerns welfare. Some researchers attribute the level of family poverty to a decline in welfare support. Advocates of welfare argue that poverty was reduced when women had access to the cash assistance formerly provided by the Aid to Families with Dependent Children (AFDC) program, supplemented by still existing programs such as food stamps and Medicaid. By contrast, others argue that welfare encourages women to leave economically secure relationships to establish single female-headed households. Critics of this welfare

dependency view respond by pointing out that programs are being cut at a time when the family poverty statistics indicate that they are needed most.

A third strand of debate is whether poverty can be alleviated by an improvement in women's earnings. In June 1963 the government passed the Equal Pay Act, which stated that every man and woman performing substantially equal work in the same establishment must be paid an equal wage. Advocates of the act stated that it would lift women, and consequently families, above the poverty line. Yet evidence today suggests that there are still marked discrepancies between male and female wages. In 1963 women earned 59 percent of what men earned; in 2000 they earned 73 percent of male wages—an increase of just 14 percent in almost 40 years.

Critics of the equal pay remedy argue that it may not be the best all-round solution to poverty reduction. They fear that if women's pay goes up, employers may find it hard to foot the wage bill and may opt to cut down on staff.

Studies show that when companies are rationalized women are more likely to lose their jobs first. Without an adequate social welfare system in place, the argument goes, the family will suffer, and incidences of poverty will increase. Organizations such as the AFL-CIO, the federation of America's labor unions, argue that besides equal pay, support measures such as government-sponsored child care, training programs, and health care are what most women need. These measures would help maintain women in the workplace and help reduce welfare dependency.

The two articles that follow examine the pro and con arguments of equal pay for men and women.

EQUAL PAY FOR WORKING FAMILIES: NATIONAL AND STATE DATA AFL-CIO

YES

AFL-CIO is the American Federation of Labor–Congress of Industrial Organizations. For detail on its 2002 Ask A Working Woman survey visit www.aflcio. org/news/2002/0507 _wwsurvey.htm.

Equal pay is a bread-and-butter issue for working families. More than two-thirds of all mothers in the United States work for pay. Two-earner families are today's norm among married couples, and a growing number of single women provide most or all of their families' support. Altogether, almost two-thirds of all working women and slightly more than half of married women responding to the AFL-CIO's 1997 Ask A Working Woman survey said they provide half or more of their families' incomes.

Little wonder, then, that 87 percent of working women in the 2000 Ask A Working Woman survey—almost every one—say stronger equal pay laws are "important," with 51 percent saying stronger laws are "very important"; 61 percent of Hispanic women and 58 percent of African American women say stronger laws are "very important."

The IWPR (www.iwpr.org) "is a public policy research organization dedicated to informing and stimulating the debate on public policy issues of critical importance to women and their families."

To better understand the wage gap for women and people of color in the United States and to better measure the price that wage inequality exacts from families and individual workers, the AFL-CIO and the Institute for Women's Policy Research (IWPR) jointly undertook a national study, including state-by-state breakouts, to analyze recent data from the Census Bureau and the Bureau of Labor Statistics.

The study confirms many recent analyses, finding that women who work full-time are paid only 72 cents for every dollar men earn—or $148 less each week. Women of color who work full-time are paid only 64 cents for every dollar men overall earn—or $210 less each week. Going further, the study uses more refined techniques to explore the dimensions, and the full cost, of unequal pay.

Working families pay a steep price for unequal pay

• America's working families lose a staggering $200 billion of income annually to the wage gap—an average loss of more than $4,000 each for working women's families every year because of unequal pay, even after accounting for differences in education, age, location and the number of hours worked.

- If married women were paid the same as comparable men, their family incomes would rise by nearly 6 percent, and their families' poverty rates would fall from 2.1 percent to 0.8 percent.
- If single working mothers earned as much as comparable men, their family incomes would increase by nearly 17 percent, and their poverty rates would be cut in half, from 25.3 percent to 12.6 percent.
- If single women earned as much as comparable men, their incomes would rise by 13.4 percent, and their poverty rates would be reduced from 6.3 percent to 1 percent.

Do you think the discrepancy between men's and women's wages is surprising? What historical reasons might there be for this gap?

The size of the pay gap varies by state

While the wage gap is much smaller than the national average in some states, the numbers do not automatically signal improved economic status for women. The primary reason for women's relatively improved status in many states is that the wages of minority men are so low. This is particularly true for the District of Columbia, Arizona, California, New York, North Carolina, Texas and Virginia.

- Working families in Ohio, Michigan, Vermont, Indiana, Illinois, Montana, Wisconsin, and Alabama pay the heaviest price for unequal pay to working women, losing an average of roughly $5,000 in family income each year.
- Family income losses due to unequal pay for women range from $326 million in Alaska to $21.8 billion in California.
- Women who work full-time are paid the least, compared with men, in Indiana, Louisiana, Michigan, Montana, North Dakota, Wisconsin, and Wyoming, where women earn less than 70 percent of men's weekly earnings.
- Women of color fare especially poorly in Louisiana, Montana, Nebraska, Oregon, Rhode Island, Utah, Wisconsin, and Wyoming, earning less than 60 percent of what men earn.
- Even where women fare best compared with men—in Arizona, California, Florida, Hawaii, Massachusetts, New York, and Rhode Island—women earn little more than 80 percent as much as men.
- Women earn the most in comparison to men—97 percent —in Washington, D.C., but the primary reason women appear to fare so well is the very low wages of minority men.
- For women of color, the gender pay gap is smallest in the District of Columbia, Hawaii, Florida, New York and Tennessee, where they earn more than 70 percent of what men overall in those states earn.

The authors make extensive use of facts and figures to support their arguments. For a state-by-state comparison table on women's pay differentials and their effect on family poverty go to www.aflcio.org/ women/exec99_ table.htm.

Unequal pay hurts men, too

Why do you think so many women work in these occupations? What other jobs do you feel might fall into the category of "women's work"?

As the percentage of women in an occupation rises, wages tend to fall. Workers who do what traditionally has been viewed as "women's work"—clerical workers, cashiers, librarians, child care workers and others in jobs in which 70 percent or more of the workers are women—typically earn less than workers in jobs that are predominately male or are integrated by gender.

- Both women and men pay a steep price for unequal pay when they do "women's work": The 25.6 million women who work in these jobs lose an average of $3,446 each per year; the 4 million men who work in predominately female occupations lose an average of $6,259 each per year—for a whopping $114 billion loss for men and women in predominately female jobs.

The authors cite precise figures in this section. Try to discover the benchmarks they use to arrive at these increases.

- At the state level, women who work in female-dominated jobs could increase their salaries from $2,112 per year in Missouri to a high of $4,707 in Delaware if they had equal pay. Annual wage gains for women in these jobs would exceed $3,000 on average in 36 states. In 34 states, wages would increase by at least $2,500 for women of color in female-dominated jobs.
- For men in female-dominated jobs, state average increases would range from $3,533 annually in the District of Columbia to $8,958 in Delaware if pay inequality was eliminated. Minority men would see increases ranging from $1,918 in Colorado to $7,996 in Alaska.

Unions mean big pay gains, smaller pay gaps

Union representation is a proven and powerful tool for raising workers' wages, particularly for those most subject to labor market discrimination: women and minorities.

- The typical female union member earns 38 percent more per week—$157—than a woman who does not belong to a union.
- Unionized women of color earn almost 39 percent more—$135—than nonunion women of color. In fact, minority union women earn $45 a week more than nonunion white women.
- Minority men who belong to unions bring home 44 percent more—$177—each week than nonunion men of color.
- Unions also help close the wage gaps based on gender and minority status for their members. Women represented by unions earn almost 84 percent as much as union men,

while unionized workers of color make about 81 percent as much as unionized white workers.

Unions have used a number of strategies to achieve pay equity increases at the bargaining table, including bargaining for pay upgrades for lower-paid classifications, bargaining for re-classifications, bargaining for upgrades for female-dominated job classifications and bargaining for pay equity studies with phased-in pay adjustments.

In the 35 years since the equal employment laws passed, women and people of color have made significant strides into the mainstream of the American workplace. But lingering unequal pay robs women and their families of economic security, doubling poverty rates for today's workers and threatening reduced retirement income and greater poverty tomorrow.

There are three clear routes to ensuring that women receive equal pay: vigorous enforcement of current equal pay laws, passage of stronger and better equal pay laws and greater protections for workers' right to organize together into unions.

Title VII of the Civil Rights Act of 1964 prohibits employment discrimination on grounds of race, color, religion, sex, or national origin. For information on other federal laws against job discrimination go to www.eeoc.gov/facts/qanda.html.

EXECUTIVE SUMMARY, POVERTY TRENDS FOR FAMILIES HEADED BY WORKING SINGLE MOTHERS, 1993 TO 1999
Kathryn H. Porter and Allen Dupree

NO

X This analysis focuses on poverty in families headed by single mothers who work. In recent years, large numbers of families headed by single mothers have moved from welfare to work. This report addresses the question whether and to what degree those who work have improved their economic situation.

No progress made

Among people in families headed by working single mothers, there was no progress in reducing poverty between 1995 and 1999, despite an expanding economy. Reductions in poverty as a result of economic growth were entirely offset by increases in poverty due to contractions in government safety net programs.

The Personal Responsibility and Work Opportunity Reconciliation Act (PRWORA) of 1996 made significant changes in the welfare system. For a summary of the act go to www.cbpp.org/ WCNSUM.HTM.

• Before counting the benefits of government safety net programs (including cash and non-cash programs such as food assistance and housing subsidies) as well as taxes and the Earned Income Tax Credit, the poverty rate for people in working single-mother families fell from 35.5 percent in 1995 to 33.5 percent in 1999. Poverty measured before counting government benefits and taxes primarily reflects the impact of changes in the economy on private sources of income, especially earnings.

For a fuller explanation of the benefits and taxes taken into consideration in this article go to www. cbpp.org/ 8-16-01wel.pdf, page 10.

• But after counting government benefits and taxes, the poverty rate among people in working single-mother families was 19.4 percent in 1999—not significantly different from their 19.2 percent poverty rate in 1995.

An earlier period of poverty reduction

This is in contrast to the earlier 1993 to 1995 period, when poverty rates dropped for people in working single-mother families, both before and after counting government benefits and taxes. During this period, which preceded enactment of the 1996 welfare law, safety net programs for low-income working families expanded and had a larger impact in reducing poverty among these families. This added to the effect of the economy in reducing poverty.

- Between 1993 and 1995, the poverty rate for people in working single-mother families edged down from 36.6 percent to 35.5 percent, before counting government benefits and taxes.
- After these benefits and taxes are counted, the poverty rate for people in these families fell more sharply, from 24.5 percent to 19.2 percent.

Among families with children that are not headed by single mothers, poverty rates dropped during the entire 1993 to 1999 period, both before and after counting government benefits and taxes.

The authors' technique is to give a general summary of a situation followed by detailed evidence using bullet points.

- Before counting government benefits and taxes, the poverty rate for other families with children dropped from 14.7 percent in 1993 to 10.6 percent in 1999. After these benefits are counted, the poverty rate for these families fell from 10.7 percent to 6.8 percent over the same period.

The widening poverty gap

In addition, the "poverty gap" for people in families headed by a working single mother has grown larger since 1995. (The poverty gap is the amount of money needed to bring all poor people up to the poverty line and measures the depth or severity of poverty.) These data show that working single-mother families that are poor have, on average, gotten poorer.

- After counting government benefits and taxes, the total poverty gap for people in working single-mother families grew from $5 billion in 1995 to $6.3 billion in 1999. By comparison, the poverty gap for people in working families with children that are not headed by single mothers fell during this period.
- Between 1997 and 1999, the number of poor people living in families headed by a working single mother declined from 4.3 million to 4.2 million. During the same period, the poverty gap for these families rose from $5.8 billion to $6.3 billion, after counting government benefits and taxes. This shows that, on average, working single-mother families that were poor became poorer.
- As a further indication of the increasing depth of poverty among working single-mother families, the average poverty

gap, as calculated per poor person in these families, rose from $1,357 in 1997 to $1,505 in 1999, after counting government benefits and taxes. In 1999, the per-person poverty gap for these families was at its highest level since 1993. By contrast, the per-person poverty gap for other working families with children remained below $1,200 and did not increase over the period from 1993 to 1999.

Holes in the safety net

A major factor in the lack of progress in reducing poverty among people in working single-mother families after 1995 was the contraction of certain government safety net programs.

- In 1995, some 46 percent of people in working single-mother families who were poor before counting government benefits were lifted out of poverty by these benefits (i.e. their incomes rose above the poverty line when these benefits were included in their income). By 1999, the proportion of people in these families who were lifted out of poverty by government benefits had dropped to 42.2 percent.
- In 1995, government safety net programs reduced the poverty gap for working single-mother families by 67.9 percent compared to the poverty gap these families faced before counting these benefits. In 1999, government benefits reduced the poverty gap for these families by 60.5 percent.

The impact of the EITC

The EITC helps low-income working families by refunding some or all of their income taxes. To find out more about EITC, go to www.chn. org/eitc/ib-eitc.htm.

This decline in the anti-poverty impact of government benefit programs occurred in spite of the increasing effectiveness of the Earned Income Tax Credit [EITC] in reducing poverty among people in working single-mother families. The increase in the anti-poverty effect of the EITC was more than offset after 1995 by a substantial decline in the impact of cash assistance and food stamps.

- In 1995, the EITC lifted out of poverty 20 percent of people in working single-mother families who would otherwise be poor; in 1999, the credit lifted out of poverty 26.7 percent of people in these families.
- But the proportion of people in working single-mother families who were lifted out of poverty by cash assistance and food stamps fell sharply, from 15.5 percent in 1995 to 10.4 percent in 1999, with the decline particularly marked in the food stamp program.
- In 1995, cash assistance reduced the poverty gap for people in working single-mother families by 21 percent; by

1999, cash assistance reduced the poverty gap for people in this group by 13.6 percent.

• Similarly, in 1995, the combination of cash assistance and food stamps reduced the poverty gap for people in working single-mother families by 35.6 percent. In 1999, these benefits reduced the poverty gap for these families by 26.4 percent. This is a drop of more than one-fourth in four years in the impact of food stamps and cash assistance on the poverty gap for people in these families.

These findings suggest that after 1995, declines in the effectiveness of the safety net in reducing poverty among families headed by working single mothers offset the effect of the improving economy, halting the reduction of the poverty rate for these families and pushing those who remained poor deeper into poverty.

The Food Stamp program was introduced by 1964 legislation and was reduced under PRWORA in 1996. "Cash assistance" refers to the Aid to Families with Dependent Children (AFDC) program, which came from 1935 legislation and was replaced under PRWORA by Temporary Assistance to Needy Families (TANF).

Summary

The issue of whether inequalities between men's and women's income is directly related to familial poverty in the United States bears examination, especially with the rise in numbers of families headed by a single woman.

In the first article the labor federation AFL-CIO argues that "equal pay is a bread-and-butter issue for working families." Citing statistics from its 2000 Ask A Working Woman survey, the organization first argues how important stronger equal pay laws are to women. The authors then use the results of a joint study carried out by the AFL-CIO and the Institute for Women's Policy Research to illustrate general pay differentials between men and women, how they can vary from state to state, and the economic effect pay inequalities have on working families and men doing "women's work."

In their "Poverty Trends for Families Headed by Working Single Mothers, 1993 to 1999" Kathryn H. Porter and Allen Dupree examine how the move from welfare to work has affected the economic well-being of families headed by working single mothers. Their report gives details of poverty rates and poverty severity for such families before and after government benefits are taken into account, and before and after the enactment of the Personal and Work Opportunity Reconciliation Act of 1996. The authors conclude that poverty among working single mother families has not decreased since 1995 despite growth in the economy and cite "the contraction of certain government safety net programs" as "a major factor in the lack of progress."

FURTHER INFORMATION:

Books:

Collins, Chuck, and Felice Yeskel, *Economic Apartheid in America: A Primer on Economic Inequality and Security*. New York: New Press, 2000.

Ehrenreich, Barbara, *Nickel and Dimed: On (Not) Getting By in America*. New York: Metropolitan Books, 2001.

Useful websites:

www.aflcio.org/home.htm
AFL-CIO website.
www.cbpp.org
Center on Budget and Policy Priorities site.
www.jcpr.org
Northwestern University/University of Chicago Joint Center for Poverty Research site.
www.census.gov
Census Bureau site.
www.policyalmanac.org/social_welfare/welfare.shtml
Almanac of Policy Issues welfare page.

The following debates in the Pro/Con series may also be of interest:

In this volume:

Topic 13 Does the welfare system provide enough support for the family?

Topic 14 Should there be more childcare facilities for people in need?

In *Economics*:

Topic 6 Should welfare be abolished?

Topic 7 Is the minimum wage fair?

WOULD FEWER FAMILIES LIVE IN POVERTY IF MEN AND WOMEN RECEIVED EQUAL PAY?

WOULD FEWER FAMILIES LIVE IN POVERTY IF MEN AND WOMEN RECEIVED EQUAL PAY?

KEY POINTS

YES: Pay laws have existed since 1963, but women still earn only 73 percent of what men are paid

YES: More families are now headed by single women, so only one wage is coming in

LAWS
Would stronger pay equality laws help ease family poverty?

FAMILY
Could changes in family structure be to blame for more family poverty?

NO: The wage bill would be too high for employers to pay, and women would lose their jobs first

NO: Some families are headed by single men, and their poverty rates are less than half those of working single-mother families

YES: For working single-mother families cuts in welfare after 1995 offset any poverty reductions achieved by the expanding economy

YES: From 1993 to 1995 expanding welfare programs combined with economic growth to reduce poverty among working single-mother families

WELFARE
Could increased welfare help alleviate family poverty?

NO: Increases in welfare would only lead to increased welfare dependency

POPULATION IN THE 20TH AND 21ST CENTURIES

"Development is the best contraceptive."

—INDIAN DELEGATE, 1974 UN WORLD POPULATION CONFERENCE

Background

For centuries humankind has worried about whether the world's population would exceed the planet's resources. Various people over the ages, beginning with Thomas Malthus (1766–1834), the British social economist, have predicted that population would eventually exceed resources unless something was done to restrict population growth. Malthus argued in his 1798 *Essay on the Principle of Population* that if the population continued to increase unchecked, it would eventually exceed the food available and cause widespread famine and death. Although Malthus's "doom and gloom" predictions did not come true, other theorists have joined him in arguing that the global population must be controlled, especially since advances in sanitation, medical and scientific knowledge, and developments in food distribution have led to lower infant mortality rates and people living longer and generally healthier lives around the world. The 20th century saw an unprecedented rise in population: in 1900 there were fewer than two billion people living on the planet; by 2000 there were more than six billion. Some organizations, such as the Population Reference Bureau, estimate that if the current trends continue, by 2014 there will be around seven billion people on Earth. This huge growth has led to further discussion about whether the Earth can sustain its population, and if not, what can be done to help save humankind.

The case of Paul Ehrlich

In 1968 U.S. academic Paul Ehrlich published *The Population Bomb*, which claimed that the Earth would suffer from chronic overpopulation, food shortages, and mass starvation in the future. Ehrlich claimed that the United States' optimum population was around 150 million; he called for population policies, including awarding "responsibility prizes" to couples who went at least five years without having children or to men who got vasectomies. He also suggested setting up a federal bureau of population and environment to reduce population growth. Although Ehrlich's predictions failed to come true, *The Population Bomb* has arguably influenced government population-control policies around the world. In the second half of the 20th century countries such as China, Iran, India, and Mauritius passed laws to regulate population growth..

Population policies

While some governments believed that a rise in the standard of living would lead to lower birthrates as people became accustomed to living well, during the late 1970s and 1980s concern increased about the negative effects of population growth on economic development. Many countries began to accept that government actions could and should slow population growth. Most population policies include promoting the use of contraceptives, maternal and child health programs to improve health, and incentives to have more or fewer children, or policies to discourage people from having more than a given number of children. These efforts have met with mixed success.

Some advocates argue that China's "One-Child Policy," introduced in 1979, was successful since it helped reduce China's fertility rate—around 6.0 per family in the 1960s—to fewer than 2.0 in the 1990s. However, the methods used to bring about this reduction have been widely criticized. They were reported to include forced abortions and sterilizations, beatings, and other human rights abuses. Similarly, between 1975 and 1977 Indira Ghandi's government in India promoted sterilization, using incentives such as free radios to entice people to take part in the policy. Some critics argue that the reported abuses contributed to the downfall of Ghandi's government and created a backlash against family-planning programs in India that has taken years to overcome.

A few countries, in contrast, see their fertility rates as too low and would welcome faster population growth. In 1997, 23 countries reported to the United Nations that they had explicit policies to increase birthrates. Many governments in Europe and the former Soviet Union worry that low fertility will cause rapid population aging and an eventual decline in population size.

The United States

During the 1960s several industrialized countries began to work together to develop programs to help slow population growth. By the end of that decade the United States had emerged as a leader. In 1969 the United States helped create the United Nations Population Fund (UNFPA), which provides international leadership on population issues and is a key source of financial assistance for family-planning programs in poor countries. The United States provided most of its funding until around 1985, but between 1986 and 1992 it withheld all contributions to UNFPA approved by the Congress in response to reports of human rights abuses in China. In 1993 President Clinton restored U.S. funding to UNFPA on the condition that no U.S. funds be used in China. In 1999, however, Congress again banned contributions as a result of concerns about a new UNFPA program in China, but allocated $25 million for 2000/2001 on the condition that the contribution be reduced by any amount the UNFPA spends in China. In recognition of the importance of its work in helping control population, approximately $34 million was allocated to the UNFPA in 2002, but President George W. Bush's administration delayed the release of funds and did not request any funds for the organization in its 2003 budget.

Topic 16

SHOULD GOVERNMENT POLICY DICTATE THE SIZE OF FAMILIES?

YES

"IRAN'S BIRTH RATE PLUMMETING AT RECORD PACE: SUCCESS PROVIDES A MODEL FOR OTHER DEVELOPING COUNTRIES"

EARTH POLICY INSTITUTE, DECEMBER 28, 2001

JANET LARSEN

NO

"HOW TO PRODUCE HUMAN BEINGS"

THE FREEMAN, MARCH 1980, VOL. 30, NO. 3

P. DEAN RUSSELL

INTRODUCTION

In the last two centuries the world's population has increased enormously. In 1800 there were around one billion people in the world; in 1900 the figure had risen to 1.65 billion, and by the end of the 20th century it had increased nearly sixfold to pass the 6 billion mark in 2000. This enormous growth has resulted in serious concerns about the ability of global resources to sustain the world's population.

While natural events such as famine and disease have to some extent checked population expansion, there is still much heated debate over the best way to tackle the "population problem." Although environmental education and contraception advice are among the methods advocated by interest groups, many people believe that government intervention, through a combination of legislation, social incentives, and educational packages, is the only way forward.

Yet, while government population control has been successful in reducing birthrates in countries such as China and India, it has attracted severe criticism from international civil liberties and human rights groups. They argue that government interference in people's families is an infringement on the basic rights of individuals. But if that is not the answer, what is?

One of the most influential figures in the population debate was English economist Thomas Malthus (1766–1834), who argued that unless birthrates declined through abstinence or birth control, humankind was doomed. He predicted that the world's population would increase at a far higher rate than the food supply. Yet as it transpired, 19th-century technological advances helped stabilize the balance of population and food supply. However, population growth still remained a concern. It was only after World War II that governments worldwide started to take measures to control the size of their populations. Environmentalists began to predict that the world's population would soon exceed its resources if something was not done to prevent it. When the influential American activist Paul Ehrlich warned in his book *The Population Bomb* (1968) that 65 million Americans might be starving to death by 2000, it brought the issue home with brutal force.

> *"[Survival is] the perpetual struggle for room and food."*
> —THOMAS MALTHUS,
> BRITISH SOCIAL ECONOMIST

While Ehrlich's predictions have failed to come true, partly due to a combination of agricultural, scientific, and technological innovations, together with increased environmental awareness, the global population has still continued to rise.

China and India have the largest populations. Between 1949 and 2000 China's population increased from 541 million to 1.26 billion, and India's from around 370 million to more than 1 billion. Thus governments started to look to population policies to avoid potential global catastrophe (see pages 200–201).

In developed countries people are tending to have fewer children than ever before, but they are also living longer. Those who cannot support themselves can usually rely on some form of welfare to keep them housed and fed. Yet this is not the case in most developing countries. While religious, social, and cultural thinking plays a part in resistance to reducing the size of families in those countries, child mortality rates are high. To compensate, parents have more children to support their families. Because of the high birthrates prevalent in developing countries, some governments, such as China and India, have implemented population policies since the 1970s. In China, for example, the average woman's fertility rate was around 6.0; by the 1990s it had fallen to 2.0.

However, some of these apparent success stories also have their downsides. For example, as P. Dean Russell discusses in the second article, although China's "One-Child Policy" — which restricts the national birth average to 1.6 and involves issuing permits to control the marriage age— has decreased China's birthrate, it has also been criticized by organizations such as Amnesty International for human rights abuses, including forced sterilizations, abortions, and adoptions. Yet the intention of these policies is primarily economic: to reduce population and raise the standard of living while achieving political stability.

Critics also worry about the issue of eugenics, which means an attempt to improve the "quality" of a race. This policy was part of the rationale for Adolf Hitler's systematic extermination of the Jews, Slavs, gypsies, and any other groups seen as inferior by the Nazis from 1933 to 1945. The Chinese government has been accused of similar measures. Critics also argue that governments should invest in education, which would allow access both to better jobs and to more informed reproductive decisions.

IRAN'S BIRTH RATE PLUMMETING AT RECORD PACE: SUCCESS PROVIDES A MODEL FOR OTHER DEVELOPING COUNTRIES
Janet Larsen

YES

Shah Reza Pahlavi (1919–1980) was ruler of Iran from 1941 to 1979, except for a brief period in 1953 when he was overthrown. Pahlavi's policies of social reform and modernization led to his overthrow by fundamentalist religious leaders, led by Ayatollah Khomeini, in 1979.

Iran's population growth rate dropped from an all-time high of 3.2 percent in 1986 to just 1.2 percent in 2001, one of the fastest drops ever recorded. In reducing its population growth to 1.2 percent, a rate only slightly higher than that of the United States, Iran has emerged as a model for other countries that want to accelerate the shift to smaller families.

Historically, family planning in Iran has had its ups and downs. The nation's first family planning policy, introduced in 1967 under Shah Reza Pahlavi, aimed to accelerate economic growth and improve the status of women by reforming divorce laws, encouraging female employment, and acknowledging family planning as a human right.

Pronatalism proves an obstacle to development

"Pronatalism" means being in favor of women having babies.

Unfortunately, this promising initiative was reversed in 1979 at the beginning of the decade-long Islamic Revolution led by Shiite Muslim spiritual leader Ayatollah Khomeini. During this period, family planning programs were seen as undue western influences and were dismantled. Health officials were ordered not to advocate contraception. During Iran's war with Iraq between 1980 and 1988, a large population was viewed as a comparative advantage, and Khomeini pushed procreation to bolster the ranks of "soldiers for Islam," aiming for "an army of 20 million."

This strong pronatalist stance led to an annual population growth rate of well over 3 percent. United Nations data show Iran's population doubling from 27 million in 1968 to 55 million in 1988.

During postwar reconstruction in the late 1980s, the economy faltered. Severe job shortages plagued overcrowded and polluted cities. Iran's rapid population growth was finally seen as an obstacle to development. Receptive to the nation's

COMMENTARY: Population control

The most well-known national policy to restrict family size is the One-Child Policy instigated by China in 1979. The policy decrees that parents in urban environments are allowed only one child, and those in rural areas two, but only if the first is a girl. Families with more than the alloted number of children are fined for each additional birth, must pay higher taxes, and are prevented from receiving free health care. The results were dramatic. From the traditionally large families of the past, which were also encouraged by pronatalist Mao Zedong, the current rate is now 1.8 children per woman. However, there is a downside to the policy's success in reducing family numbers. Poor families in rural areas are most likely to overproduce due to lack of education and contraception. Since they cannot afford the fines for extra children, some parents resort to abandoning the children, with many ending up in orphanages.

Mauritius

Another country that has introduced a policy to cut population growth is Mauritius. Recognizing that the population had doubled in 40 years, the country launched its "Action Familiale" program in 1965. Family-planning clinics were set up throughout the country, and women were encouraged to get jobs and marry later (previously, 90 percent of Mauritius women married before the age of 20). By 1985 only 11 percent of urban dwellers and 14 percent of rural dwellers were more than a half-hour drive from a clinic, marriage ages had gone up dramatically, and the average family size was only two, compared to the previous figure of 3.4.

problems, Ayatollah Khomeini reopened dialogue on the subject of birth control. By December 1989, Iran had revived its national family planning program. Its principal goals were to encourage women to wait three to four years between pregnancies, to discourage childbearing for women younger than 18 or older than 35, and to limit family size to three children.

Do you think such goals would be achievable in the United States?

Government family planning laws

In May of 1993, the Iranian government passed a national family planning law that encouraged couples to have fewer children by restricting maternity leave benefits after three children. It also called for the Ministries of Education, of Culture and Higher Education, and of Health and Medical Education to incorporate information on population, family planning, and mother and child health care in curriculum materials. The Ministry of Islamic Culture and Guidance was

Which do you think had more effect on parents' childbearing decisions—restricting financial help or providing information?

told to allow the media to raise awareness of population issues and family planning programs, and the Islamic Republic of Iran Broadcasting was entrusted with broadcasting such information. Money saved on reduced maternity leave funds these educational programs.

From 1986 to 2001, Iran's total fertility—the average number of children born to a woman in her lifetime—plummeted from seven to less than three. The United Nations projects that by 2010 total fertility will drop to two, which is replacement-level fertility.

"Replacement-level fertility" means that the two children take the place of their two parents.

Government and religion support family planning

Strong government support has facilitated Iran's demographic transition. Under the current president, Mohammad Khatami, the government covers 80 percent of family planning costs. A comprehensive health network made up of mobile clinics and 15,000 "health houses" provides family planning and health services to four fifths of Iran's rural population. Almost all of these health care centers were established after 1990. Because family planning is integrated with primary health care, there is little stigma attached to modern contraceptives.

In 1997 Hojjatoleslm Seyed Mohammad Khatami (1943–) was elected fifth president of the Islamic Republic of Iran.

Religious leaders have become involved with the crusade for smaller families, citing them as a social responsibility in their weekly sermons. They also have issued fatwas, religious edicts with the strength of court orders, that permit and encourage the use of all types of contraception, including permanent male and female sterilization—a first among Muslim countries. Birth control, including the provision of condoms, pills, and sterilization, is free.

Catholicism discourages the use of contraception. Are you surprised to learn that Islam supports it?

One of the strengths of Iran's promotion of family planning is the involvement of men. Iran is the only country in the world that requires both men and women to take a class on modern contraception before receiving a marriage license. And it is the only country in the region with a government-sanctioned condom factory. In the past four years, some 220,000 Iranian men have had a vasectomy. While vasectomies still account for only 3 percent of contraception, compared with female sterilization at 28 percent, men nonetheless are assuming more responsibility for family planning.

Rising literacy and a national communications infrastructure are facilitating progress in family planning. The literacy rate for adult males increased from 48 percent in 1970 to 84 percent in 2000, nearly doubling in 30 years. Female literacy climbed even faster, rising from less than 25 percent in 1970 to more than 70 percent. Meanwhile, school enrollment grew from 60 to 90 percent. And by 1996, 70 percent of rural and 93 percent of urban households had televisions, allowing family planning information to be spread widely through the media.

Depopulation needed to survive water scarcity

As one of 17 countries already facing absolute water scarcity, Iran's decision to curb its rapid population growth has helped alleviate unfolding water shortages exacerbated by the severe drought of the past three years. An estimated 37 million people, more than half the population, do not have enough water.

The lack of water for irrigation has helped push Iran's wheat imports to 6.5 million tons in 2001, well above the 5.8 million tons of Japan, traditionally the world's leading importer. Total grain production dropped steeply between 1998 and 2000, from 17 million to 10 million tons, largely because of the drought. The grain area harvested has decreased steadily since 1993, rapidly shrinking grain production per person.

Dwindling per capita arable land and water supplies reinforce the need for population stabilization through forward-thinking family planning programs. Had the Iranian population maintained its 1986 growth rate of 3.2 percent, it would have doubled by 2008, topping 100 million instead of the projected 78 million.

Because almost 40 percent of Iran's population is under the age of 15, population momentum is strong and growth in the immediate future is inevitable. To keep growth rates low, Iran needs to continue emphasizing the social value of smaller families. Among the keys to Iran's fertility transition are universal access to health care and family planning, a dramatic rise in female literacy, mandatory premarital contraceptive counseling for couples, men's participation in family planning programs, and strong support from religious leaders. While Iran's population policies and health care infrastructure are unique, its land and water scarcity are not. Other developing countries with fast-growing populations can profit by following Iran's lead in promoting population stability.

Despite the anti-modernization stance taken by many Islamic fundamentalists, media technology has helped the government implement its family-planning policies.

Do you think mandatory premarital contraceptive counseling for couples would be possible in the West? Who might object to it?

HOW TO PRODUCE HUMAN BEINGS
P. Dean Russell

NO

X A feature of our tour of a collective farm in China was a visit to the home of a worker. To my astonishment, our host had five children.

I wondered if he was aware of the policy of the State Council's family planning department. The chairwoman, Vice Premier Chen Muhua, summed up that policy in this clear statement: "The planned economy of socialism should make it possible to regulate the reproduction of human beings so that the population growth keeps in step with the growth of material production."

For information about the policy see the box on page 205.

Five children in one family is not in harmony with the current level of material production in the People's Republic of China. In fact, the government's plan to equalize them is based on the production of no more than two children per couple-and one, or even none, is preferred.

At my request, our tour guide put this information into a question to our farmer-host. He listened carefully, smiled proudly, and replied that the official policy on his collective farm of 26,000 members is to permit the production of children until a son is born. He and his wife had produced four daughters before the son arrived. Then both were sterilized.

This policy on the production of human beings in China varies from province to province and, apparently, from collective to collective. Also the "child production allotment" appears to be larger on collective farms than in collective factories. Increasingly, however, the philosophy now followed in rural Guizhou Province is becoming the norm for the nation: "The party organizations at all levels have called on the masses to resolutely deal blows to the criminals … [who] have used the masses' old ideas," (i.e., more sons, more bliss) to sabotage socialist population control measures.

Traditions die hard, however, in any society. Prime Minister Indira Gandhi also discovered this truth when she encouraged the use of force to sterilize people who refused to comply with her plans to decrease the population in India. Her successor as prime minister, Moraji Desai, once told me that Mrs. Gandhi's compulsory sterilization policies had far more to do with her political defeat than did the charges of corruption against her administration and family.

Can you imagine any circumstances in which Americans could be sterilized by force?

Rewards and penalties

In India and China, a combination of both "carrot and stick" measures are used in the attempt to keep the production of human beings in harmony with state plans. For example, free birth control devices, abortions, and sterilizations are readily available to all. These control measures are always actively promoted and are sometimes even enforced against reluctant participants. In some cities in China, e.g., Peking, the production of a third child may bring a fine of 10 per cent of pay for up to 14 years. One-child and no-child families in China are often rewarded by the government with more housing space and better job opportunities. These cooperating parents may also get special credits added to their retirement pensions.

The expression "carrot and stick" is used to describe a situation in which a reward is given (the "carrot") along with penalties and punishment (the "stick").

Similar reward and punishment measures are used (in reverse) in western nations where the production of children is positively encouraged. For example, in Sweden the low birth rate is of great concern to the government. The allocation of scarce housing is one of several ways the government uses to reward the producers of more Swedish babies. During my two visits to Stockholm in the 1960s I found that the waiting time for an apartment was from four to ten years. But a woman could move to the top of the waiting list for scarce and low-rent housing if she became pregnant. That's a most persuasive production bonus in a society where there's a housing shortage.

In France with its declining birth rate, a friend of mine in Paris is paid more (directly and indirectly) by the government for his five children than he's paid (take home) by his employer. He once joked to me that his family is a two-income family; his wife is paid for producing more children while he's paid for producing more lectures.

In New York City, the payment of various direct and indirect subsidies to families with dependent children usually adds up to considerably more than the parent could earn at any available job. And so on, in every nation of the world, with the government applying both carrot and stick to increase or decrease the production of human beings according to state plans.

Motivation

There is a strong tendency by most persons in any society to take the job that offers the most material goods and services for the least effort. And quite frequently in various western nations, the government pays more for the production of children than the market pays for the production of goods and services.

Do you agree with the author that parents are tempted to have children as a source of income?

This "reward principle" applies to the production of anything and everything, at all times, and in all nations. For example, when the state planners in Russia wanted more food produced, they permitted private farming, market pricing, and high profits. The socialist planners knew with certainty that the Russian farmers would respond to the profit motive in precisely the same way the managers of General Motors respond to the same motive. Both will produce more of the wanted products. In Poland, I observed people standing in line for three hours at the no-profit government stores while other people were getting immediate service in the "private sector" of the economy that operates on the profit motive.

This motivation to increase production, i.e., the basic desire of mankind to accumulate products and services for survival and comfort, is not restricted to any particular economic system. It is an inherent—not an acquired—characteristic. It came with the first human being, and every one of us today was born with it in our genes. Even the persons who use force in an effort to suppress this motivating principle "to get ahead" are themselves thereby trying to get ahead of the rest of us.

Do you agree that people are born with the desire to accumulate things?

This acquisitive characteristic is responsible for all progress, including art by the old masters. The philosopher who argues how the "surplus" production should be distributed seems happily unaware that the surplus was produced by persons who expected to gain something from it personally. What did they expect to gain? Ask any producer, including yourself. While the answers will vary widely, they will all involve self-interest (including self-glorification and immortalization) in one way or another.

Do you agree with the author's cynical view that all people are motivated primarily by self-interest?

As my minister sincerely denounced the "root of all evil" in his sermons, I continued to help him in his search for a larger church that paid its pastor more money. I recommended him because he was a high producer and a good man in every sense of the word. He, too, wanted (and I think, deserved) more of the world's products and services.

What do you want more of? Babies? Tobacco? Chrysler cars? The secret of how to get them produced is known to everyone, in Russia as in the United States. Just pay a bigger bonus in one form or another, including the government's support of prices higher than the market would tolerate.

Leave the choice to the individual

What do you want less of? Babies? Rental housing and apartments? Investment in machinery? The secret of how to decrease production is also known to everyone, in China as in the United States. Just penalize such production in one way or another, including the government's setting of prices lower than the market would offer.

Personally, I'm not in favor of our government's rewarding or penalizing the producers of any product, most especially the producers of human beings. That's a bit too close to "playing God" for my taste. Perhaps we collectively (through our government) would be well advised neither to reward nor to penalize anyone for having or not having babies. Perhaps that decision should be left with the individuals who are directly concerned, and with no one else.

In retrospect, I just can't imagine that any government planning agency would have permitted me (unit number 11) to be added to the existing 10 children already produced by a dirt-poor family in the Virginia mountains. Even the worst of the bureaucratic planners couldn't make such an obvious blunder as that.

Does the fact that the author is the eleventh child to be born into his family give more or less strength to his argument?

I think of that when I take the government–granted income tax deduction for my own children. If I ask the government to reward me with tax rebates (and other subsidies) for producing human beings, I have no moral ground to stand on when the government planners decide to penalize me for it. If they have the right to do the one, then most definitely they have the right to do the other.

Summary

People are becoming increasing concerned about population growth, particularly about whether the planet will be able to sustain the number of people living on it, and whether governments should play a role in controlling their populations. The first article, by Janet Larsen, concentrates on the example of Iran and the measures taken regarding population control and the size of families by successive, radically different governments from 1967 onward. In 1967 the shah's government adopted a liberal western model, aiming to aid economic growth and women's choices. After the shah's overthrow in 1979 the strongly traditionalist Islamic leadership rejected the western model. At war with its neighbor Iraq through much of the 1980s, it even encouraged childbearing to provide potential soldiers for the future. At the end of the war the leadership realized that Iran's population growth was unsustainable by the country's limited natural resources and instituted an extensive education program to encourage parents to limit the size of their families. The author asserts that Iran's population will now be better adapted to its resources. In the second article P. Dean Russell shows some of the different motivations of parents to have children in a variety of developing and developed countries. He first observes how, in China and in India, strong government measures to control the size of families may not be at all popular with parents. He then contrasts government rewards and penalties used to encourage parents to limit the size of their families in these countries.

FURTHER INFORMATION:

 Books:

Brown, Lester R., "Stabilizing Population by Reducing Fertility," *Eco-Economy: Building an Economy for the Earth*. New York: W.W. Norton & Company, 2001.

 Articles:

Hoodfar, Homa, and Samad Assadpour, "The Politics of Population Policy in the Islamic Republic of Iran," *Studies in Family Planning*, March 2000, Vol. 31, No. 1. Wright, Robin "Iran's New Revolution," *Foreign Affairs*, January/February 2000.

 Useful websites:

http://www.populationaction.org
Population Action International website.
http://www.popcouncil.org
Population Council website.
http://www.prb.org
Population Reference Bureau website.

http://www.un.org/esa/population/unpop.htm
United Nations Population Division.

The following debates in the Pro/Con series may also be of interest:

In this volume:

 Topic 10 Does sex education work?

In *Environment*:

 Topic 2 Should the human population be stablized?

In *Economics*:

 Topic 5 Does government intervention do more harm than good?

SHOULD GOVERNMENT POLICY DICTATE THE SIZE OF FAMILIES?

YES: The Earth only has finite resources, and the population will eventually exceed its food and water supply if nothing is done to stop its growth

YES: These measures are only introduced when necessary and as a last resort, and the international community monitors their use

PUBLIC GOOD
Will the planet's resources run out if the population is allowed to grow without controls?

NO: Factors such as later marriages, contraception, and standard of living are naturally slowing down population growth

ABUSE
Is there any way to stop governments from abusing human rights through population control policies?

NO: Scientists are coming up with all kinds of new inventions to improve crop yields and genetically engineer foodstuffs

NO: The Nazi experimentation with eugenics shows that it is easy for a government to use population polices to further its own ends

SHOULD GOVERNMENT POLICY DICTATE THE SIZE OF FAMILIES?

KEY POINTS

YES: Everyone should have the right to have children without interference

YES: In some countries children are the only economic means of support for their parents, the elderly, and the infirm

CHOICE
Is the choice to have children an individual's basic right?

NO: The good of one's country should come first; if population growth is holding back economic growth, it must be controlled

NO: There is little point in having children if there are not enough resources to adequately feed or shelter them

GLOSSARY

abortion the termination of a pregnancy either by surgery or by administering drugs. If a pregnancy ends spontaneously before 24 weeks, it is called a spontaneous abortion or miscarriage.

abstinence refraining from sexual activity. Abstinence-education programs aimed at teenagers attempt to prevent pregnancy and sexually transmitted diseases.

adoption to voluntarily take a child of other parents as one's own child. *See also* closed and open adoption; race-matched adoption.

AIDS acquired immunodeficiency syndrome; when a person's immune system becomes severely weakened by HIV, he or she is said to have AIDS. Someone with AIDS develops serious infections caused by organisms that are normally harmless to healthy people. *See also* HIV.

American Civil Liberties Union an organization that aims to preserve the constitutional liberties of everyone in the United States, regardless of race, creed, or color.

anti-Semitism prejudice against Jews because of their creed, race, or ethnicity.

Baby Boom a significant rise in the birthrate following World War II.

behavioral therapy therapy that tries to modify inappropriate behavior. It is often used in conjunction with cognitive therapy, which explores the causes of such behavior.

bigotry the state of having intolerant and prejudiced beliefs and opinions.

closed and open adoption from 1940 until 1980 closed adoptions were the norm—no identifying information was exchanged between birth and adoptive families. Now that the stigma of unmarried parenthood has diminished, open adoption has become acceptable—both parties maintain contact, and visits may be arranged.

cohabitation the practice of two people living together as if a married couple.

contraception the deliberate prevention of conception either by killing sperm before they reach the egg, by stopping the fertilized egg from growing in the woman's uterus (womb), or by stopping egg or sperm production.

corporal punishment the disciplining of children by hitting, caning, or spanking them in schools or the home.

Department of Health and Human Services a government agency that aims to protect the health of the nation by providing essential health services—particularly to disadvantaged people.

DepoProvera a progesterone-based drug normally used as a contraceptive that is given as a shot in the arm or buttocks. It stops the ovaries from releasing eggs.

earned income credit a federal tax credit for certain people who work and have earned income under a certain level. If the earned income credit exceeds the amount of tax owed, claimants receive a tax refund.

Eighth Amendment this constitutional amendment bans "cruel and unusual punishments" and states that "excessive bail shall not be required, nor excessive fines imposed."

Equal Pay Act this act came into force in June 1963. It stated that every man and woman performing substantially equal work in an establishment must be paid an equal wage.

feminism a movement that actively supports women's rights and opportunities.

hate crime an offense motivated by prejudice based on ethnicity, religion, sexual orientation, or disability, for example.

HIV the human immunodeficiency virus, which infects cells in the immune system until AIDS develops. The time between infection and the onset of AIDS varies from 1 to 14 years. *See also* AIDS.

homophobia a fear of, or discrimination against, homosexuals or homosexuality.

industrial revolution a rapid change in a country's economy caused by the introduction of power-driven machinery or by major changes to the machinery used in manufacturing. In eighteenth-century Europe the process was fastest in England.

Islamic revolution a revolution that took place in Iran, led by the fundamentalist religious leader Ayatollah Khomeini. It began in 1979, and during a 10-year period most western-influenced policies were reversed.

mentor a person who guides and counsels someone else.

minimum wage the federal minimum wage provisions are contained in the Fair Labor Standards Act, and in 2003 the rate was $5.15 per hour. If a state has its own minimum wage provision, an employee is entitled to the higher of the two rates.

misogynist someone who hates women.

monogamy the custom of being married to one person or having a single mate at the same time.

morning-after pill emergency contraception that must be taken within 72 hours of unprotected sex to be effective.

nuclear family a family group consisting of the father as provider and the mother as carer of the children and home.

pedophilia a sexual perversion in which adults are sexually attracted to children.

posttraumatic stress disorder a disorder that occurs after someone experiences a mentally or emotionally stressful event in which personal safety is at risk. Symptoms include panic attacks and nightmares.

poverty gap the amount of money required to bring all people up to the poverty line: the level of income below which someone is poor according to government standards.

prejudice an opinion formed about someone, something, or a group that is not based on knowledge of the facts but on irrational hatred, intolerance, or suspicion. *See also* anti-Semitism; bigotry; hate crime; homophobia; sexism.

race-matched adoption the matching of adopting parents with adopted children of the same racial origin.

recidivism a person's tendency to relapse into a previous mode of behavior, particularly crime.

sex education the process of acquiring information and forming attitudes and beliefs about sex, sexual identity, and intimate relationships.

sexism prejudice against women.

sexually transmitted diseases diseases contracted through sexual contact, such as AIDS, syphilis, gonorrhea, chlamydia, genital herpes, candida, and genital warts.

Social Security Act passed in 1935 after the Great Depression, this act set up general welfare provisions and a social insurance program to pay retired workers aged 65 or older an income after retirement.

stereotype a commonly held view that may be oversimplified or prejudiced.

strange situation test a test designed to study attachment patterns in young children, based on the idea that those with insecure attachments to their mothers demonstrate avoidant behavior.

stun gun a weapon that administers an immobilizing electric shock.

transcultural a joining of different cultures, as in transcultural adoptions, in which parents adopt children of a different culture.

transracial a joining of different races, as in transracial adoptions, in which parents adopt children of a different race.

triumvirate a commission, association, or ruling body of three.

vasectomy an operation to sterilize a man.

welfare assistance in the form of money or necessities for people in need.

Welfare Reform Bill a bill setting out strict requirements that recipients work in exchange for welfare benefits. It also imposes a maximum limit of five years.

Acknowledgments

Topic 1 Does Society Support Family Values?

Yes: From "Chapter 3, Communities: Communities Connect Families and Schools" by Jennifer Ballen and Oliver Moles in *Strong Families, Strong Schools* (http://eric-web.tc. columbia.edu/families/strong). Courtesy of the U.S. Department of Education.

No: From "The State of Marriage and the Family" by William J. Bennett, in *The Broken Hearth: Reversing the Moral Collapse of the American Family,* New York: Doubleday, 2001.

Topic 2 Is the Family the Source of Prejudice?

Yes: From "Lessons: Understanding Prejudice" by M'Lynn Hartwell (www.wearetraversecity.com/resources/lessons/lesson4.htm). Copyright © 2001 by M'Lynn Hartwell. Used by permission.

No: "Disliking Others without Valid Reasons: Prejudice" by Clayton E. Tucker-Ladd in *Psychological Self-Help,* 1996–2002, Mental Help Net (mentalhelp.net/psyhelp/chap7/chap71.htm). Reprinted with permission of Clayton E. Tucker-Ladd.

Topic 3 Is Marriage Essential to the Modern Family Unit?

Yes: From "The Importance of Marriage" by Familyfirst.org (www.familyfirst.org/capitolwatch/0899.shtml). Reprinted with permission of Familyfirst.org.

No: From "Rosie's Story" by Rebecca Raphael, ABC News.com (abcnews.go.com/sections/primetime/ABCNEWSSpecials/primetime_020313_rosiegayadoption_feature.html). Copyright © 2001 by ABC News. Used by permission.

Topic 4 Is the Two-Parent Family Best?

Yes: From "Single-Parent Families in Poverty" by Jacqueline Kirby, *Single Parents Living in Poverty*, Vol. 1, Issue 1, Spring 1995 (www.hec.ohio-state.edu/famlife/bulletin/volume.1/bullart1.htm). Reprinted with permission of *Single Parents Living in Poverty.*

No: "Single Parent Adoptions: Why Not"? by Cake, Hanson, and Cormell (adoption.about.com/library/writes/uc120801a.htm).

Topic 5 Do Gay Couples Make Good Parents?

Yes: From "American Civil Liberties Union Fact Sheet: Overview of Lesbian and Gay Parenting, Adoption, and Foster Care, 1999" (www.aclu.org/issues/gay/parent.html). Copyright © 1999 by American Civil Liberties Union. Used by permission.

No: From "Homosexual Parenting: Placing Children at Risk" by Timothy J. Dailey (www.frc.org/get/is01j3. cfm). Used by permission of the Family Research Council.

Topic 6 Should Couples Be Able to Adopt Children of a Different Race?

Yes: From "Adoption and Race" by Elizabeth Bartholet (www.pactadopt.org/press/articles/adopt-race.html). Reprinted with permission of Elizabeth Bartholet and Pact Press (www.pactadopt.org).

No: "Transracial Adoptions Encounter Opposition" by Clark Kauffman, November 13, 2000, DesMoinesRegister.com (www.demregister.com/news/stories/c4788998/23454.htm). Copyright © 2000, reprinted with permission of The Des Moines Register.

Topic 7 Should Fathers Have More Parental Rights?

Yes: From "Fathers Matter" by Jayne Keedle, *The Hartford Advocate* (www.hartfordadvocate.com/articles/fathersmatter.html). Reprinted with permission of *The Hartford Advocate.*

No: "The Women's Vote, A Newsletter: Covering Issues Relevant to Women" by Beth Owen, February 1996, The Committee for Mother and Child Rights, Inc. (mothersrights.tripod.com/index1.html).

Topic 8 Should Parents Be Held Responsible for the Behavior of Their Children?

Yes: "Delinquent Parents Spawn Teenage Criminals" by Raffique Shah, June 17, 2001 (www.trinicenter.com/Raffique/2001/Jun/17062001.htm). Reprinted with permission of Raffique Shah and www.trinicenter.com.

No: From "Yes, I Am Pleading for My Son's Life" by Tim Sullivan and Jim Lehrer, Online Focus: Oklahoma Bombing Trial, June 11, 1997 (www.pbs.org/newshour/bb/law/ june97/mcveigh_6-11.html). Reprinted with permission of newshour.org.

Topic 9 Should Schools Be Allowed to Use Corporal Punishment?

Yes: "Corporal Punishment Makes Impression" by Tom Larimer, *Daily News Journal*, Murfreesboro, TN, March 4, 2001 (www.corpun.com). Copyright © 2001 by *The Daily News Journal* and *The Rutherford Courier.* Used by permission.

No: From "The Influence of Corporal Punishment on Crime" by Adah Maurer and James S. Wallerstein, Project NoSpank, 1987 (www.nospank.net/srch.htm). Reprinted with permission of Project NoSpank.

Topic 10 Does Sex Education Work?

Yes: "Sex Education Pays" by The British United Provident Association (BUPA) Medical Team, May 31, 2001. Reprinted with permission of The British United Provident Association (BUPA), (www.bupa.co.uk/health_news/310501sex.html).

No: "Fact Sheet: Does Sex Education Work?" by Pamela DeCarlo, Center for AIDS Prevention Studies (CAPS), University of California, San Francisco (www.caps. ucsf.edu). Reprinted with permission of CAPS.

Topic 11 Should Teenagers Have a Right to Contraception without Parental Consent?
Yes: "Parental Consent and Notice for Contraceptives Threatens Teen Health and Constitutional Rights" by the Center for Reproductive Law and Policy, April 2001 (www.crlp.org/pub_fac_parentalconsent.html). Reprinted with permission of the Center for Reproductive Law and Policy.
No: From "Data Confirms That the Abstinence Message, Not Condoms, Is Responsible for the Reduction in Births to Teens" by Peter Brandt, National Coalition for Abstinence Education, May 17, 1998 (www.abstinence. net/Article Detail.cfm?ArticleID+168). Courtesy of the National Coalition for Abstinence Education.

Topic 12 Should the Elderly Pay for Their Own Health Care?
Yes: From "Will America Grow Up before It Grows Old"? by Peter G. Peterson, The Atlantic Monthly, May 1996 (www.theatlantic.com/issues/96may/aging/aging.htm). Copyright © 1996 by Peter G. Peterson, as first published in The Atlantic Monthly. Used by permission.
No: "Second Opinion" by Jonathan Cohn, The New Republic Online, June 25, 2001 (www.thenewrepublic. com/express/cohn062501.html). Reprinted by permission of The New Republic, copyright © 2001, The New Republic, Inc.

Topic 13 Does the Welfare System Provide Enough Support for the Family?
Yes: "What Is the Family Support Movement"? by NC Family and Children's Resource Program, Children's Services Practice Notes, Vol. 5, Issue 1, April 2000. Reprinted from Children's Services Practice Notes Newsletter, copyright © 2000 by the Jordan Institute for Families at the University of North Carolina at Chapel Hill

School of Social Work, http://ssw.unc.edu/.
No: From "How Welfare Offices Undermine Welfare Reform" by Marcia K. Meyers. Reprinted with permission from The American Prospect, Vol. 11, Issue 15, June 19–July 3, 2000. The American Prospect, 5 Broad Street, Boston, MA 02109. All rights reserved.

Topic 14 Should There Be More Childcare Facilities for People in Need?
Yes: From "New Statistics Show Only Small Percentage of Eligible Families Receive Childcare Help,"Press Release, December 6, 2000 (acf.dhhs.gov/news/press/ 2000/ccstudy.htm). Courtesy of U.S. Department of Health and Human Services.
No: "Wanted: Mother" by Susan Benitez, Woodbury Reports, 1999–2001. Used by permission.

Topic 15 Would Fewer Families Live in Poverty If Men and Women Received Equal Pay?
Yes: "Equal Pay for Working Families: National and State Data" (www.aflcio.org/women/exec99.htm). Copyright © AFL-CIO, www.aflcio.org. Used by permission.
No: "Executive Summary, Poverty Trends for Families Headed by Working Single Mothers, 1993 to 1999" by Kathryn H. Porter and Allen Dupree, Center on Budget and Policy Priorities, August 16, 2001 (www.cbpp.org/ 8-16-01wel.htm). Courtesy of Center of Budget and Policy Priorities.

Topic 16 Should Government Policy Dictate the Size of Families?
Yes: "Iran's Birth Rate Plummeting at Record Pace: Success Provides a Model for Other Developing Countries" by Janet Larsen, Earth Policy Institute, December 28, 2001 (www.earth-policy. org/ success/ ss1.htm). Courtesy of Earth Policy Institute.
No: "How to Produce Human Beings" by P. Dean Russell, The Freeman, March 1980, Vol. 30, No. 3. Copyright © 1980 by The Foundation for Economic Education, Inc. Used by permission.

Brown Reference Group has made every effort to contact and acknowledge the creators and copyright holders of all extracts reproduced in this volume. We apologize for any omissions. Any person who wishes to be credited in further volumes should contact Brown Reference Group in writing: Brown Reference Group, 8 Chapel Place, Rivington Street, London EC2A 3DQ, U.K.

Picture credits

Cover: Corbis: John Henley; **Art Explosion:** 6/7, 200/201; **Corbis:** Flip Schulke 25; **Imagingbody.com:** 158; **Rex Features Ltd:** 128, 136/137; Timepix 107; ZZ/KMK/PGR 81; Richard Jenkins: 46/47; **Ronald Grant Archive:** 93, 116; **Topham Picturepoint:** The Image Works/Ellen B Senisi 179; The Image Works/Steven Rubin 167

SET INDEX

Page numbers in bold refer to
volume numbers; those in *italics*
refer to picture captions.

A

abortion 1:188-201; 7:148; 11:144
  legalizing the abortion pill RU-486
    10:9, 48-59
  violent protest by antiabortionists
    7:141, 142-50
  see also Roe v. Wade
accountability 3:68-69
acid rain 4:86-87, 110, 138-39
ACT-UP (AIDS Coalition to Unleash
  Power) 10:41
acupuncture 5:66; 10:88, 92, 97
Adams, John 2:103; 7:20
address, terms of 12:78, 82
Adolescent Family Life Act (AFLA;
  1981) 11:127
adoptions
  gay couples as parents 11:16-17,
    40-43, 44, 48-49, 62-73
  single-parent 11:48, 56-59, 60
  transcultural 11:82, 84, 85
  transracial 11:49, 74-85
  in the United States 11:57
advertising 3:203, 205; 6:88-99
  body image and 6:74-77, 82
  and business ethics 3:171,
    198-209
  negative 3:199
  and objective journalism 6:87,
    126-37
  political 6:87, 138-49
  tobacco 3:171; 6:87, 104, 112-23,
    125
  to children 6:86-87, 100-111
affirmative action 1:9, 72-85
Afghanistan
  drugs and terrorism 8:152-53
  Internet usage 6:171
  prisoners of war in 9:179, 180-87
  U.S. foreign policy and 8:25, 43
  War on Terrorism 8:166-67,
    184-85, 190-91
AFL-CIO 8:67
  and equal pay for women 11:189,
    190-93, 198
Africa
  foreign aid for 8:115-16
  privatization in 3:44
  reparations to 1:179-81
  Third World debt 3:158, 161
African Americans
  the Constitution and 7:64-65
  and corporal punishment
    11:120-21
  and crime 9:8
  and illegal drugs 7:69; 9:129-30
  prejudice against 11:23
  in prisons 7:67-69
  racial profiling of 9:126
  single mothers 11:53-54
  and transracial adoption
    11:74-75, 80-82

Tulia trial 11:23
  see also civil rights; segregation;
    slaves/slavery
Agnew, Spiro 2:206, 208
agriculture *see* farming
aid, foreign 4:38, 39; 8:112-23
  see also relief bodies
AIDS *see* HIV/AIDS
AIDS Prevention for Adolescents in
  School 11:132
Aid to Dependent Children (ADC)
  7:83
air pollution 4:139
  "pay to pollute" systems 4:86-97
  see also acid rain; global warming
alcohol, advertising 6:104-5
Algeria, terrorism 8:165
Allende, Salvador 8:125
Allport, Gordon 11:28
Al Qaeda 8:23, 25, 111, 153, 179,
  190-91; 9:214
  prisoners of war 9:179, 180-88
Alzheimer's disease 10:80
Amazon.com 3:48, 49, 54-55, 57, 58
Amazon rain forest, and capitalism
  3:23, 24-25, 32
American Arts Alliance 12:35, 36-39
American Association of Retired
  People (AARP) 1:18
American Civil Liberties Union
  (ACLU) 1:100-101
  and abortion 1:190-93, 198;
    7:147-48
  and antiabortion violence 7:145,
    146-49, 150
  and artistic freedom 12:47, 48-51,
    56
  and the death penalty 9:120
  and disability rights 7:89, 94-97, 98
  and English language 1:87, 92-95,
    96
  and gay adoption 11:63, 64-67, 72
  and gay marriage 1:61, 62-65
  and gays in the military 7:104-5,
    113
  and hate speech 1:139, 140-43,
    148; 7:129, 131
  and Internet censorship 6:155,
    158, 160-63, 164
  and medical marijuana 5:113,
    118-20, 122
  and pornography 7:156-57
  and racial profiling 9:131
  and sex education 11:127
  and warning labels on music
    12:203, 208-11, 212
American Dream 1:8; 6:90
American Family Association
  6:162-63
American History X (film) 12:149,
  163, 164-72
American Liberty League 2:143
American Management Association
  (AMA) 7:194, 195
American Medical Association (AMA)
  5:127-29; 10:62
American Revolutionary War 7:10, 12

Americans with Disabilities Act
  (ADA; 1990) 7:89, 95-97;
    12:158
Amin, Idi 8:88
Amish, and education 1:51, 115,
  117-23, 124
Amnesty International 9:115, 166,
  168, 179
Andean Regional Initiative 8:151, 157
Angkor Wat 12:87, 88
animals
  cloning 4:174-85; 5:22-23, 26,
    34-35, 165, 174
  ethical dilemmas and 4:123
  medical research on 5:63, 150-61
  sacrificed in the Santeria religion
    7:115, 116-19, 124
  in zoos 4:123, 162-73
  see also wildlife
Annan, Kofi 8:51, 55-56
anthrax, in the mail 8:166
antibiotics, in farming 4:48; 10:151,
  152-53, 160
antidepressants, overprescribed?
  10:162, 164-75
anti-Semitism 7:135; 11:23; 12:214
antitrust laws 3:172
apartheid 1:126, 131
Aquinas, Thomas 5:61
Arafat, Yasser 8:193, 194, 209
Arbenz Guzmán, Jacobo 8:126, 127
architecture, and Nazi politics
  12:177, 178-81, 186
Argentina, privatization in 3:43
argumentation skills 3:60-61
aristocracy 2:16
Aristotle 3:60; 6:37, 43
arms industry, U.S. 8:63, 73
arthritis 10:120
artificial insemination 4:182, 183
artists
  installation artists 12:12-15, 20
  politics of 12:174-87
  responsibility 12:190-201
arts 12:8-9, 110-11, 148-49
  benefit the rest of the school
    curriculum? 12:149, 150-61
  can pornography be art? 12:111,
    136-47
  censorship 6:17-19, 20; 12:48-51,
    58-59
  corporate sponsorship 12:9,
    96-107
  and creativity 12:8-9, 22-33
  does art matter? 12:10-21
  First Amendment protects artistic
    freedom? 12:9, 46-59
  is rap an art form? 12:111, 124-35
  modern art 12:11, 21
  political correctness and 12:80
  and politics 12:174-87
  and racism 12:149, 162-73
  response to September 11 attacks
    12:9, 10-20
  should artifacts be returned to
    their original countries?
    12:84-95

218